Post-Military Society

# Post-Military Society

## Militarism, Demilitarization and War at the End of the Twentieth Century

Martin Shaw

Polity Press

Martin Shaw is hereby identified as author of this work in accordance with
Section 77 of the Copyright, Designs and Patents Act 1988.

First published in 1991 by Polity Press in association with Basil Blackwell

Editorial office:
Polity Press
65 Bridge Street
Cambridge CB2 1UR, UK

Marketing and production:
Basil Blackwell Ltd
108 Cowley Road
Oxford OX4 1JF, UK

ISBN 0 7456 0198-7
ISBN 0 7456 0199-5 (pbk)

*British Library Cataloguing in Publication Data*
A CIP catalogue record for this book is available from the British Library.

Typeset in 10½ on 12 pt Sabon
by Graphicraft Typesetters Ltd, Hong Kong
Printed in Great Britain by TJ Press, Padstow

This book is printed on acid-free paper.

# CONTENTS

Preface                                                            vii

Acknowledgements                                                    ix

**1  Militarism and Militarization**                                 1
Disciplinary Approaches                                              4
Definitions                                                          9
War and Industrial Society                                          15
Total War and Classical Militarism                                  19
Theory and the End of the Cold War                                  23

**2  Contexts of Military Power**                                   30
The State System                                                    32
International Relations and World Economy                           37
The 'World Military Order'                                          43
Politics of Military Power                                          50
Military Power as a Means of War                                    54

**3  Post-Military Society**                                        64
Variants of the 'Militarization' Thesis                             66
Sociological Alternatives                                           73
Conscription in Europe                                              83
Limits of Third World Militarism                                    93

**4   Militarism in Post-Military Society**                    109
Comparative Issues in Western Societies               110
Militarism and National Myths                         113
Nostalgia Militarism and Media Wars                   126
The Military in Post-Military Society                 134
Post-Militarism in Europe                             155

**5   Post-Military Citizenship**                              163
Demilitarization in Europe                            164
Conscription and Citizenship                          174
The Nation-State and Post-Military Society            177
A New World Order?                                    180
The Two Faces of Post-Military Society                184

**6   Postscript: The Gulf War and Post-Military Society**     192
Violence and Post-Military Society                    195
Post-Military Societies at War                        203
War and Militarism after the Gulf                     207

Index                                                 217

# PREFACE

This book has been written during some of the most turbulent years of modern times. It was conceived as the Second Cold War of the early 1980s gave way to the cautious optimism of mid-decade détente. The first draft was substantially completed early in 1989, only to be overtaken by the Eastern European revolutions which ended the Cold War. It was rewritten early in 1990 in an appropriately optimistic vein – again only to be quickly overshadowed by the Gulf crisis. It is finally being sent to press as it becomes clear that the war of January–February 1991 opened a Pandora's box of conflicts in the Middle East. If I have learnt anything from writing this book, it is that in world affairs we must now expect the unexpected.

It may be thought folly, in such circumstances, to write a book on this subject at all, when publication leaves a gap of months or even years between writing and reading. It may be thought even greater folly to try to fix the flux of world events in any sort of theoretical categories. And yet times of such great upheaval, even more than others, demand radical explanations. No one can foretell the future but we can, and must, try to interpret the directions – contradictory as they seem to be – in which we are travelling.

This I have tried to do with the concept of 'post-military society'. By this I mean, not that the military and militarism are disappearing – whether or not we wish this to happen, it is clearly not the case – but that we are moving away from the mid-century condition, in which they dominated all social relations and cultural forms in a direct and often oppressive manner. Society has developed beyond the military and militarism as they have been understood in most of the twentieth century, and this change, uneven and contradictory as it is, must be taken account of in any attempt to understand the very different military, political and social realities of the coming decades.

This book, then, is about the changes which lie behind the dramatically shifting headline relationships between war, militarism and society. In this sense, the oscillations between optimistic peaceful and pessimistic warlike scenarios – although they have certainly affected the presentation of the argument – are largely beside the point when it comes to the argument itself. Fundamental changes in the relationships of military and social realities have occurred and are occurring: the description, analysis and theoretical interpretation of them are what this book is about. We must guard against interpreting these changes in a deterministic sense, for no one can tell precisely how they will work out in the future. Indeed, to a considerable extent that depends on us, the people as well as the leaders of states. We shall be better able to influence events, however, if we understand where we are coming from. I hope that this book will contribute something to this process of recognizing the shifts which are taking place in realities which affect us all.

Martin Shaw
Hull, April 1991

# ACKNOWLEDGEMENTS

This book has been long in gestation, and many people have contributed, often without knowing, to its delayed birth: notably the editors of books and journals and the convenors of seminar series who have invited me to contribute my ideas, and students on my undergraduate Sociology and postgraduate Security Studies courses at Hull, who have most consistently provided me with critical reactions to my changing thoughts. My specific intellectual debts are, I hope, explicit in the text.

I am especially indebted to Tony Giddens, who commissioned and edited this book, for his patience and guidance, and to my colleagues in the Department of Sociology and Social Anthropology at Hull, who have long supported me in what must often have seemed a rather offbeat specialization. In the Gulf war discussion which concludes the book, I have drawn in a preliminary way upon research carried out together with Roy Carr-Hill, research co-ordinator of the School of Social and Political Sciences at Hull, and funded by the Joseph Rowntree Charitable Trust (full discussions of this work will appear elsewhere in due course). I am grateful to both for enabling me to test empirically some of the theoretical ideas developed here, and to Roy especially for a stimulating partnership.

My deepest gratitude is to Joanna, for her love and support, and to Thomas, Robin and Isabel, whose interest sustains my belief that the issues addressed here are of more than academic interest.

# 1

# MILITARISM AND MILITARIZATION

There is greater uncertainty today about the roles of war and military institutions in human society, than at any time in the twentieth century. This is not just the product of the 'end of the Cold War', but results from the contradictory features of the entire Cold War period since 1945. It was the first half of the century which gave it the tag, 'century of total war'. Since mid-century states and societies have lived in the shadow of the world wars and the changes they brought about in economies, political institutions and social relations, together with the totally novel technology of the nuclear arms race. We have been in what has commonly been seen as a 'post-war' period. Only in the 1990s is it now possible to pose the question whether 'post-war' is genuinely giving way – or can give way – to a world which has settled accounts with the legacy of war. Whether this new stage will merely be characterized by new forms of military conflict, or whether it will in some sense be positively 'post-military', is the crucial issue of our new times.

The period since mid-century can best be seen as a transitional period between the unprecedented militarism of the first half of the twentieth century and the uncertain, but clearly very different world of the twenty-first century, the foundations of which are being laid in the 1990s. This transition has been marked, of course, by a dramatic global military build-up. On most of the obvious measures, there has been an extraordinary growth in military power. Global arms spending has been increasing at

around 3 per cent annually in real terms, and is currently estimated at over $900 billion. The number of nuclear warheads has
moved rapidly upwards. There has been a notable diffusion of
military expenditure; although still massively concentrated in the
northern industrial world, the share of Third World states increased rapidly in the 1970s and has remained at a higher level.

The trend of actual wars, moreover, although always more
difficult to quantify, has included some disturbing instances. The
conflicts between the USSR, China, Vietnam and Kampuchea at
the end of the 1970s refuted any idea that 'socialist' states were
less warlike than 'capitalist' states. The involvement of the superpowers (and of Britain and France) in Third World conflicts,
increasingly with more sophisticated and better armed opponents,
aroused justified fears about the linkages between regional
wars and a possible East–West conflict. The nuclearization of the
Third World has created a military potential of fundamental significance, even if has not been realized as quickly as some had
feared. The long-running Iran–Iraq war in the 1980s, and the
Gulf War of 1991 which followed it, have highlighted the danger
war continues to pose to societies.

Nevertheless the nuclear age, to use a label widely adopted in
the last four decades, has undoubtedly been very different from
the era of the two world wars. The restructuring of the world
system around two dominant blocs and the change in military
technology contributed to a longer period without global war.
The military impasse of nuclear arms has been so widely recognized that the leaders of the superpowers, possessors of so much
overkill, themselves acknowledged (even before the end of the
Cold War) that nuclear wars could not be fought.

The outbreak of peace at the end of the 1980s should not make
us overlook the very recent peaks of tension, in the so-called
'Second Cold War' of the earlier part of the decade. Nor should it
permit us to neglect the actual wars being fought in many parts of
the globe, the ways in which the causes of wars continue to be
reproduced in international relations, or the immensely dangerous
potential of the arms build-ups across the world system. Those
who analyse military power, rather than political rhetoric, cannot
fail to be cautious (often, indeed, pessimistic) about the prospects
for peace. But it would be equally foolish to ignore the positive
consequences of a major period without war along the central
fractures of the international system, and even more mistaken

to underestimate the critical transformation which occurred in 1989–90. In one sense the 'long peace' was, like other periods of peace, an extended phase of preparation for war. But in another it could be said that it has allowed developments to take place which now provide, with the end of 'post-war', a possible basis for a more positively peaceful world and genuinely demilitarized societies – notably in Europe. These developments have been as much socio-economic as political or military, and for this reason especially it is important to make a sociological evaluation of current trends.

The basic objection to the 'militarization' thesis (which will be examined in more detail later) is that it has looked at the global military situation from too narrow a viewpoint, emphasizing weaponry rather than political relations, and tending to ignore socio-economic developments. Against the background of the global arms trade and nuclear arms race in the 1970s and 1980s, it is not surprising that many of those who analysed military power came to deeply disturbing conclusions, arguing that there was a trend towards the 'militarization' of the world. But this concept, widely used, has not so often been clearly defined. Stated in the most general terms it seems to mean that military power is generally growing and therefore has greater influence in states, societies and the international system. Andrew Ross has noted, however, that there are two distinct concepts of militarization: the more restricted notion of 'military build-up' and the wider concept of a process leading to 'militarism' in the sense of a preference for violent and military means or 'militarism of the mind'.[1] The thesis generally seems to assume the first meaning, and indeed it is in terms of this that it is most plausible.

'Militarization' is actually used in a variety of senses, describing many divergent realities, and it could be argued that the concept is very much an ideological tool of anti-militarist analysis – used to cover a variety of aspects of military power which cause concern – rather than a scientific concept. The idea of a *process* of growth in military power expresses the alarm which many feel about the role of military power in the world. The lack of clarity about its meaning indicates, however, a widespread failure to insert analyses of military power within a coherent social and political theory. This in the end diminishes rather than enhances the critical potential of the analysis. We should not accept the often unstated assumption that in order to develop a radical analysis of a phenomenon such as military power, one must be prepared to argue for the existence of a worsening trend in what one is criticizing.

The militarization thesis expresses, at best, one side of a complex set of relationships. Its one-sidedness is more apparent now than it was in the 1980s, perhaps, because of the manifold effects of East–West détente. It is important, however, to note that this one-sidedness is not just a matter of a particular evaluation of military realities, but reflects the lack of a sociological dimension. In this sense, the militarization thesis can be taken as representative of a wide range of approaches to war and the military which fail to take account of their social aspects (understood in the widest sense). This book adopts a rather different intellectual and disciplinary approach from many other writers in the field, by emphasizing precisely these aspects which have been neglected. Later in this chapter I shall return to some peculiarly sociological issues which are involved in evaluating the new, 'post-post-war' stage in international relations and society. Before we do this, however, it is important to set out some general issues of the approach that is being adopted, and to define some key concepts which underpin the analysis in this and later chapters.

## DISCIPLINARY APPROACHES

There is of course no shortage of books about war, military affairs and defence. These subjects dominated the 1980s, especially because of the crises in East–West relations and the nuclear arms race in the early part of the decade. Much of the current literature reflects this concern, but there is also an increasing amount of writing about the wars actually being fought in the Third World. At the same time, the interest in past wars, both in this century and in more distant times, remains as strong as ever. Much of this literature has been dominated, however, by preoccupations either with military forces (weaponry, manpower, etc.) or with policies (strategy, diplomacy, international relations). The focus is all too narrowly on the immediate realities of military power and its political context. Important as these are, it is necessary to examine them in a wider social and economic setting. Interestingly, this is more often achieved by those who study actual wars than by those studying contemporary war-preparation. Perhaps it is the case that when wars are actually fought, the interaction of military affairs with socio-economic relations in general is much more evident than it is in the more circumscribed studies of international relations and strategy.

This book aims therefore to make a distinctive contribution to the literature: it is about the role of war, war-preparation and activity and ideas related to war in contemporary societies. It is based on the assumption that war involves a set of social processes, related to other processes within societies. It seeks to examine the ways in which war, military institutions and military culture are both produced by, and influence, social relations. The perspective on war which is adopted is a broadly sociological one. There are, of course, many viewpoints in sociology, and there is no intention here to enter into the general controversies of the subject. We shall encounter some of their ramifications when we discuss the sociological debates about war: for although sociologists have written far too little on the subject, they have formulated quite contrasting views on the problem. Since, however, many readers with an interest in war and military affairs may have little acquaintance with sociology, and since many sociological readers may have given only modest thought to problems of war, it will be necessary to make some basic definitions of subject matter and approach.

Studies of war and militarism have often developed on the fringes, rather than at the centre, of the major intellectual disciplines. Central though the experience of war and war-preparation has been to society in the twentieth century, it has been determinedly marginalized in our intellectual culture. Sociology's neglect has been remarked whenever its writers have finally brought themselves round to the subject. This has, however, been far from an exceptional situation. Indicative, perhaps, is the volume of keywords compiled by Raymond Williams – a writer who straddled literature, sociology and politics with great authority – which simply does not include 'war' or 'militarism' among the central concepts of our age.[2] To confirm the typicality of this experience, simply turn to the index of almost any general book on culture, society or politics and observe the gaps where these terms should be.

The paradox of this silence is that those who perpetuate it will often use the term 'post-war' to mark off the modern age. The key cut-off point in our history is 1945, acknowledged as readily

by those who were then unborn as by an older generation for
whom it was a formative experience. The Second World War has
so obviously shaped the world in which we live, and the nuclear
arms race has so obviously overshadowed it, that one wonders at
any social or cultural studies which do not acknowledge these as
central realities. Similarly, it is difficult to credit the range of
contemporary Third World studies which is structured by the
dichotomy of 'development' and 'underdevelopment', dealing
only in passing with the reality of Third World wars which have
killed millions and crippled societies year in, year out since 1945.

The colossal understatement at best, and amnesia or indiffer-
ence at worst, where war and militarism are concerned is one of
the most striking features of contemporary intellectual culture.
Indeed this is highly relevant as evidence on the major problem of
this book, the extent of militarization in contemporary societies.
It is as though one of the theses of classical sociology, which
envisaged industrial society as non-militarist, has been implicitly
and often unknowingly accepted as reality by many participants
in our culture. We do not have to accept this evaluation at face
value, but it certainly needs to be explained.

It is in contrast to the low profile of military concerns in the
mainstream of social and cultural thought, that specialized studies
of war and war-preparation have burgeoned. Strategic, military
and defence studies provide a massive stream of information
about the inner workings of the military machines, the roles of
forces and weaponry, and the potentials for war and avoidance of
it. Such disciplines have tended, however, to share the bias towards the East–West conflict, at the expense of 'hot' wars in the
Third World – except where these provide testing grounds for the
latest high-technology weaponry. They have tended, even more,
to reflect rather than explain the divorce of armed forces from
society. Only where strategy is informed by military history, as in
the work of Howard,[3] does a broader social perspective tend to
emerge.

It can generally be said of strategic studies that while they
provide a standpoint from which to approach war and war-
preparation, they do little to enable us to discuss militarism and
militarization. The same is largely true even of some academic
disciplines which clearly go beyond the immediacies of the war
and military processes. International relations, for example, has
generated the most comprehensive historical and statistical sur-

veys of wars. But international relations approaches generally situate wars only in the system of states, not in the wider social framework, and measure wars according to duration and numbers of troops and casualties, not the extent of economic, social or political mobilization. International relations goes beyond the military perspective to the international political context, but typically is less interested in the connections of international with domestic politics, let alone social relations. Mainstream political science, on the other hand, deals with the domestic roots of defence policy. But as Roberts argues, there is a failure to integrate the perspectives of international relations and comparative politics.[4] Both reflect the intellectual compartmentalization which characterizes political science as a whole. Only recently has international relations theory addressed the issue of the state in a way that has drawn on the most important modern sociological theorizing: this new development is discussed further at the end of this chapter.

The perspectives of peace studies, on the other hand, can at their best encompass many of the questions that strategic and international relations theorists omit. Writers in this field acknowledge, above all, the need for different attitudes towards solving international disputes, and the role of social movements in fostering these. Peace studies do not, however, themselves form a highly coherent intellectual discipline. Even when peace studies go further than the role of 'alternative' strategic studies or international relations, their sociology often seems limited and *ad hoc*. In particular, peace studies rarely aspire to the historical breadth and width of the mainstream social sciences at their best. In analysing the prospects of peace in the current international and social situations, writers in peace studies have not usually seen it as necessary to present a coherent historical model of the relations of war and society, capable of understanding past wars as well as current dilemmas. This lack of historical perspective often weakens the credibility of peace studies, in proposing ways in which society can avoid in the future the conditions which have led to war on countless occasions in the past.

Serious thinking about war and peace must clearly cross the disciplinary boundaries of both the traditional social sciences and the newer specialized fields of studies. In arguing for a sociological perspective there is no intention to claim any exclusive insights, let alone any superior achievement. It is important, however, to developed an approach to war that enables us to understand its relations with society, in the broadest sense: to discuss the social causes and effects of war as well as the narrower military and political aspects. Many of the materials for such studies may come from historians, social and economic as well as political and military. The historical imagination has frequently been cross-fertilized with the sociological, and some of the best studies of war and society have come from historians.[5]

What is needed, as I have argued elsewhere, is the development of a historical sociology of war. Such a sociology of war must be comparative in the broadest possible sense, concerned with the role of war and militarism both in different historical phases and civilizations, and with different societies in the modern world.[6] At the heart of both these sorts of comparison, however, are likely to be questions about the relations between industrialism and warfare. Has industrialism made societies more or less warlike? What do we make of the variety of experience of war and militarism in contemporary societies? These are core issues for this book, and on these, at least, mainstream sociological theory offers important directions which we need to consider.

This chapter contains, therefore, a discussion of the nature of war, militarism and militarization as social phenomena. It continues with an outline of various ways of approaching the problems, showing how the sort of sociological approach adopted here differs from other, possibly more familiar, ways of thinking about war. Then, moving into the sociological debate, we consider the main alternative perspectives on war and militarism in modern societies which are offered by classical and contemporary theorists. In the concluding part of the chapter these models are assessed in the light of the historical experience of warfare in the twentieth century.

At this point, the main argument of the book is first presented in a general way. It is suggested that the first half of the century saw an unprecedented relationship between social and military development. In the context of 'total war', society became militarized, and war socialized, in a new way. The problems of understanding war, militarism and militarization in our own time are defined in relation to this. How far are we still under the sway of the 'totalization' of warfare? How have nuclear weapons altered the relationship between war and society in the industrialized world? How far is war in the so-called Third World reproducing the earlier European experience? How does *our* time pose the issue which has preoccupied social thinkers since the early nineteenth century: the relationship between industrialism and militarism? Are societies becoming more or less militarized, and what are the implications?

## DEFINITIONS

Before we can begin to pose these questions knowledgeably, we need some working ideas about what war and militarism actually are. We have so far used these terms loosely, and assumed the relationship between them. But there is hardly a consensus on their meaning and usage. Concerning war, perhaps, there is some rough and ready agreement that it involves the use of force, fighting and killing, by organized groups. But what is its relationship to states? War, arguably, existed before states; and many wars today are fought by non-state groupings (but do they invariably aspire to statehood?). Clearly there are close relationships between warfare and the state, but it is less clear that these define either.

If there are problems with an age-old concept like war, a term like militarism, which is more recent derivation, poses even more complex difficulties. It can be used to refer generally to war-preparation, or more specifically to ideological mobilization. Vagts, in a classic work, confines the term to those sorts of ideology which actively glorify warfare; war-preparation which does not promote war itself with this enthusiasm is not, in his terms, militarist.[7] Some might suggest, in contrast, that war-preparation is by definition 'militarism'. If this is not the case, is the term 'war-preparation' itself satisfactory?

All these discussions clearly overlap with political debate. In the politics of most societies today, the war-preparations of the potential adversary are clearly defined as 'militarist'. 'Our own' military activities, however, may not even be counted as war-preparation; they are more likely to be seen as part of a 'defence' or 'deterrence' policy, the professed aim of which may be to avoid war rather than to fight it. So to equate 'military' and 'militarism' will be seen in many quarters as quite unwarranted.

For the purposes of social science, we clearly require generic terms which are not simply tools of political ideology. Of course, it is hardly possible to devise a new, entirely neutral terminology: social science uses and refines terms which are in wider use. (An attempt to introduce a complex new terminology in this field was made in a classic work by Andreski; while the ideas of his book are still current, its terminology never caught on.)[8] It is necessary to give everyday and politically used words a more precise meaning than they usually have, so that the discussion can proceed with reasonable clarity. At the same time, it is necessary to face up to the substantive judgements involved in the choice of terminology. These judgements are chiefly theoretical, but they may have have political implications.

In this book it will be assumed that *war* is the systematic and extensive use of violence as a means of policy by an organized social group claiming (but not necessarily exercising) legitimate control over a given territory, against another such group (or groups). This definition does not suggest that all wars are mainly about the control of territory, which clearly is not the case. It suggests, however, that the protagonists in wars may be defined as social groups and institutions which possess or claim legitimate control of territory, and whose conflicts thus actually or potentially bring control into question.

This definition suggests a close but not fixed relationship between war-making and statehood: it includes actual states and would-be states, pre-state peoples, and forces within societies seeking to overthrow the existing government or state-forms, where these reach the stage of civil war. It is most obviously open to objection in that it could exclude violent conflicts involving non-territorially fixed peoples, such as hunter–gatherers and nomads. In this sense it is a definition formulated with an eye to the era of states, and is more helpful in marking distinctions between war and other forms of violence in state-bound societies. Thus class or racial violence which does not bring into question the form of state, and hence legitimate control of territory, is not war. Similarly, what are called 'economic', 'political' and 'ideological' warfare are not distinct forms of warfare, separate from organized violence, but adjuncts (albeit increasingly important ones) to the essential business of war.

There are, of course, still grey areas, such as the boundary between terrorism and civil war, but there must be in any such definition. Researchers such as those on the US Correlates of War Project have found enormous difficulty in deciding what counts as

a war.[9] Important as such classification may be, what is essential
for our purposes is a definition which enables us to generalize
about the major wars and forms of war, not one which allows us
to adjudicate all the marginal cases.

We shall also insist on the importance of the term *war-
preparation* to refer to all social activities leading, or designed to
lead, to war. War-preparation includes all forms of organization
capable of producing war, irrespective of whether there is any
intention or desire to use them. Thus the creation or maintenance
of military forces is seen as war-preparation, even if their main
purposes may be defined as 'defensive' or 'deterrent'. This makes
sense because the organizing principle of military force itself is
war: a defensive or deterrent force must still envisage war as its
potential use, in order to fulfil its defensive or deterrent function.
'Defence' and 'deterrence' may be real and important aspects of
the use of military force (although their relationships to, respectively, aggression and war-fighting must always be investigated).
They are, however, but parts of the business of war, not substitutes for it. We must distinguish here between the features which
define war-preparation as such, and the ways in which this is
politically and ideologically explained.

The distinction between war-preparation and *militarism* is
easier to define in principle than to apply in practice. War-
preparation is as old as war itself, while militarism, as we have
already noted, is a modern term, which came into prominence
with the development of industrialism and capitalism. Militarism
clearly concerns the relationship of war-preparation and society.
For the early social theorists of industrial society, militarism
denoted the pervasive influence of military principles and ideas
in pre-industrial society. According to their optimistic view, these
were becoming increasingly redundant in industrial society. On
the contrary, Marxist theorists argued that militarism was a
feature of the social organization of all class societies, and that
capitalism produced its own especially active form.

Although the term is applied differently in the two cases, militarism has (apart from a common negative connotation) a common meaning, suggesting an influence of military organization
and values on social structure. Clearly it is possible to posit a
situation, such as the sociologists of industrial society envisaged
for the future but some historians see in past periods of limited
war, in which military organization is ongoing but has relatively

little influence on social structure. In this case the distinction between war-preparation and militarism is relatively clear. In modern warfare, however, war-preparation has come to include social, economic, political and ideological mobilization. In total war there is hardly any feature of society which is not affected by war and war-preparation. It can be argued that warfare has then become central to social development. In this case, the distinction between war-preparation and militarism becomes abstract; the one necessarily involves the other. The chief issues are the extent and forms of militarism, rather than its existence.[10]

This way of looking at things assumes, of course, that the definition of militarism is not a matter of aggressiveness, or of glorifying war and military institutions. Unless therefore one is a strict pacifist, militarism is not a matter of good or bad, but of how far military organization and values (which sometimes may be justified and necessary) impinge on social structure. Neither is militarism a purely ideological force. The ideological impact of war-preparation is only one part of its influence on society. We may distinguish therefore between militarism, in general, and *militarist ideologies*, which are belief systems that give a high value to military activities.

This distinction goes against a good deal of writing which assumes that militarism is essentially an ideological phenomenon, but it is important for a number of reasons. First, it gives us a general term for the influence of war-preparation on society (militarism). Second, it enables us to compare societies in which war-preparation has a major influence, whether or not militarist ideologies are prevalent, and thus enables us to analyse such forms as the 'democratic militarism' of the Anglo-Saxon world, as forms of militarism. Third, it enables us to separate out the ideological from the wider social dimensions of militarism, allowing specific treatment of each.

In practice, of course, these meanings often overlap, and it is difficult to adhere precisely to the usages proposed. But these distinctions have a further merit, for the purposes of this book, of allowing us to pose the definition of *militarization* in a sociological sense. As we have noted, this is used in many, often conflicting ways in the current literature. Ross's survey summarizes many of those which are available.[11] They can be categorized by the level of social and political formation which is alleged to be 'militarized': thus we have militarization of international relations (identified with warlike or violent propensities), of state expenditures and bureaucracy, of political life and forms of government, of society, of ideology. All these are in principle admissible uses, but we need to be selective if we are to have a concept which can help us to analyse and explain.

Ross proposes, as we have seen, to separate militarism and militarization, arguing that it is the conflation of the two which has confused the argument. He argues for a distinction between militarization as a process leading to militarism, which he no longer wishes to call 'militarization', and as 'military build-up', which is now to be the key definition of the term. In distinguishing between militarism and militarization he argues that 'there is likely to be a mutually reinforcing, reciprocal relationship between military build-up and militarism, not simply the unilinear, causal relationship found between the first form of militarisation – process – and militarism, in which process militarisation results in militarism'.[12]

Here the confusion of terms is becoming almost unbearable. In order to make a valid analytical point, that military build-up need not lead directly to militarism, Ross tries to sever the conceptual relationships between militarism and militarization. This is not only unnecessary, since the point can be made in other ways, but also confusing, since the growth of militarism is something which would be described as 'militarization' in everyday language. It also abstracts militarization from the major set of relationships, the interrelationships of war and society, which have dominated and transformed the history of war (and of societies) in the twentieth century. Societal, political and ideological militarization are not optional extras in the analysis of modern warfare, but integral and essential components of such analysis. To separate militarism and militarization conceptually, because military build-up now sometimes occurs without a corresponding process of societal militarization or development of militarism, actually makes it more difficult to categorize the current trends.

A more useful way of posing matters is to say that an increase in the level of war-preparation (military build-up) does not necessarily entail militarization (growth of militarism). Indeed increasing war-preparation, in terms of enhanced (especially nuclear) weaponry, etc., has actually corresponded to a partial *demilitarization* of society in the nuclear age. The distinction between war-preparation and militarism is of key importance here. The issue is precisely how far and in what ways, in any given society, war-preparation has actually produced militarism. A society in which war-preparation is extending militarism experiences militarization; but it is equally possible for war-preparation to proceed with a declining effect on society, that is to say, accompanied by demilitarization.

Less dramatically, we might argue that there have been contradictory processes of militarization and demilitarization as the forms of war-preparation have changed. Militarization at one level has been accompanied by demilitarization at others: for example, militarization of elite politics or economic strategy has gone hand in hand with demilitarization of mass employment, life and politics, if the former impinge only indirectly on the latter. The combination of militarization and demilitarization may point to the need for new concepts to supplement these in analysing contemporary relationships between war, the military and society. The concept of 'armament culture', for example, discussed most extensively by Luckham,[13] may partly displace the older notion of militarism, as we shall see in chapter 3.

This way of posing matters points up another essential issue: militarism and militarization do not depend simply or directly on the role of the *military* in society. Of course, where the military is large and powerful, drawn (particularly by conscription) from many layers of society, militarization is likely to be extensive. But to the extent that war-preparation becomes central to society, it may become effective through other institutions. For example, C. Wright Mills argued that the military had grown in power in post-Second World War America. But he also argued that military issued had become central to the system of power as a whole in US society.[14] This centrality was manifested in government and economy as well as in the position of the military: there was in effect a militarization of power and economy (although *not* necessarily a societal militarization in the sense of growth of militarism). This second argument was the more fundamental, but has tended to be eclipsed by criticisms of the first, which should really be seen as a supporting argument. Thus militarism can be strong, even where the power of the military is limited; and conversely a powerful military does not necessarily involve extensive militarization of society. In many African societies, for example, military rulers dominate societies through political means essentially similar to those of authoritarian civilian regimes.

It is useful to mention some subsidiary concepts which are

important to analyses of militarism and militarization. To start to discuss the relationship between 'elite' and 'mass' relationships to war and war-preparation brings up the question of *military participation* and *mobilization*. Military participation was seen by Andreski as the key to the relationship between war and social change.[15] Marwick has modified this argument, to suggest that it is not simply the level of participation in the armed forces, but the level of societal 'wartime participation' that is crucial.[16] The concept of participation is ambiguous, being capable of both neutral and positively evaluated meanings, and there may be a sliding between the two. Societies or social groups 'participate' in wars under coercion, but also sometimes with a strong ideological identification and with expectations of benefiting from wars. They are mobilized, but often they also mobilize themselves. Both 'participation' and 'mobilization' are double-edged concepts which are important to the discussion of militarism and militarization.

This preliminary unpacking of concepts, arbitrary as it may be in certain senses, is designed to assist in clarifying the substantive questions with which this book is concerned. Although the discussion has concentrated on the relationships of war-preparation, militarism and militarization, the relationship of these concepts to that of war itself is also an extremely problematic area. This is because the dichotomy of war and non-war (leaving aside the concept of peace at this stage) affects war-preparation and all aspects of military relations in society. War-preparation and militarism are vastly different in a situation of actual war, compared to a non-war situation. This is especially true of modern total war: militarization is far greater in the active as opposed to the latent stage. This distinction is particularly important to understanding the ways in which intellectual approaches to war and militarism have developed among various disciplines and interest groups. To clarify further the contribution of the approach in this book, we now turn to look at some of the main sociological perspectives.

## War and Industrial Society

Sociology, like the rest of the social sciences, is a product of the rise of industrial capitalist society in the West. Its early intellectual affinities lay partly with the conservative reaction to market relations (a reaction which has been eclipsed in recent times by the rise of 'neo-liberal', free-market conservatism). In many respects, however, its early theorists fully shared in the optimism of the nineteenth century. Industrialism, writers like Saint-Simon, Comte and Spencer believed, was fundamentally transforming society and, in so doing, eliminating warfare between states. Whatever else they might disagree about, the early sociologists saw industrial society as an inherently transnational order in which inter-state rivalry and warfare would disappear, with military institutions losing their dominant position. In Mann's phrase, they held to an 'optimistic theory of pacific capitalism': demilitarization was a law of industrial society.[17]

There were, Mann reminds us, writers like Gumplowicz and Hintze who asserted the vitality of militarism. The mainstream of sociological writing (in the way this has been defined subsequently in the English-speaking world) has, however, retained the idea of a basic opposition between militarism and industrial capitalism. Even Marxists have tended to think in these terms, preserving (despite the theory of imperialism) the notion of a capitalist rationality inimical to militarism. Marx himself left militarism out of his theory of capitalism: the logic of capital was the production of surplus value through exchange, with the market replacing relations of coercion. Although later Marxists have seen militarism as a product of capitalism, with capitalist states fighting wars to enhance the world-market share of 'their' national capitalists, the idea of different logics for capital and state power has tended to remain.

The 'optimistic theory' has of course been dealt enormous blows by the twentieth-century history of industrial society. Even as the classical sociologists were formulating their concepts of non-militarist capitalism in the nineteenth century, the 'industrialization of warfare' was under way, as McNeill has described.[18] Successive wars, beginning with the American Civil War and culminating in the world wars, have demonstrated the unprecedented military potential not only of industrial technology, but also of the social organization of industrial society. The era of large concentrated populations and workforces, dominated by huge corporate and state bureaucracies, climaxed in mass warfare on a global scale. In this sense, the 'pessimistic theory of militaristic capitalism', favoured by some radicals and Marxists, has fitted better with historical experience.

While no one can doubt that the era of industrial capitalism has seen unparalleled warfare and militarism, there are objections to explaining this in terms of industrialism or capitalism. Giddens has argued that industrialism, capitalism and state military power are distinct 'institutional clusterings' in society, and that 'none is wholly reducible to any of the others'.[19] Mann argues that militarism '*is* a central part of modern society' but 'its centrality does not derive from either capitalism or industrialism' but 'from geopolitical aspects of our social structure which are far older than capitalism'.[20]

The argument of these writers is that we must make a clear distinction between socio-economic and political aspects of social structure. As Mann emphasizes, a nation-state system based on warfare was in place before capitalism developed, and constituted part of the framework for that development. While industrial capitalism has clearly generated an enormous increase in the scale and impact of war, the causes of wars continue to arise from conflicts in the state system rather than directly from capitalism. The socio-economic system is not directly militarist; it sustains the war and militarism (which are not properly distinguished, a weakness to which we shall return) generated by the relations of states.

This distinction of capitalism and state war-making is advanced by Giddens as part of a 'contemporary critique of historical materialism'. Its influence is also to be found, however, in writing more clearly influenced by Marxism, often as a unargued assumption. As an example we have the statements of Anderson that the prevalence of war-making 'does not correspond to a capitalist rationality' and that the calendars of war 'are foreign to capital'.[21] And there is a thought-out 'Clausewitzian Marxist' version of the position in the work of Kaldor, who emphasizes 'the separateness of state activity and the mode of production' and the distinct momentum of a 'mode of warfare'. She sees the rigidities of the military process as conflicting with the logic of capital accumulation, and war itself as the result of a tension between warfare and capitalism.[22]

While, therefore, the simple notion of 'pacific' industrialism has been refuted, an analytical distinction between industrial capitalism and militarism has been widely maintained. Indeed, while Mann is essentially agnostic about their substantive relations, Giddens has suggested that there is what we may describe as a rational core to the thesis of a 'pacific' industrial capitalism. He sees it as expressing a truth about the relationship between state and society, although proponents of it were led to erroneous conclusions about inter-state relations. Modern states, he believes, are essentially demilitarized in the sense that they dominate 'their' societies internally in a non-military fashion. When the state monopolizes violence really effectively, it no longer needs to *use* it in any very extensive way against groups within the population. In particular, the success of the state's claim to control the means of violence 'radically lessens the dependence of the state apparatus upon the wielding of military force as a means of its rule'. Even military regimes normalize their rule by relying less on the means that brought them to power.[23]

Giddens argues therefore that a fundamental shift took place in the relationship between warfare, states and societies with the rise of industrial capitalism. States gained unprecedented control over societies, largely completing their internal 'pacification' and establishing clear territorial boundaries. Violence within states became highly controlled compared to all previous eras. The greater control of states over societies, which limited violence within them, created at the same time a capacity for greater violence by states against one another. It is not that there is a fixed level of violence in society which has to be expressed, whether internally or externally; but the process of pacification, part of which was the establishment of what Marx called the 'dull economic compulsion' of the wage relationship, coincided with a vast increase in productive power, both human and mechanical. The availability of such resources to states meant a leap in the levels of violence possible in a more consistently 'outward-pointing' militarism.[24]

This is an extremely useful thesis, whch expresses both the tension between and the combination of the logics of capitalism, industrialism and warfare. But it is historically too great a simplification of the changing relationships of war, state and society, and therefore limited, we shall argue, as an analytical framework for discussing contemporary militarism. Two central difficulties can be identified. On the one hand, although populations may be seen as pacified, when they are incorporated in the modern state and productive systems, they are also (by contrast with traditional rural populations) concentrated and mobilized. This, after all, is the reason Marx saw the modern industrial working class as capable of a new, more disciplined kind of revolutionary violence than previous subordinate classes. In this he was not entirely wrong, as the history of the early part of the twentieth century shows. On the other hand, nothing has more concentrated and mobilized the populations of advanced industrial societies in this century than the process of fighting wars. The mobilization of societies for wars has been a double-edged process, leading to revolutionary movements of a kind which ordinary economic crises have not produced. This was something which Marx generally did not anticipate, but it gave his theory an unintended (and therefore problematic) relevance.[25]

The 'pacification' of societies by states has therefore to be seen as a very much more problematic process than Giddens suggests. Although populations may have been controlled, for the most part, without the use of military force, the class contradictions of which Marx wrote were real. They did sometimes achieve violent expression; and the task of preventing that was a major problem for states. Moreover, the concentrated external military power which states possessed generally required, before the invention of nuclear weapons, extreme societal mobilization. States sometimes used this to divert popular energies from class issues; but mobilization itself concentrated class political forces which, especially in the context of military failure, were able to challenge the existing form of state power. Revolutionary violence, it is true, has proved not to be a threat to the state as such, as Marx and others hoped; but it has altered the geopolitical relations between states as well as the power relations within them. In this sense, the separation Giddens makes between internal and external aspects of nation-states is less complete than he suggests; this is a point of considerable importance for understanding both. We shall now look at this in turn from two points of view: that of developing a sociological conception of militarism and militarization, and that of international relations theory, concerned with understanding inter-state relations.

## TOTAL WAR AND CLASSICAL MILITARISM

In distinguishing between internal pacification and external warmaking, Giddens underestimated the problems which war-making can, in turn, pose for social order. The distinction between war-preparation and militarism, which we made earlier in this chapter, was not clarified, with consequent weaknesses in the substantive argument. It is correct to argue that social order no longer depends, in most nation-states, mainly on military power. It is also true that military power is now, more than ever, a force directed primarily to the external conflicts of states. But the consequence of outward-pointing war-making and war-preparation, on the unprecedented scale made possible by industrial technology and social organization, was (in the first half of the twentieth century) a unique militarization of society. Contemporary analyses of militarization generally neglect this recent historical experience, and fail to compare current developments to – or show how they have developed from – earlier forms of war-preparation and militarism. To understand this we need more concrete historical concepts of the relationships between war, militarism and society.

If we can identify, as Kaldor suggests, a 'mode of warfare', or in Giddens's terminology, an 'institutional clustering' around warfare, the core of this, in industrial capitalist societies, is the military itself and the military–industrial sector. And yet while, at some times and in some countries, these are both relatively discrete institutional areas, in the development of modern warfare they have tended to extend their influence deep into society. In actual wars, and periods of intense war-preparation, they have dominated society: the logic of war has become the driving force of social change. In the first half of the twentieth century, war was of a new type, *industrialized total war*, with profound implications for society as a whole. There developed what can be described as a distinct mode of warfare, 'total war', and this mode of warfare determined much else in society.

Early industrialized war-preparation (from about 1840 onwards) was highly labour-intensive, like early industrialization generally, which was taking place across Europe and North America in the same period. The machines with which industrialization provided armies and navies did not supplant soldiers and sailors; on the contrary, they required greater masses of men to fight and of men and women to supply them. The rapidly growing populations of the industrial and agricultural revolutions were fed into a new mode of warfare made possible by industrialization and state control over society. Industrialized war became 'total war' in a double sense, both because mechanized weaponry and transportation enabled 'total' killing and destruction, and because expanded state control (or surveillance) of societies enabled 'total' economic and ideological mobilization.

Total war transformed industrial capitalism and socialism alike. States took control over economies as well as societies: state ownership, regulation and intervention became a basic pattern of capitalist economies – in direct consequence of total war. The contradictions of wartime participation led to opportunities for socialist movements, both revolutionary and reformist, which were never produced by economic crisis. And yet both kinds of socialism were marked, as twentieth-century capitalism has been, by the statism of total-war mobilization. The 'total' character of war mobilization was also reproduced in new 'totalitarian' models of state power, among which 'socialist' variants were some of the most extreme and the most militarist.[26]

The social and political logic of total war interacted with a strictly military logic of escalating murderousness. Once economies and societies had become part of the supply side of war – a 'home front' producing the shells, tanks and moral support needed by mass armies in a war of attrition – it also became necessary in military terms that they became targets of attack. There rapidly followed the perfection of technologies, such as tank, chemical and above all aerial war, which increased the mobility of armed forces and enabled attacks on the hinterlands of all but the most remote combatants. Through the two world wars, therefore, total war became literally genocidal. Warfare had to be, could be and was directed against the peoples themselves, since their productive capacity and ideological morale were essential military factors.

Total warfare involved from the outset a process of ideological mobilization. The late nineteenth and early twentieth centuries were the heyday of a new sort of popular militarism, closely linked to imperialism and nationalism, which developed with mass communication and education.[27] The grisly results of this militarist culture in the First World War naturally brought into question some of its enthusiasms. Militarist ideology was never revived in quite the same simple nationalist forms; it gained new strength from the contest of revolution and counter-revolution which also issued from the war. The militarism of the 1930s, by contrast with that before 1914, was overlaid with the conflict of Fascism, socialism and democracy: international conflict was fused with ideological war.

The warfare of the two global contests therefore involved a great militarization of societies at all levels. Economy and culture, as well as politics and ideology, became part of total-war mobilization. Whole peoples 'participated' in war, leading, as the theory of 'wartime participation ratios' suggests, to radical (but not always beneficial) social change. At its strongest, this participation was part of a dialectic of social revolution or reform, leading to social change within the statist framework of war mobilization. We can therefore identify revolutionary and democratic–reformist variants of total-war militarism. At its worst, however, war participation meant mass enslavement, even extermination, within militarism which was utterly destructive and devoted in the most ruthless bureaucratic way to aggrandizing the power of ruling groups.

The variety of experience of total-war militarism is something which needs to be stressed against any simple notion, whether of social improvement through war participation or of the evils of militarization. And yet the overwhelming fact of militarism, in its different forms, was there as a powerful factor in all early and mid-twentieth-century societies. The years before 1914 were dominated by the build-up to war, their popular nationalism and militarism utterly innocent of the slaughter to come. The First World War involved the most dramatic transformation of world society in history: an unprecedented international upheaval in social structure, state organization, economy, class struggle. The 'inter-war' years were but a period of war-preparation, in which the political fissures opened by the first war fed into the unresolved conflicts of states and led towards a new general conflict. The Second World War was an even more global struggle, more politicized, more destructive, even more complete in its mobilization and murderous effects on civilian populations. The decade after the war saw the rapid development of a new 'Cold War' of East and West, with swift rearmament and remobilization even before demobilization was complete.

At the end of this half-century of classical militarism, the world in the early 1950s seemed almost as militarized as at any time in the previous half-century, and this militarism seemed as likely to lead to a new global conflict. The issues in the second half of the twentieth century have appeared therefore to be much the same as in these earlier periods. An arms race threatened to lead to nuclear war between the USA and the USSR, just as a naval arms race led more than seventy years ago to war between Great Britain and Germany. Military conflict overhung society as it had throughout the century, defining the ultimate limits of culture.

The main difference – and of course it was overwhelming – appeared to be the finality of the nuclear outcome.

The nuclear age had altered more, however, than the ultimate stakes. It modified the ground rules of the world military order and the way in which war and war-preparation affected societies. In particular, it undermined classical militarism and its role in society. It is the argument of this book that while the militarism of some Third World societies reproduces the militarism which predominated in Europe in the first part of this century, the advanced industrial world (especially in Europe) has been undergoing a profound transformation in the relationship of warfare and society. Even in the Third World, to the extent that modern weaponry and forms of military organization have been adopted, the signs of this change are apparent. We have seen a differentiation and specialization of militarism, which amount to a partial *demilitarization* of societies.

As the danger of nuclear war has grown ever more awful, so the experience of militarism in Western societies has paradoxically become more indirect and vicarious. Most members of these societies have not experienced them as militarized. There has therefore been a huge disjunction between the knowledge people have had of the ultimate dangers of nuclear war, and the general irrelevance of this to their daily lives. As war-preparation has become separated from the areas of social life which involve the majority of society, so it has become more politically insulated from mass involvement, although retaining an abstract ideological potency.

## THEORY AND THE END OF THE COLD WAR

This transformation of militarism, with the partial demilitarization rather than militarization of society, has not only been inadequately understood in social theory; it is also relevant to the ways in which international relations theory has begun to incorporate sociological understanding of state power.

International relations theory, as we have already noted, has generally been based on the largely unstated assumption of a separation between the state system and societies. Indeed this has been taken so far that critical international relations theorists have recently taken an interest in sociological writing about the state, as a corrective to the one-sided perspectives prevalent in their own discipline. They have therefore discovered, in Marxist writings and even more in the work of Giddens and Mann, a useful infrastructure for their own theory. Linklater, for example, has seen recent sociology as an advance on both 'realist' and Marxist positions in international relations. Indeed he sees a 'realist dimension' in the claim (made by the new sociological theory) 'that war and international conflict have been far more important determinants of world history and social evolution than Marxism has allowed'.[28] But sociological approaches cannot, he continues, be equated with realism since they adopt the position of 'critical social theory'.

The separation between internal and external aspects of the nation-state, untheorized by international relations, is given a specific foundation in historical sociology. It is seen by Giddens as a consequence of the specialization of military power, due to the functional differentiation of the 'surveillance' and 'war-making' sides of the state. It is linked by Mann more specifically to the development of nuclear weapons: 'Contemporary weaponry has intensified the state's privacy, as military secrets are jealously protected and as abstruse computer-simulated war-games dominate the training of élites.' Publics in the nuclear age have, he argues, little knowledge of or interest in 'the private geopolitical strategies of state élites'.[29]

The danger is that sociological and international relations theory are not simply moving closer together but may actually pass each other in opposite directions. International relations theorists, on the one hand, in searching anew for the social roots of international conflict and military realities, may look for social-reductionist solutions which increasingly have been rejected in sociology. Social theorists, in recognizing the autonomous significance of state and military power, may have separated them too much from social relations. Giddens's argument, as we have already seen, in identifying military power as 'outward-pointing', neglects the 'inward-pointing' processes of militarization. Mann's position, which is more closely focused, also makes an excessive separation of geopolitics and social relations.

This is by no means a wholly abstract issue. The end of the Cold War raises particular questions of interpretation that demonstrate the concrete importance attached to it. One major issue is the role of social movements in international relations. Realist

writers in international relations theory have always emphasized
the autonomy of states as actors in the international system. The
new social theorists, more surprisingly, seem to have conceded
this point. Giddens seems to deny the capacity of other social
forces to affect inter-state relations decisively, when he argues
that 'no plausible "dialectical counterpart" to the progressive
accumulation of military power seems to exist'.[30] Mann puts
forward a similar case when he argues that 'class politics and
geopolitics are separable', and that the historical linkage 'between
national and transnational class struggles, and international geopolitical confrontation' can (and should) be rendered obsolete.[31]

Clearly, the types of social inputs into international relations
Mann has in mind are the conflict between 'capitalism' and
'socialism', and the way in which the East–West conflict has been
seen in some quarters as an extension of class struggles between
the working-class movement and capital. On the first issue, the
East–West conflict has been partly a conflict of interests, as Mann
suggests, between two superpower states and their blocs; but it
also involved, if not a conflict between capitalism and socialism,
then a conflict between two socio-economic systems, the regulated
free-market capitalism of the West and Stalinist 'state socialism'.
The overthrow of the Stalinist political system has been simultaneously the opening up of Eastern Europe and the USSR to
Western capitalism. On the second point, although Mann is right
to dismiss the hackneyed ideologization of the Cold War in terms
of class interests, there *were* social and political conflicts within
Eastern and Western states which interacted with the inter-state
conflicts. Narrowly, class conflicts over wages and social conditions may have had little effect on international relations, but
broader social movements have clearly influenced the East–West
conflict.

This is a complex issue: states retain a great deal of autonomy,
as realists and new social theorists alike assume, and may for the
most part conduct their affairs in the sort of 'geopolitical privacy'
to which Mann refers. But under certain conditions, social movements may have important and even decisive impact. The Western
European peace movements of the early 1980s clearly failed in
their immediate and short-term aims of forcing NATO states to
abandon cruise missiles. The initiative for arms control and disarmament eventually came with a change of political regime in
the USSR, and for motives connected primarily with the domestic

economic cost of the arms race. But the peace movements could nevertheless claim to have influenced state actors at a number of levels: possibly in that their mobilisation emphasized to Gorbachev and his supporters, before they took power, the anachronism of Brezhnev's European policy; certainly in that they prepared Western opinion to be sympathetic to Gorbachev's initiatives; and finally, and most importantly perhaps, in that they stimulated small but influential unofficial peace movements in Eastern Europe in the early 1980s, which in turn influenced the democratic revolutions of 1989.

The case of the Eastern European democratic upheavals is an even more crucial example of social movements' influence on international relations. Certainly US–Soviet détente clearly prepared the way for the Eastern European changes, and Gorbachev's policy of non-intervention by the USSR was a necessary condition for them to occur at all, let alone peacefully succeed. Nevertheless, this greatest single break in the Cold War system occurred through popular action. Stalinism in East Germany, Czechoslovakia and Romania was not 'reformed away' by the party-state, but overthrown by the people. Even where, as in Hungary, Bulgaria, Yugoslavia and Albania, the party took greater initiative in reform, the pace was clearly set by oppositional alliances and embryonic parties. The Berlin Wall was not removed by East–West negotiation, but broken through as a result of the action of the people, on the streets of Leipzig, Berlin and other cities.

These experiences clearly question the received wisdom of both international relations and social theory. There is a more complex interaction than has been allowed, between social forces and inter-state relations. As far as international relations theory is concerned, it has been demonstrated once and for all that there are actors other than states in the international system. As for social theory, clearly there has been an overemphasis (in reaction to Marxist socio-economic determinism) on the autonomy of the geopolitical, and an over-simple view of the 'external' character of military power.

These points are relevant to an even larger issue which needs re-examination in the light of the changes which have taken place. Classical social theory, as we have seen, raised the possibility that industrial society would be inherently pacific. We know now that no simple connection can be made: Marxists have argued that, in its capitalist form, industrialism leads to competition which leads to military rivalry; Mann has argued that industrialism and capitalism are irrelevant except to the technology of war, that geopolitics is what counts; and Giddens has argued that pacification is internal to the nation-state, while externally there exists the war-regulated anarchy familiar to international relations 'realists'.

The new international situation of the 1990s raises the prospect that a 'peaceful' industrial society might come into existence throughout the northern hemisphere. This could incorporate North America, both former halves of Europe, the USSR, Japan and Australasia – and even extend to include other areas of the Pacific Rim, Asia and Latin America which are increasingly participating in the global industrial economy. Within this industrial world, political conflicts may in future be resolved through a network of security agreements, increasingly institutionalized through formal arrangements. War may become increasingly unthinkable between states within these institutions. Instead, complex political understandings will facilitate increasingly open trade and economic interdependence, which in turn will reinforce security interdependence and work against reliance on war and military rivalry. The model for this new world will be the economic union of Western Europe which, in less than half a century, has turned former military enemies into closely interconnected partners.

This prospect, of course, is not inevitable: if the vision of a war-free industrial society is realized, this will not be the automatic result of technology, market relations or the capitalist social system (in this sense no one should revert to the nineteenth-century models). If it is achieved, it will result (as the European Community has) from political agreements between states. It will involve abrogating much of the autonomy of separate nation-states, and creating supra-state structures of complex kinds, in which part of the power classically centralized in each nation-state is transferred to higher-level structures. In Mann's terms, geopolitical rivalries will be overcome by agreement, so that industrial capitalism can develop without being confused by interstate military rivalries.

In Giddens's terms, pacification is being extended from the level of single nation-states to larger units, such as the European Community, and the potential exists to extend this to the much larger world of northern industrial society. It is even possible to envisage that if this richer, more powerful half of world society sustains this development, it will in the longer run transform international society as a whole, leading to a hitherto unthinkable pacification of the Third World as well. It must be stressed, however, that such developments can occur only as a result of political agreements: they must involve a partial pacification of nation-states themselves by supranational state institutions. There is no automatic social trend that will produce a peaceful world in the twenty-first century: only a possibility which states may be able to realise, and which social movements can influence states towards.

If this sort of development occurs, the role of military power in society could be altered enormously in the medium and longer term. Military power exists, in the last analysis, to further the interests of states in the state system: its role will alter if there are fundamental changes in that system. Its consequences for relations within societies, with which this book is concerned, will equally be altered, in ways which will be of central importance to both sociology and international relations. The middle chapters of this book attempt to analyse the relationships between military power and society as they have developed in the 'post-war' period. I shall return in the final chapter to some of the very radical ways in they may now change.

# Notes

1  Andrew Ross, 'Dimensions of militarisation in the Third World', *Armed Forces and Society*, 13 (1987), pp. 562–4.
2  Raymond Williams, *Keywords* (London: Fontana, 1976).
3  For example, Michael Howard, *War in European History* (Oxford: University Press, 1976); *The Causes of Wars* (London: Allen & Unwin, 1985).
4  Darryl Roberts, 'War and the historical formation of states: evidence of things unseen', in Martin Shaw and Michael Banks, eds, *The State in International Relations* (Hemel Hempstead: Harvester–Wheatsheaf, 1991).
5  For example, Arthur Marwick, *War and Social Change in the Twentieth Century* (London: Macmillan, 1977) and William H. McNeill, *The Pursuit of Power: Technology, Armed Force and Society since AD 1000* (Oxford: Blackwell, 1982).

6 Martin Shaw and Colin Creighton, 'Introduction', in Creighton and Shaw, eds, *The Sociology of War and Peace* (London: Macmillan, 1987), pp. 1–13.
7 Alfred Vagts, *A History of Militarism, Civilian and Military* (1937) (London: Hollis & Carter, 1959).
8 Stanislav Andreski, *Military Organisation and Society*, 2nd edn (Berkeley: University of California Press, 1968).
9 Melvin Small and J. David Singer, *Resort to Arms: International and Civil Wars 1816–1980* (London: Sage, 1982).
10 For a fuller discussion of total war, see below and also Martin Shaw, *Dialectics of War: An Essay in the Social Theory of War and Peace* (London: Pluto, 1988).
11 Ross, 'Dimensions of militarisation'.
12 Ibid., p. 564.
13 Robin Luckham, 'Of arms and culture', *Current Research on Peace and Violence*, VII, 1 (1984), pp. 1–64.
14 C. Wright Mills, *The Power Elite* (New York: Oxford University Press, 1956) and *The Causes of World War Three* (London: Secker & Warburg, 1959).
15 Andreski, *Military Organisation and Society*.
16 Marwick, *War and Social Change*.
17 Michael Mann, 'Capitalism and militarism', in Martin Shaw, ed., *War, State and Society* (London: Macmillan, 1984), p. 25.
18 McNeill, *The Pursuit of Power*, chaps 7–8, pp. 224–307.
19 Anthony Giddens, *The Nation-State and Violence*, vol. 2 of *A Contemporary Critique of Historical Materialism* (Cambridge: Polity, 1985), p. 5.
20 Mann, 'Capitalism and militarism', pp. 28–9.
21 Perry Anderson, *Lineages of the Absolute State* (London: New Left Books, 1974), pp. 31–3.
22 Mary Kaldor, 'Warfare and capitalism', in E. P. Thompson et al., *Exterminism and Cold War* (London: Verso, 1982), pp. 261–88.
23 Giddens, *The Nation-State and Violence*, p. 192.
24 Ibid.
25 Engels did indeed foresee something of this: see the discussion in Shaw, *Dialectics of War*, pp. 51–3.
26 I have argued this more fully in *Dialectics of War*.
27 John MacKenzie, *Propaganda and Empire: The Manipulation of British Public Opinion 1880–1960* (Manchester: University Press, 1984).
28 Andrew Linklater, *Beyond Realism and Marxism* (London: Macmillan, 1990), p. 168.
29 Michael Mann, 'War and social theory', in Creighton and Shaw, eds, *The Sociology of War and Peace*, pp. 67, 70.
30 Giddens, *The Nation-State and Violence*, p. 326.
31 Mann, 'War and social theory', p. 71.

# 2

## CONTEXTS OF MILITARY POWER

Throughout the twentieth century societies, and the human beings who make them up, have existed in a framework of nation-states. Despite a profound internationalization of economy and culture, political boundaries are still, for the majority of purposes, the boundaries of societies. Most of the activities within societies are conditioned by the international framework of states. War and militarism, in particular, do not emerge directly from the internal relations of societies, however much they may be influenced by them. They, more than most social activities and institutions, are the products of the international state system. In order to understand the pattern of war, war-preparation, militarism and militarization in society, we need first to examine the nature of the international order.

Although war-preparation has become a basic part of economic and social structures, it remains first and foremost a means of state power. However destructive its consequences for society, war as a social institution continues to exist because it is still regarded by states as a necessary extension of policy. If, as can well be argued, war is increasingly a social anachronism, the problem will not be resolved simply by pointing this out. War will be ended, if at all, only when states (and those who wish to establish or take over states) no longer see any necessity for or advantage in organized violence. This obviously requires alternative methods of resolving conflicts in the international system.

These fundamental truths, which underlie much writing in

strategy, international relations and peace studies, need to be remembered in a sociological study of war and militarism. The direct rationales for war and war-preparation arise from the interests and policies of states (and aspirant states) in relation to one another. This is the starting point for analysis, and this is why this chapter is about the international system in general and the military order in particular. We need to understand how the international relations between states have changed in order to grasp the pattern of war and war-preparation, and with them the social relations of warfare.

The international political and military orders are not, however, self-sufficient arenas of rivalry between states. As state power has grown in magnitude and in its ability to dominate society, it has also become more dependent on society for its resources. All-out warfare in particular has shown that a state is only as powerful as its economy; and in order to mobilize its economy to the full a state needs to mobilize its society in the cultural, political and ideological senses. States often face the fact that although military power is directly concentrated in state institutions, socio-economic power is both more dispersed and more dependent on international relationships outside the control of an individual state. Although societies are indeed bounded by states, they are also interconnected by many relations which undermine the integrity of individual states. To understand international relations in the political and military senses, we need to understand too the international economic and cultural contexts in which these are situated.

If the international state system is the best starting point for understanding war and militarism, this reflects analytical convenience rather than a belief that these can be explained wholly in terms of the state-system. We need to bring socio-economic relations into the picture from the outset, in order to give a full picture of how and why relations between states have changed. A further complication is that militarism itself enters into socio-economic relations: for example, an overconcentration of economic resources in the military may weaken an economy; or the militarization of a society may restrict its capacity for scientific or technological innovation. In the long term such factors will in turn have political and military implications. In this light it becomes clear that any starting point is in a sense arbitrary, since the interrelationships between military, political and socio-economic forces are such that each constantly affects the others.

In choosing the state system as our starting point, therefore, we are simply beginning from the level of the world order which most directly generates war and militarism. We are recognizing that it is states, not societies or economic systems, which prepare and fight wars for their own ends. It is states which, first of all, concern us: but states operating in a socio-economic context, and states whose military activities will feed back through socio-economic mechanisms into their abilities to sustain themselves in the longer term.

## THE STATE SYSTEM

States do not exist in isolation from one another: there is no such thing as 'the state', beloved of political, sociological and Marxist theory. Rather, there are systems of states, or state systems, within which the relations of states shape the form and internal organization of each particular state. The European state system which evolved from the Middle Ages, with regular warfare as a means of resolving conflicts, led to the creation of modern nation-states. Nation-states linked society and state in a more active relationship, the closer identity often bonded by war. The transition to a Europe of nation-states was accelerated in the nineteenth century under the impact of the French Revolution and the continental wars that followed it. Although there was no major European war in the century between the conclusion of the Napoleonic Wars and the outbreak of the First World War, a system of nation-states was consolidated through several limited continental wars and the uninterrupted process of colonial conflict.

The socio-economic changes brought about by the rise of capitalism, and later industrialism, clearly fed into this system of nation-state militarism. The new urban masses were the main social bases of patriotism (whether revolutionary or not), and the improved means of transport and communications enabled the rural population to join in. Increased populations as a result of expanded agricultural and later industrial economies swelled armed forces, first in France, later throughout the continent. The growth of bureaucratic organization enabled states to manage, however erratically at first, the mobilized populations and more especially the new mass armies. Later in the century, railways, telegraph, the mass production of weaponry and iron warships transformed the prospects for war. Mass newspapers and mass political parties showed new ways to popular mobilization.

If economic changes created new mechanisms for war, they also changed the relations between states in the international system. Whether or not, as the argument between Marxists and non-Marxists often goes, states were actually fighting for economic interests, rapid economic changes certainly transformed the balance between them. The rise of Britian to global hegemony in the first half of the nineteenth century was based on its industrial and commercial supremacy. The rise of Germany as the major continental power, eclipsing Russia, which had dominated after 1815, was as surely based on the industrial advance of the one and laggardliness of the other. And finally, the displacement of all the European powers by the USA after 1945 was founded on American economic superiority, which was already a fact before 1914.

If economic power is the necessary foundation for military and political power, there is, however, no automatic transformation of the one into the other. The time-lag between the USA's achievement of economic leadership and its assumption of world supremacy reflects the enormous series of events that had to occur for the translation of economic into political power to become reality. Above all, of course, it was the two world wars which enabled the USA to achieve this dominance. It is worth noting, moreover, that US supremacy did not result from a specific strategic goal of US leaders; both world wars were initiated by rival states and it was the actual process of war which enabled, indeed to some extent forced the USA to realize its potential for global power. War was the means for the most profound alteration of the world political system. While economics provided the basis, it would be foolish to underestimate the extent to which it was political and indeed military struggle which actually forged the nature of the post-war world system. War actually changed the economic and social systems of the competing states quite as much as it was conditioned by them.

It is important therefore to see the extent to which political, economic and social change was *led* by war, a possibility which is hardly envisaged by most social theory. The Second World War completed a number of fundamental processes of change which had begun, but remained inconclusive, as a result of the First

World War. At the level of socio-economic structure, the war led to extensive statization and the adoption of Keynesian policies of economic management. Internationally, the war undermined the positions of all the major European powers and Japan, either through defeat or (as in the case of Britain) through dependency on the major victors. The war left one dominant global power – the USA – and only one serious if much weaker rival: the USSR. Nevertheless the war, in decisively weakening the old European empires and in blocking the emergence of a Japanese empire in Asia, paved the way for the emergence of a much larger number of states than had previously existed. Some of the new states were of potentially great importance in the world system.

If the post-war state system was bipolar, it was based on an essentially unequal bipolarity. It was not just that in the early post-war years the USSR was recovering from appalling devastation, whereas the USA was building on an unprecedented wartime boom. Nor was the inequality simply one of military technology, although the USA possessed the atomic bomb, which the USSR, in the late 1940s, was still working to develop. More fundamentally, the US economy was the largest and most advanced in the world, the Soviet far smaller (in terms of total product) and technologically backward. The USA dominated, through its direct military and economic power and through its allies, not only Latin America, but now also the major part of Europe, and much of Asia, the Middle East, Africa and Australasia. The USSR was basically a regional power with an influence in those parts of Europe and Asia adjacent to its own borders.

Both the USA and the USSR, as a major powers in the first decade after the war, based their strength on the same kinds of force which had triumphed in 1939–45. Both maintained a huge preponderance of what are now called 'conventional' forces, with massive conscript armies and basic, mass-produced weapons-systems. The development of atomic weapons, which had clearly charged the ultimate deciding factor in war, did not yet have a major effect on the overall scale and character of armed forces, which continued to resemble those of the world war. The two superpowers (as they came to be called) consolidated their positions by constructing alliances, and tested the balance of power: in Europe in the Berlin blockade and, in the Far East, in the Korean War. Although atomic weapons were available, they were not used.

The superpowers took over the position of dominant imperial powers in the post-war world. The old European imperialisms, many of whose colonies had been occupied by the Axis powers during the war, faced new pressures for independence from within. The challenge to, in some cases defeat of, and eventual withdrawal from empire faced all the European colonial powers from the 1940s to the 1970s. The process of decolonization varied considerably not only between empires but also between colonies in the same empire, and was a major (but not universal) cause of wars in the period after 1945. Britain was in some respects a more 'enlightened' decolonizer than others, and avoided the major conflicts that embroiled, for example, the French in Vietnam and Algeria, or the Belgians in the Congo. It has been estimated, however, that Britain was involved in no fewer than eighty-eight wars between 1945 and 1982.[1]

The empires of the new superpowers were of a different character from those of the old colonialisms. The USSR, itself internally a continuation of the old Tsarist empire, consolidated satellite states in the countries of Eastern Europe which had been liberated by the Red Army, primarily as a strategic buffer against future Western attack. At the point when this was achieved, in the early 1950s, the USSR appeared to dominate a unified 'Communist bloc', including China (where the Revolution triumphed in 1949) and other states such as North Korea, North Vietnam and Albania where Communist parties had achieved power independently of the USSR. But no sooner had this bloc been created than it began to fissure: Yugoslavia broke away in the late 1940s, and by the late 1950s China had broken with the USSR, and several Eastern European peoples had rebelled (albeit unsuccessfully) against Soviet domination, leading their governments to seek greater autonomy from Moscow in order to preserve some legitimacy for Communist rule.

The American 'empire' was far more extensive, but also much looser than the Soviet, and also began quickly to fragment. At its peak, in the early years after 1945, the USA clearly controlled most of the non-Communist world, industrialized and non-industrialized alike. Japan and West Germany were first occupied and then, when the trappings of statehood were returned, denied the possibility of becoming independent military powers. The rest of Western Europe accepted US economic, political and military leadership. The USA took over, in whole or part, the role of the

European powers in many of the territories that were decolonized: in Vietnam, fatefully, this meant taking over a war against the forces of national liberation. But as the USA recognized – in pursuing mostly indirect economic and political domination rather than colonial or military control – the problem of hegemony in the post-1945 world system was far from simple. Moreover, the dynamism of the Japanese and West European economies, once initial post-war recovery was achieved, meant that strong interests, independent of the USA, soon asserted themselves within the Western alliance. While Japan and West Germany were militarily restricted, France and Britain were less restrained in asserting independent military interests. The last spasms of these old imperialisms, which continued in the 1980s, may also be seen as the first expressions of a new Western European power.

More dramatically, US hegemony in the wider world system has been contested and has declined with the rise of a wide range of new powers. Third World states have come in many shapes and sizes, and it is hardly possible to encompass the entire pattern of international conflict in the Third World in a single trend – as, for example, when Marxist writers talk of the 'revolutionary struggle' of the Third World against US imperialism.[2] The process of state formation has sometimes taken a revolutionary form, and has often involved conflicts with US interests. But Third World revolutions have generally been more nationalist (and recently, Islamic) than socialist; revolutionary struggles are now often against existing independent states, including Soviet-backed regimes, as well as against US-backed neo-colonialism. US hegemony has been undermined, not principally by revolutionary struggles or by the extension of Soviet influence (which has been limited and problematic), but by the emergence of a larger number of relatively autonomous state powers with the capability for independent action in the international system. The USA and the USSR have each attempted to manipulate the complex forces at work for their own ends, but ultimately neither has been able to control the processes of international relations as a whole.

The major trend in the international system has therefore been towards fragmentation. In place of a the bipolar system, with clear US hegemony, which existed in the early years after 1945, we have a multi-polar world, in which there are many important and relatively autonomous centres of state power. The competition between the superpowers is still the dominant conflict, but it interacts with many other conflicts between states. The USA is still the major world power, and the USSR still the only other superpower (if now only in terms of nuclear weapons), but many other states have considerable leverage, economic, political and/or military. The crisis experienced by the USSR at the beginning of the 1990s has brought its status into question: the USA appears manifestly stronger, while states such as Japan and Germany (and the European Community as a whole) have clearly greater economic strength than the USSR, but the new pattern of global political and military power is still very fluid. In the Third World, states which in global terms possess very modest resources may nevertheless play a significant or even major role at a regional level, as Iraq has shown. With the dissolution of the Western colonial empires, the number of states increased, and although there are many small states intrinsically incapable of playing a dominant role, the larger Third World states increasingly have the potential to determine events in a regional context, which in turn may have a global impact.

## INTERNATIONAL RELATIONS AND WORLD ECONOMY

The relationships between economic, political and military power are, as we have argued above, crucial but never simple. The USA's military might, and hence its ability to determine much of the post-war order, rested on its economic superiority. The defeat of Germany, and the decline of Britain and France as global powers, reflected the economic weakness of these European states compared to the great North American economy. And yet the USSR was also able to emerge, despite economic backwardness, as a major victor and potential superpower.

The post-war changes have also been paradoxical, considered in the light of the relationships between economic and military power. The USSR has realized its potential as a superpower, partly owing to economic development but even more because it has devoted an above average part of its national economy to military purposes. The military share of the Soviet national product has been estimated at 12 to 15 per cent gross national product, compared to 6 per cent in the USA, although official

Soviet estimates now suggest a figure of 9 per cent.[3] The higher
expenditure on the military reflects not the expansionism often
conjured in Western propaganda, but the fact that the Soviet
economy is barely half the size of the USA's. Despite the extra
priority of military expenditure in the USSR, in absolute terms it
still falls behind that of the USA. The striking features of the
Soviet military–economic relationship are, on the one hand, that
it has managed to support superpower status at all, but on the
other that this has imposed colossal burdens. Gorbachev's disarmament policies of the late 1980s were clearly designed in large
part to free resources for economic renewal, which has been held
back by excessive military burdens.

In contrast, Japan, with an economy superior to the USSR's in
its total product – and vastly superior in its productivity – plays a
very restricted global role. Despite its status as one of the world's
major economies, Japan remains a political and military subordinate of the USA. The effects of military defeat, and the
trauma of the atomic bombs, remain. More even than Germany,
which is a major force in NATO, hosts US and British nuclear
weapons, and whose collaboration with France is essential to the
slowly emerging European military system, Japan continues to be
denied (and to deny itself) an independent global role. Although
Japanese military expenditure and the percentage of national
product devoted to it are rising, they are smaller than those
of any other major Western country, and the use envisaged for
military power is far more restricted. Japan exercises a world role
overwhelmingly through its economic penetration, which has
increased in the developed countries of Europe, the USA and
Australasia, and in many less developed countries, especially in
Asia, alike. Much of the political and military potential of Japan
remains, therefore, dormant: American leaders complain of this,
as in the Gulf War, but it is the continuing result of the defeat
they imposed on Japan in 1945.

In a paradox which is of central importance to current international relations, Japan has, however, benefited from its denial of a
military role. The Japanese economic 'miracle' rests in good part
on the fact that it has been able to invest in its civilian economy
resources which, elsewhere, are diverted to the military. Less than
1 per cent of Japan's research and development, for example, goes
into military work, compared to around 30 per cent in the USA
and the UK. These figures, as Weston and Gummett have argued,
do not in themselves explain Japan's superior economic per-

formance, but they are a striking reflection of its demilitarized consumer-goods economy which has been so successful in international competition.[4]

A similar, if less extreme, pattern can be found in Germany, whose economy has come to dominate Western Europe and has become, like Japan's, a serious rival to the USA. The economic success of West Germany, compared to France and – even more – Britain, can be explained to a considerable extent by the more drastic reconstruction required after 1945, and the restriction of its military expenditure, which removed a burden on German state expenditure which its rivals continued to bear. The reunification of Germany in 1990 has, however, removed the remaining formal constraints on German independence, and the new German state can be expected to edge cautiously towards a greater global role, both autonomously and as the leading state within a more politically cohesive European Community.

France and the UK stand out as states with medium-sized economies which have retained, and aspire to continue, major political and military roles on a global as well as regional scale. Combining residual colonial roles with nuclear arms, these two states have been involved in military operations, from the Pacific and the Falklands in the 1980s to the Gulf in 1991, bringing them like the superpowers into conflict with budding regional powers. But neither country has the economic resources to sustain a comprehensive independent military role indefinitely, and it has been argued (especially in the case of Britain) that a high military spending profile has been a cause of economic decline.[5] The important long-term question is how the ambitions of the existing European nuclear states mesh with the emerging economic union of Western Europe, in which Germany must have a major role. A united Western Europe, even more than Japan, has a major geopolitical and military potential.

The economic revival of Japan and Western Europe (especially Germany) has brought into question the political and military leadership of the USA. The USA remains by far the strongest single economy, and has sustained historically unprecedented military budgets for more than four decades. But the uneven distribution of military costs among Western states has created tensions within the West. Japanese, Western European and recently East Asian firms have eaten into markets previously dominated by US interests. The USA has recognized the economic threat, in its attempts to make Japan and Western Europe incur more of the costs of 'defence', for example in the NATO policy of raising national military expenditures by 3 per cent per annum in the early 1980s, and in the billions of dollars extracted from Germany and Japan in 1990–91, as a substitute for direct military involvement against Iraq. There was also an element of economic warfare, against Western Europe as much as the Soviet bloc, in the trade boycott imposed after the Polish coup of 1981 and in US opposition to the Soviet–West German gas pipeline. Whereas Western Europe, especially Germany, has a major interest in East–West trade, direct US–Soviet trade is a relatively minor interest, and cutting East–West economic links always harmed Western Europe far more than the USA.

In order to sustain a massive expansion of its military budget, the USA under Reagan developed an enormous budget deficit, raising interest rates worldwide. In the end, this proved unsustainable, leading to the international stock market crash of late 1987. As for the USSR, so – if in a less extreme fashion – for the USA: massive military spending has created economic problems that have forced political leaders to look for ways of reducing it. Thus there were, on both sides, economic reasons (although they were not the only reasons) for the unprecedented disarmament process of the late 1980s. But it cannot be assumed that states will always recognize and act on a potential mismatch between economic and military resources; the temptation to overreach militarily is always there, especially for a dominant imperial power.[6] Short of an all-out war in which all major states are forced to increase their military burdens correspondingly, rearmament may remain unilateral and thus damage the economic interests of the heavily armed powers.

The changes in the world economy since 1945 have included major transformations of what, for want of a better term, we still call the Third World. The largely non-industrialized continents (Asia, Africa, Latin America) were, of course, by no means uniform in their level of economic development in 1945. The idea of an impoverished Third World exploited by the developed West was a gross simplification even at the height of its popularity in the 1960s. The huge disparities in growth rates in the 1970s and 1980s have led to attempts to separate out groups of states according to their level and form of development. The continued growth of some relatively advanced larger states in Latin America and the rapid industrialization of some smaller East Asian states has led to the distinction between 'newly industrializing countries' (NICs) and the larger number of poorer, 'underdeveloped' states. At the same time the vast increase in oil prices in the 1970s (only partly reversed in the 1980s) gave rapid new economic leverage to the oil-producing states in the Organization of Petroleum-Exporting Countries (OPEC).

The NICs and OPEC countries are both groups of states whose economic success has created a political and military potential. Nevertheless, many NICs and OPEC states (including some of the richest in per capita terms) are small states with little or no capacity for regional domination or even influence. Aggregate economic resources, rather than per capita wealth, remain more reliable indicators of geopolitical significance. This is not least because military strength in the Third World still depends to a much greater extent than in the industrialized north on sheer manpower, which in turn depends on population.

Thus among Middle Eastern OPEC countries, populous Iran developed (under the Shah) into a formidably armed regional power, a 'sub-imperialism', to quote Halliday.[7] When the Islamic Revolution temporarily undermined this military strength, Iraq attempted to take over its neighbour's role, attacking Iran in 1980, and (partly to offset the disastrous economic effects of this first war) annexing Kuwait in 1990. The wealthiest oil state (Saudi Arabia), on the other hand, with a small population, has remained militarily vulnerable despite its ability to buy the most advanced Western military technology. The massive US-led operation to restore Kuwait and defend Saudi Arabia in 1990–1 was the culmination of their historic weakness *vis-à-vis* their more populous and therefore militarily powerful neighbours, which has been visible since the 1970s.

The largest non-OPEC countries, not usually classified as 'newly industrializing', are also militarily most important. China, with a population easily exceeding those of the USA, USSR and European Community combined, cannot but be a great power; likewise India, Pakistan and Indonesia, although all very poor countries in terms of living standards, are important regional powers. Even Vietnam, which has neither a large population nor a buoyant economy, is nevertheless a regional power to be reckoned with in South East Asia.

Taken together, there are therefore three main trends which indicate a transformation of the position of the Third World in

the global system. First, often taken for granted but a precondi-
tion for other changes, has been the achievement of independent
statehood in most territories. This is the most fundamental form
of fragmentation in the world system, which has multiplied the
number of states to the present total of around 165. Formal
political independence, while it hardly guaranteed real economic
independence (so far the radical critiques of the 1960s were
correct), nevertheless provided a framework in which, given other
favourable conditions, major changes could occur. It was a necessary if not sufficient condition of economic, political and military
development. Second, there is the achievement (very much against
the hypotheses of 1960s dependency theories) of a substantial
degree of economic development in many parts of the so-called
Third World. Third, there is the emergence of regional, and in
some cases potentially global, political–military powers among
these states.

While formal political independence is near-universal, however,
economic growth and geopolitical–military power are extremely
uneven in their development. There is, moreover, no simple or
direct association between the incidence of these two trends.
Economic development in the NICs has taken place against the
background of a situation in which, in the 1980s, overall growth
rates in developing countries have been lower than those in the
industrialized world. In many poorer countries, growth rates have
fallen and even become negative; in many of the OPEC countries,
too, the 1980s have been a decade of crisis as oil prices have
plummeted from the heights reached in the 1970s. The growth of
military power has been directly affected by these trends, as we
shall see. But it is affected by other factors, such as population,
regional rivalries and major power involvement, which are not
dependent simply on economic growth. The NICs of the Pacific
Rim are small, even city-states (such as Singapore and Hong
Kong), and therefore inherently unlikely to become regional
military powers.

The processes of economic, political and military change in the
Third World must therefore be looked at specifically, taking
account of the interactions between different forms of power
in various national and regional contexts. The complexity and
variety of these situations make the concept of a Third World a
loose residual category, not an analytical tool, which becomes

apparent once we look more closely at the patterns of war and military power in the contemporary world.

## THE 'WORLD MILITARY ORDER'

The global distribution of military power, which is at the heart of the 'militarization thesis', is often presented as constituting a 'world military order'. Where this term is used, as for example in the collection by Kaldor and Eide,[8] it is rarely defined. The theoretical purposes of the available presentations of military statistics are often unclear. Indeed the more authoritative sources, in eschewing bias, are often at pains to deny any purposes beyond 'information'. And yet the ways in which we present information clearly reflect the way in which we perceive the world. The Yearbooks of the Stockholm International Peace Research Institute (SIPRI), to take as an example one of the most respected sources, contain a great deal more information about military expenditure and about weaponry than they do about armed forces and military personnel.[9] This seems to reflect an implicit belief that technology is of greater importance than manpower in modern warfare – which may be true of war involving the super-powers and other advanced industrial states, but is not necessarily so valid for many intra-Third World conflicts. This may reflect, therefore, a theoretical bias towards the nuclear arms race, and possibly towards the arms trade rather than actual wars in the Third World. It may also reflect the political perspectives of the concern with disarmament (overwhelmingly focused on weapons rather than size of armies) in peace research.

What this example shows is not, of course, that the actual facts provided by SIPRI are suspect or bias; some other major sources are considerably less explicit about their purposes than SIPRI but still provide useful and reliable information. It does mean that information about the world military order usually reflects un-stated ways of conceptualizing it. Analyses of this order can be divided, from a theoretical point of view, into those which view military facts as aspects of international economic relations, as aspects of international power relations between states, and, finally, those which look at them from the standpoint of their implications for possible wars. Only the last can strictly speaking be said to constitute a distinct 'world military order'. And yet analyses, both in the main statistical sources and in the academic literature, tend to conflate these dimensions of military power.

The problem arises because of the nature of military power. All forms of power have manifest and latent functions, direct and indirect consequences, and implications for institutional orders other than those within which they are most obviously exercised. But military power is unique in that its most direct and manifest function, the waging of war, is relatively infrequent. Small and Singer's mammoth study of wars in the nineteenth and twentieth centuries found that only five nations were involved in an average of more than one war per decade.[10] Many wars, moreover, are relatively minor and involve only a fraction of a state's armed forces. And even within wars, often only a small part of the time in which forces are deployed is spent in actual fighting. So that battle, which military theorists from Clausewitz onwards have seen as the essence of war, occurs rarely; even war is fairly uncommon in the existence of most armed forces.

Most armed forces therefore exist within states which are not at war, or even likely to go to war in the foreseeable future. Military power is thus evaluated, by states and also by the military itself, in economic and political as much as strictly military terms. For states, the costs of military power (both to themselves and relative to their rivals), or its role in international and domestic power relations, may be quite as important as its use in war. The military's ability to gain resources (weaponry, manpower) or political power may be quite as important a consideration for its leaders as its preparedness for battle.

Much of the available information about and analyses of military power reflects these often competing perspectives, but without distinguishing between them. Of course, one would not wish to suggest that economics, politics and war are ultimately wholly separate realities. Just as military power has economic and political significance outside war and potential war situations, so economic power is a critical factor in war, and war can indeed be seen as 'the continuation of policy by other means' (although, as Clausewitz well knew, it is much more than an extension of politics). But these three forms of activity – economics, politics and war-making – have different ends and characteristic means, and we can examine military power in relation to each in turn.

Many analyses of the world military order are focused on its economic dimensions. *The Military Balance* begins its country-by-country surveys with information about defence expenditure in the context of gross domestic product, inflation, debt and population.[11] Only then does it provided details of military personnel and holdings of weapons. The *SIPRI Yearbook*s are generally even more concentrated on world military expenditure, arms production and the arms trade, at the expense of, as has already been mentioned, information on military personnel, although the military potential of advanced weapons systems is always very well covered. A whole school of defence analysis, notably from left, is concerned with the political economy of military expenditure. There seem to be two main motives for this: the specific Marxist-inspired theoretical belief that economics should be the prime mode of explanation of militarism (as of social and political phenomena in general); and the wider concern with the diversion of resources from economic development, the relief of global poverty and other social problems.

Spending figures show the relationships between economic and military power. In 1988, according to SIPRI, gross figures for military expenditure of the major Western countries (in billions of 1986 US dollars) were USA 267, France 29, West Germany 28, the UK 26 and Japan 21.[12] These figures, which show that US spending is nine to ten times that of each of the three major European military powers, and more than twelve times greater than Japan's, give a rough general measure of overall military capacity. That these disparities in military expenditure clearly distort underlying differences of aggregate economic power is shown by the proportions of gross domestic product devoted by each power: the USA's might reflects both its gross economic superiority and a higher level of military spending (6 per cent); the UK achieved near-parity of military spending with its European rivals only by virtue of devoting 4.4 per cent compared to France's 3.8 per cent and West Germany's 3 per cent; Japan, with its very strong economy, needed to devote only 1 per cent of gross domestic product (GDP) to military purposes to come close to the major European levels of gross military expenditure.[13]

Another measure SIPRI provides is per capita military expenditure; this reflects a combination of military commitments and economic strength, and is interesting to study in relation to the proportion of GDP devoted to military expenditure. In Europe some the highest percentages of GDP are achieved by less affluent countries: for 1988, Greece 6.6 per cent, Turkey, 4.1 per cent, East Germany 5 per cent. Of the major Western European countries, only the UK approaches these levels of spending. These high proportions of GDP do not, however, result in the highest levels of per capita spending; nine Western European countries (NATO and neutral), led once again by the UK, were ahead of the first of these 'high' military spending states (East Germany) in an earlier SIPRI survey.[14] These facts illustrate the fairly obvious but important points that the most advanced Western economies support high levels of military activity without, as economies, becoming dominated by military expenditure; while weaker economies, such as those of Eastern and southern Europe, and even more in the Third World, can sustain high levels of military activity only by means of devoting much larger shares of national economic activity to military purposes.

These contrasts are central to a number of dimensions of the economics and politics of military power. In East–West competition, the fact that the USSR needs to devote an estimated 9 to 15 per cent of GDP (depending on the estimate one finds most reliable) to come near to matching the USA's military effort, based on 6 per cent of GDP, implies (whatever the precise Soviet figure) a huge military 'distortion' of the economy, which in turn affects its viability in a competitive world economy. In intra-Western competition, the lower levels of military expenditure in some Western European countries, and even more Japan, compared to the USA, have contributed (as we have noted) to the growth of economic and political conflicts in the Western world.

The significance of such divergences continues when we extend our analysis to the Third World. In general, Third World military expenditures remain at less than a fifth of the world total, and even those of the most powerful states do not regularly match those of the major Western states, let alone the superpowers. Nevertheless, using SIPRI figures – and acknowledging that these are 'data with a high degree of uncertainty' – Middle Eastern states have achieved expenditure levels in peak years close to those of Japan and the Western European powers. In 1979 Iran may have spent nearly $16 billion (at 1986 prices) compared to less than $15 billion for Japan and $22–26 billion for the three major European powers. In 1984 Iraq may have reached $22 billion (Japan, $17 billion; three Europeans, $26–27 billion in the same year); Saudi Arabia may have spent $21 billion in each of 1982 and 1983.[15] Late 1980s figures were tending to be lower, but the result of the Iraqi invasion of Kuwait has been to produce massive rearmament in Saudi Arabia, including a single arms deal totalling $20 billion being negotiated with the USA at the time of writing.

The more impressive levels of military spending in some Third World countries are achieved by devoting huge proportions of GDP to military ends: in the case of Middle Eastern states such as Israel, Iraq, Syria and Saudi Arabia, levels of 15 to 25 per cent (or even higher) are common. (Outside the Middle East, only one or two countries involved in civil wars, such as Angola and Nicaragua, devoted comparable levels of GDP to military purposes in the late 1980s.)[16] The economic significance of such levels of military expenditure is of course always relative and contextual, and is different in actual war compared to periods of 'peace'. In the situation of global and total war in 1939–45, in which national economies were war economies, historically very high levels of military expenditure obtained. Only when an economy like Germany's reached a level of a production for direct military purposes equal to around 70 per cent of all economic activity did this impose an intolerable strain on the civilian economy; by comparison, economies like the USA's and UK's, in which around 40 to 50 per cent of total production was devoted to the war, were quite viable.

In Third World wars, especially those which tend towards total war for the combatant nations but are limited in geographical scope, a very high level of military expenditure is likely to damage a national economy compared to others which are not involved in the war. A great deal obviously depends on the initial condition of the economy: the effects on the Tanzanian economy of the 1976 invasion of Uganda were acute because of its poor and fragile state at the outset of the war; the effects on the Ethiopian and Sudanese peoples of the civil wars in their countries have been catastrophic in the 1980s. Iran and Iraq both suffered critical economic crises during and after their eight-year war.

The economic effects of military expenditure outside actual war situations have been more controversial, with some economists arguing that a higher military burden actually has a positive effect on economic growth. A recent study concludes that despite some spin-offs from the defence sector to the civilian economy, 'In general, the econometric analysis suggests that when all the effects (spin-off, mobilization, allocation and so on) are taken into account, the net effect of defence spending on growth is negative. The result is robust and seems to hold for a large sample of LDCs.[3] A further part of the same study, using an 'entitlement approach' to welfare, concludes that 'military spending must be detrimental to economic well-being, although it does have some positive economic benefits'.[17] There are obvious exceptions to this, such as Israel and South Korea, where there has been an association of high military spending and rapid economic growth, but these are cases where there has been a large external subsidy to the military effort.

A striking result of West's study reinforces the evidence from Europe we have already cited, that the less affluent countries tend to have higher proportional military expenditures. His conclusion is that:[18]

> Among oil-importing developing economies, the richer countries (upper-middle income) tended to have lower defence burdens, and lower growth rates of defence burdens, relative to the poorest countries (low and lower-middle income). It seems that poverty per se is not sufficient to restrain military spending nor is defence a luxury good whose share [in GDP] is reduced as income falls.

The larger military establishments and arsenals of some of the better-off Third World countries are achieved, therefore, with less military domination of the economy than those of many of the poorest countries.

These conclusions are reached by means of comparative statistical, macro-analyses of national economies. An alternative, more qualitative approach is to look at the relationships between military–industrial sectors and the rest of the economy. Kaldor has described the nature of modern military technology as increasingly 'baroque'.[19] She argued that, largely because the most advanced weapon systems had not been fully tested in war since 1945, the tendency had been for armed forces and arms-producing firms to seek constant refinement of ever more complex systems. The results were systems which were so sophisticated that they required more and more maintenance to remain operational, and were likely not to work when finally exposed to battle. The other side of this ever-growing sophistication of weaponry was a declining fit between military and civilian technology. Whereas the typical weapon systems of classical total war – the machine gun, tank and bomber – were mass produced in a similar way to major civilian commodities, the missile systems of the late nuclear age involved technologies far beyond direct affinities with civilian production. Military technology, which led the economy in the Second World War, had now become a constraint on economic growth.

Kaldor argued that this conclusion does not apply only to Western countries like the USA, which led in military technology. The world military order, with the competitive pressures on states to match one another's arsenals, meant that anachronistic military technology was widely diffused. The Soviet economy, even more than the American, was distorted by investment in baroque military technology. In Third World countries the import of Western military technologies was often all the more discordant with economic development. For a country without an advanced modern industrial sector to import expensive modern weapons systems, or indeed to attempt to develop its own sophisticated military sector, created a huge divergence between the military and civilian economies. At the very least, it diverted scarce foreign currency into the military sector, often without any appreciable spin-offs to civilian economic development.

Nevertheless, the increased military spending of Third World countries in the 1970s, which overall was only slightly reversed in the 1980s, fuelled a very substantial increase in the global arms trade. The oil price boom, which created a fairly sudden and very substantial influx of petro-dollars into a number of states in the Middle East and elsewhere, was a major factor in expanding demand for arms. This growth was not confined to OPEC countries, however, and reflected a general rise of competitive military ambitions in Third World states. The diffusion of more advanced military hardware became both a major market and a major means of political leverage for arms-producing states.

The main suppliers in the arms trade are the superpowers, the major Western European states and China. Between 1982 and 1986, according to SIPRI, the USA accounted for 34 per cent of total arms exports, the USSR for 30.5 per cent, France 12.1 per cent, the UK 5.5 per cent, West Germany 4.4 per cent, China 3.1 per cent and Italy 2.5 per cent. Globally, 69 per cent of arms exports went to Third World countries. The UK (66 per cent),

West Germany (63 per cent) and, most importantly, the USA (only 51 per cent) saw a lower than average percentage of their exports going to the Third World. However, the USSR (with 76 per cent, the largest arms exporter to the Third World), France (86 per cent), China (97 per cent) and Italy (98 per cent) all exported arms overwhelmingly to Third World countries. On the one hand, this reflects the existence of a large market within the West for the most sophisticated US, UK and West German arms. On the other, it follows from the policy motivations of the arms-producing states: for political as well as commercial influence in the Third World, in the cases of the USSR and China, and for sheer commercial benefit, in the cases of France and Italy. In France, above all, a massive industry has been built on the Third World arms trade. British weapons, generally more sophisticated and higher priced, have found a less ready market, although there has been an attempt in the 1980s to design weapons especially for the Third World market.

Despite the decline of oil prices, all but one (India) of the five biggest arms importers in the mid-1980s were still Middle Eastern states (Iraq, Egypt, Syria and Saudi Arabia). These states, more-over, took between them an increasing share of the Third World trade (47 per cent between 1982 and 1986), their increased imports masking a general decline, especially in Africa and Latin America. An increasing number of Third World states have, however, begun to establish their own arms industries, either to mass produce cheap basic weaponry or to produce weapons (including nuclear arms) that the major arms producers will not so readily export. Some Third World countries have themselves become arms exporters (Israel, Brazil, Egypt, Singapore, Indonesia) or re-exporters (Jordan, Libya, North Korea, South Korea). These are significant mainly in cases (such as Iran and Iraq during their war) in which, for political reasons, the major exporters restrict their supplies. Total Third World arms supplies were 3.3 per cent of global exports in 1982–6: a significant percentage but, even taken together, still small by comparison with the major suppliers.[20]

## POLITICS OF MILITARY POWER

Many of the economic contradictions of the international distribution of military power reflect political rather than specifically war-related realities. These are of two main kinds: those related to international politics, and those reflecting national political situations. Although military force always has a potential for use in war, there are many situations in which states maintain military power as much for political reasons as for military effect. Particularly because of the characteristic difficulty of regularly using much military force, even definitions of its potential military use often reflect political goals rather than a rational military assessment.

Nowhere is this more true than in the relationships between the nuclear-armed states, both the superpowers and the other established nuclear states. Although nuclear weapons certainly have actual and potential military functions, both as deterrents and in the use that is envisaged in war, it is highly arguable that these military functions are subordinate to essentially political and ideological purposes. This is true, not so much in the rational Clausewitzian sense that war is an extension of politics by other means, but in the sense that nuclear weapons have a political and ideological significance essentially separate from any rational military use. The collapse of the Cold War, which has deprived nuclear war-plans of any political rationale, has increased this separation of weapons from strategy, leaving them as totems of superpower or great power status – a status which, on any other measure, seems to be less and less valid for the USSR.

Thus in the nuclear arms race between the superpowers, the competitive development of weaponry has been only partly related to the specific military advantages of different systems, or to the purposes they serve within a framework of deterrence. It has also reflected the thrust from scientific and technological development, and above all the political relationships between the powers, the way these are conceived ideologically, and the role of weapons in them. Thus it has been a political need, although this has taken different forms in each case and at different moments in the history of the arms race, for each power to be seen to be equal, or superior, to the other in weaponry. This, combined with the incremental impetus of weapons development, helps to explain the development of nuclear weaponry beyond what is rationally 'usable' or even what is rational in terms of deterrence.

The possession of giant, militarily dubious nuclear arsenals has had the political function of defining US and Soviet power, not only to their political–military elites themselves and to each other, but also to their subordinate allies, to states outside the blocs, and to the peoples of the superpowers. Nuclear weapons define their pre-eminence in the global order, and legitimate their power systems to their own peoples. In these senses they are of enormous importance in the world political system, transcending economic power (which would make Japan and West Germany superpowers), and displacing social conflicts within the superpower states.

Lesser powers also seek the political status afforded by the possession of nuclear weapons. The UK's decision to develop its own atomic bomb reflected an assumption of great power status and military–technical leadership. It followed the exclusion of the UK from nuclear collaboration with the USA after the Second World War, and its purpose was partly an assertion of British power and independence from the USA. The military definition of the function of the British bomb, consolidated in the late 1950s, followed from its development as a symbol of national power. Militarily, British nuclear weapons are still largely superfluous to NATO's immense US nuclear arsenal. The 'independence' of Britain's 'deterrent' is much more of a political symbol than a military reality, defining the UK's special role in the Western bloc and offsetting its economic inferiority to Germany and France and its relatively marginal role in the European Community. As such it is also a powerful symbol in British internal politics.

Essentially the same considerations apply to French and Chinese nuclear weapons. Although military rationales exist for them (in relation to the vastly superior arsenal of the USSR), they function much more as symbols of great power status, both *vis-à-vis* powerful neighbours and in the context of domestic politics. The unity of French parties around the *force de frappe*, like the Atlanticist nuclear consensus in Britain up to 1980, demonstrates the ideological importance of military power in national as well as international politics.

The political importance of weaponry could almost be said to be inversely proportional to its possibilities for use. Nuclear weapons are such a potent ideological force precisely because it is so difficult to conceive of their rational military use. Nuclear deterrence, while it makes some sense in relation to the use of nuclear weapons by other states, is so disproportionate to most non-nuclear situations that it has very limited applications. As is clearest in the British and French cases, nuclear deterrence is less of a military strategy and more of a doctrine of national power.

Nuclear weapons are also a symbol of national power in the Third World, and reasons of national prestige and ideology are a major factor in the drive of states to acquire them. In the absence of effective measures of disarmament, promised by the nuclear-armed states at the time of signing the Non-Proliferation Treaty, many additional states have seen nuclear weapons as a symbol of international status. Many of the states which are acquiring a nuclear weapons capacity are also, however, those involved in active regional conflicts, and we should not neglect the military purposes in their policies. In the Middle East, especially, the development of Israeli nuclear weapons (now well documented if not officially acknowledged) and of a Iraqi nuclear potential (thought to be only a few years from realization prior to the Gulf war) has had an obvious capacity to lead to use in war.

More generally, the growth of military power in the Third World has often been seen by Western critics primarily as a force for the suppression of popular discontent. The increasing aspirations of some of the more powerful states to regional dominance, and the pattern of Third World wars which is discussed below, should caution against such purely internally based explanations of military force. The majority of Third World states that have increased their military strength in the last twenty years have done so because of regional rivalries, competition and perceived threats. Much of the sophisticated weaponry which has been imported is bought primarily with a view to conflicts with neighbouring states, although the same technologies are often used to counter insurgent movements within national state boundaries. Iraq, for example, having used chemical warfare against Iran, turned the same means on its rebellious Kurdish minority in 1988; and having failed to use its forces effectively in the Gulf war, turned them with murderous effect on the Kurds and other opponents of the regime in 1991.

Nevertheless, military power clearly plays different roles in the political systems of many Third World countries from that which it plays in most industrialized societies. In northern industrialized states the military is everywhere a powerful interest group, claiming huge resources and able through its economic and political leverage to influence defence and foreign policies. In the superpowers, especially, the military is immensely strong: in the USA, through the 'military–industrial complex', and in the USSR, through a powerful military sector which has had a prime claim on economic resources. But it remains, in both systems, essentially subordinate to political power, and is powerful primarily because the states are superpowers locked into military rivalry. Only at the margins of the industrialized world, in the 1960s and 1970s in Spain and Greece and in the 1980s in Poland and Turkey, has the military played a direct political role. By contrast, in many parts of the Third World, the military is a major or dominant political force. As I argue more fully at the end of this chapter, this reflects the economic and political conditions of many states rather than their external conflicts.

## MILITARY POWER AS A MEANS OF WAR

The global distribution of military force is, we have seen, a reflection of much more than the potential for war. The 'world military order' is an integral part of the international economic and political order, and military power must be understood in its many different functions. However, although military force is often little used for long periods, and thus appears to be primarily an economic or political fact, it always has its potential for use in war, and must always, in the last analysis, be examined in this light.

The possibilities of war inherent in the world military order today are often difficult to grasp, hidden as they seem to be by the complex of international relations. Studies of the patterns of actual wars in recent decades can tell us only a limited amount, since the vast majority of the armed forces and weaponry available to states have not been committed in war. The previous peaks, or depths, of war experience can give only limited indications, because of the revolution in weaponry since 1945.

The range of theoretically possible wars is enormous, given the complexities of a fragmentary international state system with so many members, the variety of issues between them, and the range of weaponry and forces available. Most attention has been focused on what may be called the 'maximum possible' concept of war, namely, a nuclear war between the superpowers and their allies. There is general agreement on the obvious: that an all-out nuclear war would unleash massive, more or less instantaneous 'overkill'. In such a war, the majority of members of the combatant societies would be killed, most of the infrastructure of industrial civilization destroyed, and major damage would be done to the environment of the planet.

There is dispute about particular theses – for example, the 'nuclear winter' argument that nuclear attacks on industrial centres would create large clouds of dust which would block out the sun and plunge the world into sub-zero temperatures even in summer. But there is widespread agreement that even a nuclear war involving relatively limited forces (compared to the arsenals that are available) would unleash utterly unprecedented and globally disastrous killing and destruction. Openshaw et al.'s study of the effects of nuclear war on Britain examined a range of possible attacks and (without taking account of the possible effects of a 'nuclear winter') showed that all involved immense numbers of human deaths and massive societal damage.[21] Although Britain may not be entirely typical, in that it is a small densely populated country, studies have suggested similar effects even for much more dispersed societies like the USA and the USSR.[22]

Although there is little scientific disagreement that even the most limited nuclear war would be a major disaster for the whole of industrial civilization, and hence for world society, political and military leaders and thinkers, especially in the USA, have clearly continued to believe (until the end of the Cold War) that war between the superpowers could be limited in such a way that it remained thinkable – and winnable. The US strategic doctrine of 'flexible response' has envisaged a graduated use of different kinds of both conventional and nuclear weapons. US leaders indicated in the early 1980s that they believed in the possibility of a limited nuclear war confined to the European theatre.

As for the USSR, its political leaders have consistently refused to admit any possibility of a graduated or limited war, and have argued that any nuclear war would be a global disaster. But the USSR has continued to plan for nuclear war, and possesses a similar range of forces to those of the USA. US strategic planners may well be right to argue that in practice, the USSR would be prepared to engage in a would-be limited conflict. They may not be so correct in believing that a conflict could actually remain limited. Wars rarely remain within the limits foreseen by politicians and strategists, and the course of a nuclear conflict in which even a single missile would inflict massive destruction is particularly difficult to predict.

NATO and Warsaw Pact planners have also carried out regular exercises for possible conventional wars in Europe. Although in many of their scenarios nuclear weapons are quickly resorted to (and indeed this is the basis of NATO policy, which envisages the first use of nuclear weapons), in others more prolonged conventional conflicts are played out. It is likely that, if the trend of recent years towards nuclear disarmament continues, military planning may emphasize the greater likelihood of conventional wars (and not necessarily East–West conflicts). Of course, there are those in the peace movements, peace research institutes and left-wing parties in Europe who advocate conventional disarmament down to minimal armed forces, allowing only a residual form of 'non-provocative' defence. But it seems unlikely that this will be realized in the next decade; that will require a further major shift, beyond the revolution of the late 1980s and early 1990s. The Gulf war has ensured that considerable forces will now be justified by 'out of area' conflicts.

Even if all the forms of disarmament currently on the agenda are realized, the danger of a major war centred in Europe will remain as a worst case. It is still possible, if increasingly unlikely, that the tendency towards integration and détente in Europe and in Soviet–US relations could again be overridden by short-term conflicts. But these would be new conflicts with a new sort of USSR: clearly the unprecedented *rapprochement* of the late 1980s no longer depends mainly on the survival of Gorbachev. The USSR, whatever the outcome of its economic and political crises in the 1990s, is certain to be a less monolithic, more open and militarily weaker state than during the last seventy years. It is no longer realistic to believe that there will be a simple reversion to the Cold War, in the way that the more limited détente of the 1970s gave way to the 'Second Cold War' of the early 1980s. So long as the conflict of interests between the USA and the USSR remains, and they each possess historically unprecedented means of destruction, the danger of a nuclear war will not disappear – but it will become an increasingly remote possibility, unless activated by conflicts outside Europe.

War between the superpowers, centred in Europe, remains therefore the most fearful but not the most likely form of war in the foreseeable future. And Europe as a whole is unlikely to become the locus even of minor wars: although historically the most war-prone continent, and although many of the national and ethnic conflicts buried by the Cold War have now re-emerged, hardly any European state, existing or potential, will have both the interest and the means to wage war against its neighbours, considering the formidable costs this is likely to impose on the protagonists. Within Western Europe the danger of war has effectively disappeared since 1945, and is being permanently prohibited by economic and political integration. In Eastern Europe the necessities of economic and political recon-struction, including links with the West that would be lost by any state which initiated war, will serve to inhibit (if not in every case prevent) the warlike development of local conflicts. Within the USSR, inter-republican and inter-ethnic rivalries are, in the last analysis, likely to be contained by central military power, if not by common economic interests. Even in south-western Europe, where the tensions loom large and the inhibitions to open conflict appear weakest, it is likely – although not certain – that Greece and Turkey will be linked eventually in the European Commun-ity, and that even fragmenting Yugoslavia will be sufficiently dependent on the Community to contain its conflicts short of war.

Actual wars since 1945 have been concentrated almost entirely in the Third World, and they are therefore likely to remain so. Virtually all wars in which the superpowers and other major industrialized states have been involved have been in the Third World, and such intervention has been a critical factor, not least in arms supply, even if the superpowers have not generally caused the conflicts which have taken place.

As we have argued earlier, statistical analysis of the pattern of wars is of limited value, since individual wars vary so greatly that a single war – the Iran–Iraq war in the 1980s, for example – can greatly skew the averages. Small and Singer, in their quantitative study of a century and a half of war, found that 'there is no significant increase in the frequency of war and ... [that] inten-sity is essentially a characteristic of individual wars rather than of years of decades'.[23] They argue that increases in the number of inter-state wars per decade, and in numbers of battle deaths, are related to increases in the number of states in the system, and in population; when allowance is made for these factors, there is no tendency for the number of severity of wars to increase. The 'widespread belief' in an increase in the number and severity of wars they put down to the effect of modern communications in making us aware of every war in any part of the globe, and,

second, to memories of two world wars which colour our understanding. Small and Singer do admit a trend in that 'more civil
wars resulting in more nation months [of war] and more battle
deaths have been fought in recent periods than in earlier ones'.[24]
But this again is explained by the much greater number of states
in which civil wars can now take place. Small and Singer give
little specific attention to the period since 1945, however, and
their tendency to 'normalize' away the apparent increases in war
intensity in this period, due to the increase in the number of
states, begs the question.

Kende's study of war in the period from 1945 to 1976 is
therefore more helpful.[25] He found a slight tendency for the
numbers of wars to decline in this period, but a more important
shift from wars between colonial powers and insurgent forces,
which were more important in the first decades after 1945, to
various types of war involving Third World states: internal anti-
regime wars; internal tribal wars; and border conflicts. The involvement of ex-colonial and other 'foreign' forces is identified as
an important factor. (As a later study of military intervention in
civil wars in the 1970s emphasizes, the interveners are increasingly other Third World states as well as northern powers.[26])
There is also a clear relationship between war-making and state-
making in the Third World. Civil war was not just a characteristic
of the colonial period, but continues within many independent
states, in which ethnic, national or regional challenges to central
state power remain. Whereas industrialized states are generally
'pacified', as Giddens suggests, in many Third World countries
the state is far from secure in its control, and genuine nation-
states have hardly been created. Social inequalities and political
divisions fuse with national conflicts to create many possibilities
of civil war.

Studies of recent wars tend therefore to divide them into 'inter-
state' and 'civil' wars. Lists of major conflicts between 1945 and
1980 are provided in table 2.1. It will be apparent that many
inter-state wars have their origins in civil wars, or that inter-state
wars are internationalized civil wars. Moreover, as a survey of
very recent wars suggests, the similarities between inter-state and
civil wars in the Third World are often as great as the differences.
As Neuman puts it, 'Although war in the Third World appears to
vary very sharply from "modern" war (that is, armed conflict
between developed countries), wars fought between uniformed

Table 2.1   Wars 1945–1980

| *Interstate* | | *Extra-systemic and civil wars* | |
|---|---|---|---|
| Palestine | 1948–9 | Greece | 1944–9 |
| Korean | 1950–3 | China | 1946–50, |
| Russo–Hungarian | 1956 | | 1967–8 |
| Sinai | 1956 | Paraguay | 1947 |
| Sino–Indian | 1962 | Indochinese | 1945–54 |
| Vietnamese | 1965–75 | Madagascan | 1947–8 |
| Second Kashmir | 1965 | First Kashmir | 1947–9 |
| Six Day | 1967 | Hyderabad | 1948 |
| Israeli–Egyptian | 1969–70 | Yemen | 1948, 1962–9 |
| Bangladesh | 1971 | Costa Rica | 1948 |
| Yom Kippur | 1973 | Burma | 1948–51 |
| Turco–Cypriot | 1974 | Colombia | 1948, 1949–62 |
| Vietnamese–Cambodian | 1975–89 | Indonesia | 1945–6, 1950, 1953, 1956–60 |
| Ugandan–Tanzanian | 1978–9 | Philippines | 1950–2, 1972– |
| Sino–Vietnamese | 1979 | Bolivia | 1952 |
| Russo–Afghan | 1979–89 | Guatemala | 1954, 1970–1 |
| Iraqi–Iranian | 1980–8 | Algeria | 1954–62, 1962–3 |
| | | Argentina | 1955 |
| | | Tivetan | 1956–9 |
| | | Lebanon | 1958, 1975–6 |
| | | Cuba | 1958–9 |
| | | Iraq | 1959 |
| | | South Vietnam | 1960–5 |
| | | Congo | 1960–5 |
| | | Laos | 1960–2, 1963–73 |
| | | Sudan | 1963–72 |
| | | Rwanda | 1963–4 |
| | | Dominican Republic | 1965 |
| | | Uganda | 1966 |
| | | Nigeria | 1967–70 |
| | | Cambodia | 1970–5 |
| | | Jordan | 1970 |
| | | Pakistan | 1971 |
| | | Sri Lanka | 1971 |
| | | Rhodesia | 1972–9 |

Table 2.1   *(Cont.)*

| Interstate | Extra-systemic and civil wars | |
|---|---|---|
| | Ethiopian–Eritrean | 1974– |
| | Angola | 1975– |
| | Timor | 1975– |
| | Saharan | 1975– |
| | Ogaden | 1976– |
| | Afghanistan | 1978–9 |
| | Iran | 1978–9 |
| | Nicaragua | 1978–9 |
| | El Salvador | 1979– |

*Source*: Melvin Small and J. David Singer, *Resort to Arms: International and Civil Wars 1816–1980* (London: Sage, 1982) Appendix A, pp. 304–7, 312–13, 323–9. Criteria of inclusion are clarified pp. 21–76, 78, 203–20. Conflicts excluded are listed pp. 339–40.

national troops or between such troops and guerrillas seem to share many characteristics.'[27] Wars, she argues, are won or lost by ground troops, not navies or air forces; state forces use guerrilla tactics and guerrillas use conventional offensives; and wars have primarily been defensive and often protracted. (This characterization hardly fits the Gulf war, of course, in which American air power was uniquely decisive.)

This argument also appears to miss the most dangerous international development of our time. Once again, the use of the 'Third World' category blurs the distinctions which should be made. Although it is perfectly correct that there are continuities between inter-state and guerrilla warfare, the rapidly growing potential for inter-state war is a crucial tendency that deserves to be highlighted rather than merged with guerrilla struggle. The larger and richer states, especially in the Middle East but also in Asia, Latin America and even Africa, now have the arsenals and the capability for mobilization to wage impressive military campaigns. Where their interests collide with one another's, or with those of northern powers, major wars, with reverberations throughout the international system, can be expected to occur.

This potential has existed since the 1960s, as the wars between China and India and India and Pakistan first indicated. It has been manifested since the 1960s in the wars between Israel and the Arab states. It was demonstrated again, between Communist states, in the Sino–Vietnamese war of 1979. Its fullest and most devastating realization so far has been in the Iran–Iraq war of 1980–8, a war which combined a 1914–18 mass slaughter with high-technology missile exchange. Because this war failed to implicate the superpowers, except at the margins, its significance has tended to be minimized. It was widely noted, after Iraq's invasion of Kuwait, that Western interests had tended to identify with the Iraqi containment of Islamic-revolutionary Iran, missing the danger posed by Iraq's own military expansion: Iraq, like Iran, was a regional power in the making, and as an Arab state had even greater potential to destabilize the Middle East as a whole.

Iraq, however, is only one of a number of states in the Middle East and elsewhere which now have the capacity to create this sort of instability in the international system. Decades of industrialization, population growth, oil revenue flows and arms sales – not to mention transfers of nuclear technology – have created the basis for serious military power in a number of states. Many so-called Third World states have sophisticated military equipment, even if they remain dependent on the advanced world for re-supply. The Argentine use of Exocets against Britain, the Iraqi and Iranian 'war of the cities', and the (however in effectual) Iraqi Scud attacks on Israel and Saudi Arabia are recent reminders that Third World wars are not all wars of attrition between masses of foot soldiers. Regional conflicts can be major, modern wars.

Just as we can trace the emerging pattern of regional inter-state wars, culminating in the Iran–Iraq war, so we can identify a pattern of conflicts between regional powers and major Northern powers, climaxing in the US-led multinational intervention in the Iraq-Kuwait conflict. Britain and France have been involved in conflicts which derive from residues of their colonial pasts, from the Suez intervention of 1956 to the Falklands war of 1982 and the tensions in the Pacific as a result of French nuclear testing. The USA, as global policeman of Western interests, has also been involved in potentially very serious conflicts with major regional powers, such as that with Iran at the beginning of the 1980s.

It is not alarmist to see the future of war in a series of conflicts on the Iraq–Iran, Anglo–Argentinian and Iraq–USA models, with the added danger of nuclearization. It is of supreme importance, obviously, that the ending of the Cold War has created the possibility of superpower co-operation and the reinvigoration of international institutions, in order to manage regional conflicts to avoid major wars, as well as preventing these from escalating into East–West conflicts. But there clearly is a potential in the Third World, not just for civil war and border disputes, but for major war of a modern kind. The nuclear non-proliferation regime may largely hold, as a recent study suggests, so long as such conflicts are contained.[28] But it would be rash to predict that nuclear weapons will not be used, in a context of a major war in the Third World, where a nuclear-capable power feels itself threatened by conventional defeat. Chemical weapons are even more likely to be used, as many states have the capability to manufacture chemical agents. Both possibilities were clearly present, if fortunately unrealized, in the Gulf crisis of 1990.

In the multi-polar world of the 1990s, both superpowers are weaker than they were at the height of the Cold War system, and some of the regional powers are formidable military factors. Even full co-operation between the USA, the USSR, the European Community and Japan, and a rapid strengthening of the United Nations, will not remove the danger this development poses. If issues arise which strain the developing new co-operation, regional conflicts in the twenty-first century could still pose a threat of global war. The end of the Cold War does not, yet, mean that we have removed the risk of the total destruction of human society: it poses the challenge in a new form. What the post-Cold War era does mean, however, is a change in the character of military confrontations, the sorts of forces which are required, and the international political regime within which they are managed. All these changes will have profound effect on militarism within societies.

# Notes

1 Background paper, 'The Falklands crisis', *State Research*, 5, 30 (June–July 1982), p. 139.
2 See for example Ralph Miliband, 'The politics of peace and war', in Martin Shaw, ed., *War, State and Society* (London: Macmillan, 1984), pp. 119–35.

3 Jonathan Steele, 'Gorbachev comes clean on Soviet defence bill', *Guardian* (31 May 1989).

4 David Weston and Philip Gummett, 'The economic impact of military R & D: hypotheses, evidence and verification', *Defense Analysis*, 3, 1 (1987), p. 63.

5 Malcolm Chalmers, *Paying for Defence* (London: Pluto, 1985).

6 This has been argued effectively by Paul Kennedy, *The Rise and Fall of the Great Powers* (London: Fontana, 1989).

7 Fred Halliday, *Iran: Dictatorship and Development* (Harmondsworth: Penguin, 1979).

8 Mary Kaldor and Asbjørn Eide, *The World Military Order* (London: Macmillan, 1979).

9 Stockholm International Peace Research Institute (SIPRI), *SIPRI Yearbook* (Oxford: University Press, annually).

10 Melvin Small and J. David Singer, *Resort to Arms: International and Civil Wars 1816–1980* (London: Sage, 1982), p. 179.

11 International Institute of Strategic Studies, *The Military Balance* (London: IISS, annually).

12 *SIPRI Yearbook 1989*, table 5A.2, pp. 183–7.

13 Ibid., table 5A.3, pp. 188–94.

14 *SIPRI Yearbook 1987*, table 6.6, p. 134.

15 *SIPRI Yearbook 1989*, table 5A.2, pp. 183–4.

16 Ibid., table 5A.3, p. 189.

17 Sadaat Deger and Robert West, *Defence, Security and Development* (London: Frances Pinter, 1987), pp. 9–10 and 13–14.

18 West, in ibid., pp. 12–13.

19 Mary Kaldor, *The Baroque Arsenal* (London: Deutsch, 1982).

20 *SIPRI Yearbook 1987*, p. 193.

21 Stan Openshaw, Philip Steadman and Owen Greene, *Doomsday: Britain after Nuclear Attack* (Oxford: Blackwell, 1983).

22 United States Congress, Office of Technology Assessment, *The Effects of Nuclear War* (London: Croom Helm, 1980).

23 Small and Singer, *Resort to Arms*, p. 139.

24 Ibid., p. 267.

25 Istvan Kende, 'Local wars 1945–76', in Asbjørn Eide and Marek Thee, eds, *Problems of Contemporary Militarism* (London: Croom Helm, 1980).

26 Bertil Duner, *Military Intervention in Civil Wars: The 1970s* (Aldershot: Gower, 1985).

27 Stephanie G. Neuman, 'Questions? Answers? Hypotheses? Lessons? A summary', in Robert E. Harkavy and Stephanie G. Neuman eds, *The Lessons of Recent Wars in the Third World*, vol. 1 (Lexington, Mass.: Lexington Books, 1985), p. 283.

28 John Simpson, ed., *Nuclear Non-Proliferation: An Agenda for the 1990s* (Cambridge: University Press, 1987), pp. 7–8.

# 3

## POST-MILITARY SOCIETY

Classical militarism was a nineteenth-century phenomenon which reached its peak in the two world wars of the first half of the twentieth century. The rise of the nation-state, the nation-in-arms, nationalism and conscription was the context for mass militarism. Industrialization, state bureaucracy and new means of mass ideological diffusion were its essential ingredients. Classical militarism evolved, from its revolutionary origins in France to the naive patriotisms of the decades before the First World War and the ideological nationalisms of the Second. Militarism, contrary to the sociological optimists, was a defining characteristic of the 'modern' industrial social order.

Social theorists of late twentieth-century societies have begun to announce the dissolution of this industrial order. The second industrial revolution, in the first part of this century, extended mass production and consolidated large-scale organizations. The so-called third industrial revolution, which we are now experiencing, is leading, it is widely argued, to 'post-industrial' societies in which mass production and centralized bureaucracy are displaced by high-technology production and smaller-scale organizations. The dynamics of commodity production, the market and the accumulation of capital remain central, but they now favour different forms of social organization and culture. This transformation of industry, society and culture is creating, moreover, a global economic order which undermines the nation-state and emphasizes the transnationalism of information, production and markets.

It is unnecessary here to go into all the merits and demerits of this argument. Clearly the thesis can be overstated: information industries are still industries, and even in advanced Western economies there are sectors where the scale of organizations is increasing. Within the emerging global economy, moreover, there are regions (such as East Asia) in which mass-production manufacturing is rapidly advancing. The transition from industrial to 'post-industrial' societies looks more like a revision of the international division of labour, with a shift to manufacturing in parts of the Third World and to information-based service industries in the advanced countries. Nevertheless, it is important that the leading industrial sectors, in the most advanced countries, are increasingly based on electronics and computers, and that with the changes in the technological base have gone important changes in social organization, culture and politics.

There was clearly a symbiotic relationship between classical industrialism and militarism. It is wrong to see militarism as simply a reflection of industrialism. Markets, capitalism and industrialism grew within the framework of an international state system, in which military conflicts already thrived. While economic and technical changes certainly had profound implications for both the international order and military organization, they can hardly be seen as a prior cause of them. Indeed, military technologies and organization often prompted or anticipated industrial innovations. Large-scale hierarchical command structures were developed in ancient armies, at a time when production was by individual peasant farmers and craftsmen, and thousands of years before they came to typify industry.[1] Modern methods of discipline were pioneered by military leaders centuries before factories became widespread. Even assembly line production was developed for the manufacture of guns in the mid-nineteenth century, decades before it became typical of industrial production. The standardized mass production which was described as 'Fordism' by Antonio Gramsci, in the 1930s, was the application to commercial production of methods which had developed largely under the impetus of arms competition before and during the First World War.[2]

The new stage of industrial society has been accompanied – indeed, as in the past, anticipated – by new forms of military technology, organization and culture. The atomic bomb was a qualitative development of weaponry based on unprecedented scientific effort, perhaps the first 'post-modern' artefact. In 1945 the means of war were already developing far beyond the standardized mass production of tanks and bombers which had matched the 'Fordist' form of industrial production. And yet, as Kaldor argues, innovation became trapped within an increasingly hidebound form of industrial organization. Technological innovation, within the corporate and state military industries of the post-war world, became a matter of exaggerated sophistication of the weapons systems derived from 1939–45. The large systems inherited from that era – the missile and aircraft carrier as well as the tank and bomber – have been refined until many of them have become too complex for easy use in battle. In conditions of disuse, owing to the nuclear stalemate, arsenals have become 'baroque'.[3] While the technologies of the 'third industrial revolution' are clearly making possible some simpler, cheaper new weapons (for example missiles like the infamous Exocet which can destroy vastly more complicated and expensive weapons-platforms), they may also be incorporated as further refinements of the established systems.

In the military field, therefore, a simple dichotomy of 'modern' and 'post-modern', 'Fordist' and 'post-Fordist' fails to work. This is not only because high technology has increasingly dominated weapons production throughout the whole period since 1945, but because innovation has been combined with a perpetuation of a statist military sector. Nevertheless, the 'mode of warfare' has evolved beyond classical total war, and war-preparation today is very different from that of the Second World War. We shall consider, later in this chapter, the different forms of militarism in contemporary societies, north and south. But first it is necessary to look at the various forms of the pervasive thesis that there has been an extension of 'militarization' in recent years. We shall look at the extent to which the sorts of evidence which are available about militarism can justify the different arguments which have been put forward.

## VARIANTS OF THE 'MILITARIZATION' THESIS

Concepts like militarism and militarization can be given a variety of different meanings, as we remarked in chapter 1. Although the links between them should be specified, they are all too often implicit and assumed. The argument that there is a process of militarization in contemporary societies takes a number of forms, dealing with matters which are logically and empirically distinct from one another. But too often the distinctions are not made, and the common use of the term 'militarization' links together some real and significant phenomena with unfounded general assumptions about the extension of militarization.

The early example of Mills's *The Power Elite* illustrates the problem. This has often been treated in sociology as offering a general model of power in Western industrial societies, to set alongside pluralist accounts and Marxist concepts of a ruling class. In fact, it is a specific, historically informed account of power in US society, and Mills's main thesis is that a ruling elite combining the political, economic and military leaderships emerged in that society in the first half of the twentieth century. It is widely recognized that Mills gave more weight to military matters than did his pluralist and orthodox Marxist 'competitors', but Mills is generally misunderstood on this issue. What is essentially a secondary, if important, argument that the power of the military itself has dramatically increased, has been substituted for the more important thesis that the whole system of power has been militarized. Mills in fact argues – and this argument is essentially independent of the question of the military – that the emergence of the USA as a superpower, possessing the atomic bomb, has pushed military issues to the centre of the system of power, as defining issues for all sectors of the power elite. A common concern with fundamental international and military questions separates the elite from the middle and lower levels of power.[4]

Mills therefore advocates a variety of militarization thesis – before it was a widespread concern – but it is a very specific sort of militarization which he identifies. The militarization that concerns Mills affects the system of power, and specifically the position of the groups which form the elite. He is not arguing that there has been a general militarization of society, except in so far as the ideas of the power elite about war and peace – what he calls its 'crackpot realism' – dominate society. But another side of his argument suggests a tension in this relationship, for he wishes to emphasize the extent to which 'publics' of concerned citizens have been excluded, by the formation of the power elite, from any participation in these key international and military areas of power.

It has to be remembered, moreover, that Mills was writing about American society. To the extent that the USA had become a superpower, other Western states had been reduced from great power status. Military subordination clearly defined the context of power and ideology in other states – explicitly in the case of West Germany and Japan, implicitly in France and Britain. In this formal sense, their systems of power were also militarized. But by the same token, it could hardly be said that elites in these countries were concerned with global military power in the same way as those of the USA. In this more important sense, Mills's concept of the militarization of power was specific to the USA, and even implied a corresponding demilitarization of power in those countries – most notably Germany and Japan – which had lost a great deal of their international military status.

Mills was writing, too, in the mid-1950s, at a time when the dominance of nuclear weaponry in the world political and military order was becoming evident, but when neither the USA nor Britain had much reduced the level of their conventional armed forces to take account of the power nuclear weapons gave them. He was also writing when early Cold War ideology retained much of the strength which it was to lose in subsequent decades. In this sense he was writing at a moment of transition in the post-war history of military preparations, and was not able to foresee the extent to which nuclear-armed states like the USA and the UK might dispense with the military participation of society.

The early example of Mills suggests that militarization can be understood in a partial sense, the militarization of a particular social institution or group rather than of society as a whole. This distinction is not often observed, however, and there is a tendency to move from specific to general senses of militarization. A good example of this is Cynthia Enloe's important study, *Does Khaki Become You? The Militarisation of Women's Lives*. The solid basis of this book is the analysis of the way in which the military, notably in the USA and the UK, has increasingly sought to control and organize the women who traditionally have served male armed forces as ancillaries and camp-followers. Looking not only at women members of the armed forces, but at wives and girlfriends, nurses and prostitutes, Enloe makes a strong case that the military increasingly seeks information and control, rather than leaving women's roles to the women themselves or outside organizations to define.[5]

Even the first half of Enloe's title is misleading, however, since the military does not seek to put all these women into uniform. The second half is more so, since it jumps from the specific groups of women whom she discusses to suggest a general 'militarization of women's lives'. This greatly overstates the links between the specific forms of militarization of several groups of women who have a direct (and subordinate) relationship to the military, and women at large who live in what is seen by the author as a patriarchal and militaristic society. It raises but hardly starts to answer the question whether a society (and its members both male and female) in which military preparations (for example nuclear weapons) have a high political and ideological priority, can automatically be described as militarized. The description, unlike the discussion of specific groups of women, seems to serve an ideological rather than an analytical purpose. But we may question whether such a use of 'militarization' genuinely serves the interests of radical or feminist anti-militarism. For if, unlike the army wives and prostitutes, most women are not directly militarized, it may be argued that this is a positive factor for opponents of militarism.

The ambiguity over whether Western industrial societies should be seen as a militarized is a prevailing feature of recent radical analyses. E. P. Thompson, for example, in his famous 'Notes on Exterminism', has argued of the superpower societies: 'The USA and the USSR do not *have* military-industrial complexes: they *are* such complexes. The "leading sector" [weapons systems and their supports] does not occupy a vast societal space, and official secrecy encourages low visibility; but it stamps its priorities on the society as a whole.' He adds: 'Science-intensive weapons-systems civilianise the military: but in the same moment more and more civilians are militarised.'[6] Here Thompson attempts to catch the paradox of modern militarism: that while warfare becomes so destructive, and war-preparation so expensive, that it has a decisive influence on society, nevertheless the military sectors of societies are not large, even in the superpowers, and even these sectors are subject to 'civilianisation'. And yet Thompson argues that simultaneously 'more and more civilians are militarised'.

Thompson's concept of civilian or societal militarization seems to be based, not so much on the fact that military expenditure may claim a priority over other forms of state expenditure, but on the deep ideological significance of military power. 'The ruling groups', he argues, 'come to *need* perpetual war crisis, to legitimate their rule, their privileges and their priorities; to silence dissent; to exercise social discipline; and to divert attention from the manifest irrationality of the operation. They have become so habituated to this mode that they know no other way to govern.'[7]

Although Thompson is right to point to the ideological priority of military demands (at least at times of international or military crisis), this is not the same as saying that the economy, or even the ideological systems of industrial societies, are heavily militarized. The buoyancy of civilian economies, consumer culture, etc., and the 'low visibility' of military issues in much ideology and politics (to which Thompson himself refers) would suggest that this is not so. The fact that some Western states have increasingly abandoned direct state ownership of major industries reflects, among other things, a decline in the domination of economic life by strategic interests. The exterminist potential of nuclear weapons usually exerts an insidious rather than a direct militarizing effect on societies and cultures. Other than in this sense, however, people in contemporary Western societies are less directly affected by military power than members of most historical societies.

When the concept of militarization is directly advanced in the literature, as it is by a very wide range of (especially radical) writers, it most often refers to Third World societies. It has been used, however, as Ross has noted in his review, in often confused ways, to refer to a wide range of phenomena. Those which he has collected include:[8]

> a process in which increasing state resources are allocated to armed forces and/or related military activities;
>
> a steady growth in the military potential of states ... usually accompanied by an increasing role for military institutions both in national ... and in international affairs;
>
> an overemphasis on the importance of armed forces [entailing] both growing military power ... and growing military involvement in, and control of, domestic politics;

institutionalised and routinised relations between states and within states, in which military behaviour comes to be preferred [and] the preference for violent courses of action at the expense of nonviolent ways of influence;

the increase in armaments, advances in the destructive character of weapons, growing number of people under arms, and dramatic increases in military expenditure.

It is obvious that some new way needs to be found to differentiate these many different aspects of military power, and to define the process which is described as militarization. Ross tries to resolve this problem by a renewed distinction between militarization and militarism. Many writers, he argues, have failed to distinguish between militarization as a process leading to militarism (militaristic behaviour, ideological militarism), and as military build-up. He implies that we shall have greater clarity if we put the first sort of development under the heading of militarism, and reserve the term 'militarization' for the second. As we have suggested, this attempt to separate militarization from militarism is unacceptable. Clearly it is possible to refer to military build-up in terms of the militarization of international relations, or of state expenditure in Third World countries. But militarization in its broadest sense is a societal process, affecting civil society as well as the state, and it is essential to examine it in this sense.

The substantive purpose of Ross's distinction is to prepare for his argument that 'it is typically not militarism, and therefore not this first form of militarisation, that is most evident in Third World countries. What is present in these countries ... is the second form of militarisation – military build-up.' This definition, he argues, unlike some other conceptualizations, is 'relatively precise and unambiguous' and 'allows us to identify operational dimensions of militarisation'.[9] Ross then attempts to quantify militarization on the basis of six categories of indicators: military expenditures, armed forces, arms imports, arms production, wars and military regimes.

It may be argued, against Ross, that if classical militarism is evident anywhere in the late twentieth century, it is in certain Third World countries, for example in Iran and Iraq during their prolonged war and in Iraq following its invasion of Kuwait.

However, Ross's point is valid: that, even in the Third World, what is generally meant by 'militarization' is in fact not a societal process but the increase in military expenditure and accumulation of armaments, which do not necessarily imply societal militarization. In the advanced industrial countries, the disjuncture between the two forms of militarization may be even greater.

Rephrasing Ross's argument, we may agree that what is most often described as militarization in the Third World (or 'global militarization') is military build-up rather than societal militarization. Although it is possible to have military build-up without militarization, it is difficult to conceive of militarization without military build-up in some form. The argument (which Ross presents) that there is a levelling off, or even a decline, in military build-up, while not conclusive, is nevertheless relevant to militarization. If societies were not militarized in the period of more rapid military build-up, they are not likely to be so in a period when military forces are expanding more slowly or not at all.

The evidence summarized by Ross supports the case that in the Third World as a whole, military build-up peaked in the 1970s and has since fallen away. (His data are for the early 1980s, but trends did not radically alter in the second half of the decade.) Annual growth rates in the military expenditure of developing countries, which averaged 7.2 per cent in 1963–73 and 4.7 per cent in 1973–83 taken as a whole, were only 2.1 per cent in 1980–3. The slowing down was apparent in Africa, East Asia, Latin America and the Middle East, but not in South Asia.[10]

Annual growth rates in the size of armed forces were much less than those for military expenditure, in itself a measure of the investment in hardware rather than men (and hence an indicator of dissociation between military build-up and militarization). The trend, again, was a decline, from 3.8 per cent in 1963–73 to 1.3 per cent in 1973–83, and only 0.3 per cent in 1980–3. In East Asia, Africa and the Middle East the size of armed forces actually declined (on average) in 1980–3, although in South Asia, again, there was a sharp increase, and in Latin America no change compared to the decade as a whole.[11]

Ross also argues, in line with the evidence discussed in chapter 2, that the rate of arms imports into the Third World as a whole had stopped increasing in the early 1980s, after the rapid increases of the 1970s. Only in the Middle East and Latin America was it still increasing in the early 1980s (but by less than before), while in East Asia, Africa and South Asia it was falling.[12] Similarly, and also in line with SIPRI figures presented in the previous chapter, Third World arms production, despite the tremendous expansion of the 1970s, represented a very small proportion not only of global arms production but also of national economies in the Third World. Israel apart, in no country did arms production represent more than 0.4 per cent gross domestic product or 1.1 per cent of total industrial production in 1983.[13]

Of his other 'dimensions of militarization' (or military build-up), Ross finds that the trends in the numbers, length and severity of wars are unclear (again, see the discussion in chapter 2). The only dimension on which there is a clear increase is in the number of military regimes, from 33 out of 110 developing countries in 1973 to 56 out of 107 in 1985 – an increase concentrated in Asia and Africa, since the military in Latin America was less prominent in the mid-1980s than a decade earlier.[14] The increase in military intervention in politics is, of course, very significant, although not conclusive in itself, for the argument about societal militarization in developing countries, as we shall see later in this chapter.

## SOCIOLOGICAL ALTERNATIVES

If the militarization thesis is now under challenge on empirical grounds in relation to the developing world, arguments which suggest that it is inapplicable to industrialized societies have been widely advanced. Indeed, while the militarization thesis reflected the combination of Third World rearmament and arms imports in the 1970s and the nuclear arms race and resulting arms explosion in the West in the early 1980s, sociologists had already advanced a very different sort of position. Between the late 1950s and the mid-1970s, coinciding approximately with the period of détente, military sociologists had developed a fairly closely knit body of comparative work. They suggested that profound changes in the relationship of the military and society were outmoding the models of military organization and ideology which had dominated in the nineteenth century and the first half of the twentieth. Instead of the militarization of society, they posited a civilianization of the military. If anything, although they did not use the term, their analyses pointed in the direction of demilitarization as the dominant trend of the entire period since 1945.

The sociology of the military has grown by the application of ideas from the sociological mainstream (e.g. organizational theory) to military institutions. While its practitioners sometimes insist that they are concerned with the sociology of war in a broad sense,[15] the evidence of a recent survey is that military sociology is largely focused on military organizations.[16] Jacques van Doorn has indeed referred to 'the sociology of the military' as 'a discipline focused on a specific social institution'.[17] There has been little direct concern with the social causes or effects of wars, which have for the most part been left to military and social historians. The wider social impact of war-preparation and miliary organization has been of interest to military sociologists, but their analysis has tended to suggest a very limited influence. Indeed, as van Doorn suggests,[18]

> Current civil–military relations in many Western countries are the exact opposite of the militarisation of politics and society. The process now taking place is one of social penetration into the armed forces, resulting in a high degree of civilianisation, isolation and alienation of the military.

Military sociologists such as van Doorn and Janowitz have analysed the causes of this situation, identifying factors such as the decline of mass armies and the professionalization of armed forces as consequences of changes in military technology as well as in social stratification, occupational formation and political culture.[19] The 'decline of mass armies' analysed by military sociologists has therefore been more than a question of size. Although armies remain enormous by historical standards, and globally armed forces were increasing in size until the 1980s, in the more advanced Western states there has been a shift from manpower to technology and from conscript to professional. With the greater reliance on technology and skilled manpower has come an increasingly managerial approach to the control of armed forces, and armies have become increasingly similar to other large-scale bureaucracies in industrial societies.

Military sociologists have therefore seen the military as an increasingly inward-looking social institution, confined to a narrow role by both its own professionalism and the normative culture of democracy. The military is less a source of influence on society at large, than a sphere which has been profoundly circumscribed by the wider society. Even conscription, which where it remains in Western European countries might appear to be a means by which the military extends its influence, is seen instead by van Doorn as a conduit for civilianization.[20]

The link between military participation and citizenship, forged in the era of mass mobilization and world wars, is therefore seen by Janowitz as declining. On the one hand,[21]

> the trend toward eliminating or reducing conscription has been a general development in Western industrialized nations with a stronger emphasis on all-volunteer professional forces ... It is difficult, under these circumstances, to define military service as an integral aspect of citizenship or vice versa.

On the other, 'Resistance to military service becomes widespread, as the logic of nationalism is questioned and the rationale for the military obscured by the reality of nuclear weapons.'[22] Military sociology has, therefore, been concerned mainly with the 'problems of legitimacy' which these trends pose for the armed forces. Divorced from society, rejected by many young people, often deprived – apart from demoralizing anti-terrorist activities – of opportunities for combat, invaded by civilian modes of organization, the military suffers from a crisis of corporate identity in modern Western societies.

There are major weaknesses in these perspectives from military sociology. First, they have tended to assume, rather than analyse, the reasons for these trends in international relations, military technology and the development of warfare. Second, and crucially from our standpoint, in its concern to see the military as the object of trends originating in civilian society, military sociology has devoted little attention to the effects of this changing relationship on societies at large. Too closely focused on the military as an institution, military sociologists have hardly tried to examine the content of the (presumably residual) military culture in societies, or the ways in which the transformation of military institutions generates new effects on other social institutions and groups. Yet, as we have seen, plausible analyses of such effects have been advanced, ranging from the general effects of nuclear and Cold War culture and ideology (Thompson's discussion of exterminism), to the specific policies for controlling groups of civilian women (Enloe's cases of militarization). Military sociology, preoccupied as it has been with the armed forces themselves, has offered no way of characterizing these or other forms of contemporary militarism.

Those sociologists who have attempted to grapple with the changing forms of military influences in contemporary industrial societies have largely been theorists of power on a grand scale. Giddens, in his definition of modern nation-states as internally pacified but externally violent, provides a useful baseline for an examination of militarism. He does not discuss, however, how the changing forms of warfare have produced different militarisms in various nation-states and periods of recent social history.[23]

Michael Mann has produced a historical typology of modern militarisms, from the 'limited wars' of the years from 1648 to 1914, to the 'citizen wars' between 1914 and 1945 and what he sees as the bifurcated militarism of the nuclear age.[24] There are some problems in the rather simplified treatment of the period of total war as one of 'citizen warfare'.[25] But he offers a provocative account of contemporary military culture and its influence on society. At its centre is a split between what he calls the 'deterrence–science militarism' of the elites and the forms of popular militarism. Where the first half of the twentieth century saw the direct involvement of the masses in war, breaking down the separation of limited war and society in the previous two and a half centuries, the nuclear age sees a re-privatization of war by the elites. War-preparation becomes not just a private but a secret activity of political and military leaders, in which populations acquiesce but do not actively participate. 'Contemporary militarism', Mann suggests, 'is not up-front. It is subtle and diverse.' In many societies the upbringing and education of young men, especially, are overtly militaristic:[26]

> But modern society is not like that. Education and the socialization of the young are large pacific. Our sports do not relate well to modern warfare, even violent ones like boxing. True, the play of young boys is often militaristic, and male notions of honour retain some of the coloration of traditional militarism. But these are elements in a diverse modern culture, not its core. Nor could they be a reasonable preparation for the highest nuclear level of warfare.

Mann sees the 'deterrence–science militarism' of the elites as common to East and West. They are concerned with 'intrinsically rational and privately planned limited wars as an instrument of policy', wars which are often 'relatively short and costless for the Superpowers' and from which 'their civilian populations are insulated'. There is a distinct military economy, with a different *modus operandi* (the cost-plus contract) from that of competitive capitalism; and a distinctive military ideology which embraces officers and military intellectuals:[27]

> Officers, especially higher commands, are introduced to complex techniques of behavioural and natural sciences. They play war-games in which computer simulation of complex chains of interaction between levels of decision-making and weapons capacity requires clear, logical thought. As this is 'to think the unthinkable' it develops a distinctive form of *esprit de corps*: 'tough-mindedness', the clear-sighted 'hawk', with the capacity to keep logic going while the bombs fall. This also seems characteristic of civilian/diplomatic advisers like Kissinger or Brzezinski – exuding a certain contempt for the 'civilians', the doves who would substitute hope and faith for *Realpolitik*.

The peoples of East and West, however, have experienced radically different militarisms. The USSR and its Eastern European allies were, according to Mann (writing in the mid-1980s), still in the grip of 'militarized socialism' (or in Soviet jargon, the 'military-patriotic society'):

> Various wartime tools of social control have been refined. These range across the whole of social life from labour brigades, factories, kolkhozes and sovkhozes with military discipline, training in mass sports with defence applications, the activities of the Komsomol, Party, trade unions, schools and the whole of the media. The lessons of what is universally referred to as the 'Great Patriotic War' are continuously reaffirmed through all the propaganda organs of the state.

This militarized socialism, Mann argued, was no longer associated with social progress and had a defensive and conservative character. But it 'has remained unscathed through the period of domination by nuclear weapons', and '*institutionalises* global militarism in the lives of the people – which is not so in the West'.[28]

In the West, according to Mann, the Second World War 'equation of citizenship with militarism has also turned defensive . . . : not further social progress, but preservation of what we have, requires military force'. But for all this, unlike the USSR, 'militarism is not central to the social structure of the West. Its major armed forces are relatively marginal to society, and there is no equivalent to militarised socialism.' Although in the abstract, much of Western public opinion may support 'deterrence–science militarism', 'it is less directly implicated than are Soviet citizens'. This sense of 'indirect participation' is conveyed by Mann's term for popular militarism in the West, 'spectator sport militarism'.[29]

Part of this militarism is a residue of Second World War citizen warfare. Beyond this residue the nation, in the West, is mobilized 'not as players but as *spectators*' in wars fought by client states with support from 'our' advisers and small expeditionary forces.

> The spectators are in fact quite well-informed about such wars. Knowledge through actual participation in two world wars among the older age-groups is transmitted to the young through comics, books, magazines, movies and television documentaries. Conscription provides experience at the 'amateur playing' level in most countries. The media are also experienced at quickly relaying abstruse military technique and performance to a mass public.

In terms of the way they become media events, wars like the Falklands or the Grenada invasion 'are not qualitatively different from the Olympic Games'. Stronger emotions are stirred but real sacrifices, even in terms of economic resources, are not demanded, except from the minority of professional troops. Mann argues, indeed, that real sacrifices could not be demanded; 'popular support is shallow and volatile' and 'if the nation is called to real sacrifice, we see that its militarism is not rooted deep', as the conscript armies of the USA in Vietnam and France in Algeria and Indo-China showed. Spectator sport militarism, like the militarized socialism of the East, may be used by elites as an ideology for domestic consumption, to increase social control and prevent change. Or, suggests Mann, if the gap between elite and popular militarisms is not total, then to some extent we may be back to 1914, where 'mass, part-manipulated electorates can push their diplomats over the brink'. In this sense the combination of deterrence–science and popular militarisms may not be so stabilizing.[30]

Mann's account of the West, it will be seen, incorporates the military sociologists' view of armed forces ('relatively marginal to society') and attempts to define the ways in which society at large is still implicated in militarism. It is a schematic view, which invites elaboration and qualification, and some of his more particular judgements may be questioned. The dichotomy of Eastern and Western popular militarisms, while substantially valid up to the Gorbachev era, is now largely redundant. The division of elite and popular militarisms, while a useful model, is not as absolute as Mann often seems to suggest: 'deterrence' (for example) exists, in a highly simplified form, as popular ideology as well as elite theory, as the British Conservatives have demonstrated in successive elections. The persistence of conscription in continental Europe is a substantial form of direct military participation, which arguably does not fit so easily as Mann suggests into the 'spectator sport' mode. The abolition of conscription in the USA, as earlier in Britain, may support Mann's judgement that 'the United States is, perhaps, the country where militarism is least evident'.[31] Undoubtedly, consumer culture predominates despite the USA's historically unprecedented arms economy. But aggressive nationalism, declining in Western Europe, is alive and well in superpower America, and the military is a far more visible embodiment of power. If spectator sport militarism has a single home, it is surely the USA.

What Mann's account of this militarism only starts to address is the nature of the military content of contemporary culture. In fact, the 'spectator sport' aspect of militarism is hardly new. MacKenzie's admirable study of imperialism demonstrates that in Britain, at least, militarism in the classical period was largely a spectator sport affair. Wars were fought, just as they are today, on the other side of the globe, with little direct cost to the imperial populace, whose participation was equally vicarious. Popular culture before 1914 was saturated with colourful and heroic military images, disseminated through many media.[32] Only later was this culture overlaid with the less easily romanticizable experience of mass slaughter in two world wars, although, as

Mann suggests, this too has been incorporated into a mass consumption ideology of war.

The difference between contemporary and classical mass militarisms is more closely captured by the concept of 'armament culture', which emphasizes the affinities as well as the discontinuities between elite and popular ideologies. The technological bias of modern armed forces is reflected, Luckham argues, in a 'fetishism of the weapon' in all levels of culture:[33]

> we are now entering a new stage in which the manufacture of warfare is overtaking man and expropriating his culture. Automated warfare and the nuclear bomb have deprived man of this capacity to strive for glory, recognition or safety through combat. At the same time weapons are shaping his consciousness through the agency of what can be called armament culture, based on the fetishism of the weapon, or rather that of the advanced weapon system. It is thus distinct from militarism or the dominance in society of warlike values, although it is *empirically* related to it.

For Luckham, armament culture is more than just the effects of armament upon culture (i.e. upon music, literature, the arts, theatre, film, etc.), it is the way in which 'Armament has entered the process of *cultural production* itself, as well as being the *product* of manifold forms of cultural activity.'[34]

The development of armament culture is one aspect of the way in which 'social relations between living human beings have come to experience as relationships between abstract qualities or things' – in this case 'between stockpiles of weapons'. The development of ever more powerful weapons has converted soldiers into operators, and civilians (as well as soldiers) into targets, of weapons systems. But the 'citizen-targets' are 'encouraged to identify with the instruments' of their own liquidation.[35] Weapons 'are readily transmuted into symbols and become constituent elements in dominant ideologies',[36] and 'become fetishes in a Freudian as well as a Marxist meaning of the term',[37] being given human, animal and cosmic names and attributes. Weapons are an extreme intance of the general technologism of modern culture, with its belief in the supremacy of the technological fix; military organizations 'a special form of the regimentation of men around machines'; and modern war 'a particularly extreme example of the belief that any problem can be solved if technology and capital are applied to it in large enough doses'.[38]

Luckham locates the sites of armament culture both in the 'armament complex' (Mann's deterrence–science militarism') and outside it. The armament complex, he writes,[39]

> is itself a sector of cultural production and reproduction. Within it occurs an articulation between the specialised subcultures of science, management, war and politics. From this interaction emerge weapons, strategies, myths and values, which are imprinted on other forms of cultural production. At the same time scientists, soldiers, politicians and others draw freely upon the imagery and assumptions of mass culture.

(An example is President Reagan's celebrated – or notorious – 'Star Wars' speech.) Luckham divides the 'organic intellectuals' of the armaments complex into three main groups: the scientific estate, the security intellectuals and the security managers. Beyond the armament complex, there are interpreters, publicists and propagandists 'who directly transmit the values and images of armament to the general public, the targets of the weapons'.[40]

The discourse of 'strategy', Luckham notes, 'borrows heavily from the rhetoric of theatre, organised sport and the capitalist market place'. (Consider 'scenario', 'theatre', 'game plans' and 'assets'.)[41] Other sorts of interpenetration include the politicization of military activity (counter-insurgency, etc.) and the militarization of policing: 'the special control groups, riot squads and anti-terrorist teams which have become such a visible part of the cultural landscape of modern cities, airports and TV programmes'.[42]

Instead of considering the culture of the armament complex as separate from mass culture (as Mann tends to) Luckham asks 'how are the specialised sub-cultures of the armament complex welded into broader hegemonic hegomic ideology? How do they penetrate political discourse and mass culture?'[43] His answer is multi-faceted: directly, 'unmediated by other cultural institutions and ideologies', through images of military power on television; through the 'marriage' of armament with other values such as nationalism; through the activities of interpreters who 'transpose

weapons and military force into the realm of political discourse';
through education, for example history texts; and through games
based on war and books and magazines about it. Not all of this
diffusion is blatant ('the influence of the armament complex on
the content of cultural production in the monopoly controlled
media is subtle and sometimes difficult to detect').[44] The autonomy of media results in the means through which diffusion takes
place being in the hands of media professionals rather than of the
armament complex, and this even allows pockets of dissent to
exist (but they tend to be marginal). As with all cultural trans-
ission by mass media, moreover, we cannot be sure how far
the products of armament culture affect the consumers, i.e. how
the messages are received.

Luckham argues that armament culture has 'global reach',
although there are important differences between advanced Western countries, the USSR and Eastern Europe, and various societies
in the Third World. The fetishism of the weapon, both in state
policies and popular culture, is a fact of life in 'socialist' societies
and in the Third World although its forms may vary. The USSR
has been wedded to the goal of strategic parity, measuring its
strength in warheads and megatonnage; Third World states, as
we have seen, have sought to secure their status by importing
military hardware. Armament culture informs the ideologies of
ruling classes, 'because it is implicit in the international state-
system by which their own claims to govern are recognised'.[45]
Weapons systems and ideas both arrive in culturally encoded packages, so that their importation requires a modification of general
culture if they are to be assimilated successfully. Luckham does
acknowledge that the overall bias of the Soviet system is different
from that of the West: 'Many observers of the communist countries', he grants, 'have been struck by their emphasis on *military* –
rather than armament-related – practices and symbols.'[46] And
many forms of Western culture are, he argues, simply unavailable
in Eastern Europe (this was written in the early 1980s). Nevertheless, he concludes, armament is internalized in a variety of ways.

Armament culture is, as we have seen, distinct from militarism
in Luckham's view, although there are points in his analysis
(when, for example, he cites the common patterns of military
hierarchy, uniform and ritual in developed and Third World
countries) where the distinction tends to be lost. Certainly it
would be possible to follow Mann's concept of 'spectator sport

militarism', and define armament culture as simply a new, more subtle form of militarism. The diffusion of armament culture could then be seen as evidence of pervasive militarization. Luckham resists this temptation, rightly in my view, because it denies the specific cultural character of armament and it presents it in an over-determined way. There are, Luckham reminds us, contradictions in the relationship between armament and mass culture, which open up possibilities for opposition to armament.

The concept of armament culture illuminates important issues which neither militarization theorists nor other alternatives to militarization fully clarify. While it is very important to distinguish it from militarism, the concept of armament culture should not replace militarism or militarization. Rather, we need to consider how armament culture has grown out of classical militarism, and how it combines with it in different societies. The spread of armament culture is a dominant trend; but militarism survives, to a varying extent, and we can identify important processes of militarization, both in the development of social institutions and in the spread of armament culture itself. The development of armament culture is not a simple process either of militarization or demilitarization, but a contradictory merging of the two. At the same time as images of weapons become diffused in all areas of culture, they often become detached from a specifically military context. This leaves a great deal in armament culture open, not just to new military definitions, and to market forces, but also to anti-military interpretations.

## CONSCRIPTION IN EUROPE

Inevitably, attempts to define forms and processes of militarism, militarization and armament culture in general may lead to formulations which sacrifice historical trends for intellectual coherence. Just as the general concepts of militarization that have been advanced simplify reality, so the alternatives we have examined are open to objections on the basis of contradictory evidence. In particular, the claims of many of these concepts to global reach can be challenged on the basis of conflicting trends in different parts or regions of the world system, and in particular national contexts.

The tendency of sociologists to theorize about societies in

general, apart from the reality of a complex, nation-state frag-
mented world system, is always dubious. In matters of war and
militarism which are directly connected to the conflicts of the
state system, clearly it is particularly questionable. And where
social scienctists do divide societies into groups, the tendency to
operate on the basis of a rough and ready division of First,
Second and Third Worlds is also inadequate – again, in this area,
even more so than in others.

It makes more sense to look at societies in terms of geopolitical
position and role than of the simple tripartite division of the
world. Thus, as Mills's analysis of the power elite acknowledged,
the role of the USA as a superpower had early effects on the role
of military power in US society. The importance of the USA has
never been as typical Western industrial state, but as the leading
and dominant state, trends in which tended to influence others.
US society necessarily presents a different pattern of relationships
between military organization and values and society, from those
of other Western states, but one which always has a bearing on
the rest. Because of its world role, economic and political life in
the USA are far more directly influenced by military power than
elsewhere. Patriotism is far more 'up front', the military has a far
higher profile, and the ideology of global confrontation is far
more pervasive. It is possible to present the dominant ideology
and culture, in Thompson's terms, as 'exterminist'. And yet the
USA, the greatest military power the world has ever seen, does
not present as a classically militarist society. Analysts since Mills
have noted the split between the higher level of power (or in
Mann's terms, the elites which participate in 'deterrence–science
militarism') and the the middle and lower levels (at which 'spectator sport militarism' is prevalent). America's is predominantly a
consumer, commodity-based culture, in which 'armament culture'
is inserted as an important 'element but not the core'. The non-
militarization (more accurate than demilitarization) of American
life is further emphasized by the move to all-volunteer armed
forces since the 1970s. Although this shift is more recent than
Britain's, and non-professional forces (the National Guard) still
have a role for which there is no British counterpart, it underlines
the move from manpower to technology, from soldiering to
weapons system maintenance, from militarism to armament culture. The general trends of which most theorists write originate in
the USA.

Other Western societies exhibit a rather different pattern. The two economically most powerful states, Germany and Japan, are heirs to the most virulent classical militarisms. But they are fundamentally constrained from reproducing them by the constitutions imposed by the USA and the other victors after the Second World War. Japan, indeed, is denied even the existence of a standing army (in name, although it possesses one in reality). Both countries (Japan especially as a result of its experience of atomic bombing) are likewise excluded from full independent participation in 'deterrence–science militarism' or the 'armament culture': they lack the nuclear weapons several lesser states possess.

It is clearly accurate to talk about extensive demilitarization of Japanese and West German societies, even if there are undoubtedly substantial ideological survivals of older militarisms in the state and among sections of the population. But despite considerable absolute military expenditures, these two powerful states are and seem likely to remain obliged to play the role of military subordinates to the USA in Europe and Asia respectively. The growth of Franco-German collaboration and common West European defence offers some outlets, but still restricted, for Germany's contained power, just as US-led activities in the Pacific offer some for Japan's. The militarism which accompanies such constrained and collaborative military power is necessarily ideologically subdued, however, even though both states possess very substantial armed forces.

The two major contrasts are Britain and France, economically weaker states but, having merged victorious from the Second World War, able to claim the status of great powers and the right to independent nuclear arms. Unlike Japan and West Germany, these two countries have been able to flex their military muscles, first in colonial wars and more recently in conflicts with independent states outside Europe. The combination of post-imperial interventionism and nuclear armament has enabled national elites to participate fully in the armament culture, and to diffuse a nationalized version of it in the political culture.

It is striking that of these two pairs of states, West Germany and France, like virtually all continental European countries, maintain conscription; Japan and Britain, in common with the USA and virtually all Western industrial states outside continental Europe, no longer have it. It is tempting to believe that direct mass military participation of the adult male population, via conscription, is not after all a major indicator of militarism. Certainly, there is no simple correlation with the strength of militarist ideologies and the armament culture, which operate as we have seen at numerous levels. Nevertheless, conscription is by far the most important form of mass military participation, and the major index of militarism in the sense of an extensive influence of specifically military culture in society. Among advanced industrial states, conscription is now entirely a continental European affair. All continental states, NATO and neutral as well as Warsaw Pact, with the insignificant exceptions of Liechtenstein, Luxembourg and Monaco, retain conscription. The other European states which do not have conscription are the offshore countries: the UK, Ireland and Iceland. None of the Western industrial states outside Europe now enforces it: Australia, Canada and New Zealand, in addition to the USA and Japan, are non-conscripters.[47]

As indicated above, neither the military sociologists with their concept of 'the decline of mass armies' nor Mann or Luckham regard the persistence of conscription in Europe as a major stumbling block to their theories. The trend in Western European armies, as well as in those of the USA, the UK and other states with all-volunteer forces, has long been identified as towards professionalism and high technology. West European conscripts can well be seen, as they are by Mann, as amateur players, extras indeed in the professional stage confrontation of the European theatre. They can also be seen as importers of civilian values into the military context, for example by demanding rights of oranization and self-expression, the denial of which is more readily accepted by professional soldiers. The persistence of this old form of military participation in Europe, moreover, hardly prevents the permeation of armament culture.

Nevertheless, this issue does raise the problem of unevenness in the transformation of militarism. Most of the theories we have considered are USA-based or centred (British writers have little difficulty, given the similarity between US and UK patterns as well as participation in a common Anglo-Saxon culture, in identifying with the typicality of American experience). This is a valid approach, to the extent that the USA dominates globally and especially in the politics of the West. But it has limitations, where states and societies are situated in a radically different way within the divisions of the world.

The persistence of conscription in Europe is determined by several different factors. First, it reflects tradition and history: many continental states, unlike the USA or the UK, introduced conscription in the nineteenth century and have practised it more or less continuously for a hundred years or more. Second, it has survived because even in the age of superpower nuclear rivalry, the perception of threat in continental countries is primarily one of invasion across a land frontier. (In societies like Germany there has been as much concern about tactical nuclear weapons used in conjunction with ground forces, as with intermediate-range or strategic nuclear missiles.) Third, it is reinforced by the persistence of local conflicts: it is no accident that Greece and Turkey have the longest periods of military service in the West, or perhaps that isolated Romania had an even longer term than other Eastern European states until its revolution.[48]

The fact of conscription is evidence, therefore, that old-fashioned mass militarism persists in Europe, but has become subdued in the West, and especially the north-west of the continent. Most Western European states have, due to size, location and the end of empires, little scope for independent military activity. Incorporation into NATO restricts both independent nationalism and militarism and the scope for Euro-nationalism and Euro-militarism (although the resistance of nation-states to the emergence of a Western European state has also been a powerful inhibition). Germany's constitutional demilitarization, moreover, acts as a brake on the independent military development of the European Community as a whole. Size and proximity to two great blocs give the conscript armies of the neutrals a strictly defensive, almost pacific character. Economic success and the growth of consumerism have put militarism in the shade, although the armament culture has had its successes. This is reflected in the varying lengths and terms of military service in European countries before the onset of détente and disarmament in the late 1980s, as table 3.1 shows.

The table of course excludes the offshore European states that have no conscription. It indicates that the tendencies towards longer terms of conscription and denial of alternative service, especially outside the armed forces, have coincided to a large extent with the differences between neutral states (which on the whole have had the shortest terms of service and best non-military alternatives), NATO states (which have had much shorter average terms and better alternatives than states in the East)

Table 3.1    Minimum length of basic military training in European
             countries during the 'Second Cold War' (1984)

| Period (months) | States |
|---|---|
| 6 | Austria,[a] Cyprus |
| 8 | Finland[a] |
| 9 | Denmark (N),[a] Sweden[a] |
| 10 | Belgium (N)[a] |
| 11 | Switzerland |
| 12 | France (N),[a] Italy (N),[a] Norway (N)[a] |
| 14 | Netherlands (N)[a] |
| 15 | Spain (N),[a] West Germany (N)[a] |
| 18 | East Germany (W),[b] Portugal (N), Yugoslavia |
| 20 | Turkey (N) |
| 24 | Albania, Bulgaria (W), Czechoslovakia (W), Hungary (W), Poland (W), USSR (W) |
| 26 | Greece (N)[b] |
| 30 | Romania (W) |

[a]    Indicates alternative service available outside armed forces.
[b]    Indicates alternatived service available only within armed forces.
(N)  North Atlantic Treaty Organization member.
(W)  Warsaw Pact member.
*Source*:  Peter Whittle, 'Conscientious Objection to Military Service', *SIPRI Yearbook 1985*, London: Taylor and Francis, 1985, table 18.3, p. 625.

and Warsaw Pact states (which as a group have had the longest terms and virtually no alternatives to military training). But it also shows an even closer geographical split, with neutral and NATO states in southern Europe having longer terms and less availability of alternatives than those in the nort-west.

To a large extent, then, differences in the extent and form of conscription within continental Europe, which can be seen as a measures of militarization, have coincided with levels of economic and social development – as well as geopolitics. The less industrially advanced and prosperous states have had the longer terms and more repressive forms of military service. Trade unionism in the armed forces, which has been unheard of in eastern and southern Europe, is also permitted within several but not all northern countries (such as Germany and the Netherlands). Civilianization is manifest, too, in the higher ratio of military-related civilian employment to armed forces personnel, in the most advanced industrial states.[49]

That conscription is a continental European phenomenon, in the first place, and varies as we have described, raises a major question against the clear division of Eastern and Western militarisms, asserted by Mann (and acknowledged to some degree by Luckham). The major differences between East and West have been reflections not only of political system but of geopolitics and levels of economic and social development. The USSR and its allies, much more than the USA or the UK, have been locked into a situation of territorial military threat. They were also, however, far more technologically and economically backward, and although this was partly offset by intensive investment in some high priority military areas, the USSR has lagged well behind the USA, and the Warsaw Pact behind NATO as a whole. The old Soviet and Eastern European political systems may well have been built, as a Mann suggests, around 'socialist militarism', but the persistence of this old-fashioned militarism in the East owed as much to geopolitics and economics as it did to ideology. Now that all of these are changing simultaneously, radical changes are occurring in the system of conscription.

It may be unrealistic to think that the pattern of conscript armies, consolidated in Europe over the four decades since 1945, will be completely overthrown in the near future. Nevertheless, the radical reduction in conventional force levels under way in the 1990s raises important questions about the future development of armed forces in the West as well as the East. Armies everywhere require fewer men, and it makes sense for governments and commanders to question whether they should still be obtained by conscription. Young people in Western societies as much as in Eastern Europe will also want to know why they should continue to sacrifice a period of their life, when the Cold War has ended and most circumstances for which forces have been designed are disappearing. The process of troop reduction and general de-escalation of military conflict in Europe is therefore reinforcing the delegitimation of armed forces, noted by military sociologists since the 1960s. The experience of peace movements in Western Europe in the early 1980s suggests a large potential for anti-military protest, which if turned against the survival of conscription could have profound consequences. A new phase in the 'decline of mass armies' has almost certainly begun, one which the 'new' threats revealed in the Gulf war will be powerless to reverse.

Any such developments almost certainly depend, however, on the deepening of processes of change in the USSR and Eastern Europe. There are important structural reasons for the USSR's radical troop reductions. The Soviet economy has for many years suffered from the large-scale siphoning of resources from civilian to military purposes. Soviet leaders, in competition with the West, are compelled by the same logic which replaces men by machines and simple machines by more sophisticated ones. In addition to these fundamental realities, they have had to face – after Afghanistan – much the same disillusionment with the military which was widespread in the USA after Vietnam, and a growing resentment towards the armed forces in the minority republics of the Union. Their former allies in Eastern Europe, especially in Hungary and East Germany, had faced opposition to military service among young people since the early 1980s; this has now spread to the USSR, including Russia itself. All these factors have pushed the related issues of conscription and the size of armed forces to the fore in the USSR, and in the ex-Communist states of Eastern Europe.

In a period of great flux, it is difficult to be sure how far and how fast changes in the Soviet armed forces, their relationship to society, and corresponding changes in Western Europe will develop. Clearly there is a developing 'virtuous circle' of demilitarization; although there may be setbacks, it is difficult to foresee either the international or national circumstances which could restore the vicious circle of Cold War militarization that prevailed for so long.

As recently as 1989, commentators on the Soviet Union foresaw only a relatively modest reform in the system of military service. Cooper argued that 'The force reductions may lead to economically beneficial changes in the system of conscription, in particular a restoration of the exemption procedures for students in higher education.'[50] This might, however, be as far as reform would go in the short run. Shenfield saw political limitations on the reduction of armed forces, in the role they have played in controlling the national conflicts in Soviet Central Asia in 1988–9. The military 'solution' adopted in these situations, he wrote, had[51] disappointing implications for Soviet society. The only institution upon which Moscow was able to rely to bring events under control was the army, which alone is run on completely centralised lines. This circumstance sets definite limits on demilitarisation. The idea of replacing the large standing army by a much smaller professional army combined with territorial militias ... must now look impractical and even dangerous for the foreseeable future.

Nevertheless, the fact that the issue of replacing conscription by purely professional armed forces could be raised seriously was an index of major transformation in the climate of military thinking in the USSR. By 1990 the centrifugal forces in the Union had come to threaten the army itself: the minority republics were demanding military as well as economic and political autonomy. Attempts to keep conscripts within their national territories went hand in hand with the demands for republican armies. (A similar process was developing in Yugoslavia, where in 1990 reformist Slovenia attempted to ban the Serbian-dominated Yugoslav army from exercising on its territory, and in 1991 the army was in direct conflict with Croatian military police.)

A wholesale transformation of the Soviet armed forces, such as would unequivocally alter the case for mass conscript armies in Western Europe, appears increasingly likely to occur during the 1990s, although the form in which they will eventually be stabilized is difficult to predict. Other forms of demilitarization have developed apace, however, with the process of economic reform in the USSR. These will reinforce the social and political momentum for demilitarization, and in turn have effects in the West. The massive defence sector was an early target of Gorbachev's reforms, and some significant forms of industrial 'conversion' (from arms to non-military production) have taken place.

This process has been assisted, ironically, by what is more usually seen as an indicator of Soviet militarism: the wide economic control of the Soviet defence ministries and armed forces. The fact that these already include a great deal of production which is not specifically military in character has meant that there is no institutional barrier to conversion. It has long been quite normal for Soviet weapons factories to produce civilian goods alongside military hardware: nuclear missile plants, for example, produce refrigerators and tractors, and because of their priority over resources and expertise, their civilian products are often better than those made outside the defence sector. Policy changes under *perestroika* have transferred responsibility for much light industrial production (equipment for food industries, household goods) to defence ministries. 'The nuclear-weapons-producing Ministry of Medium Machine-building', Cooper reported, 'now has responsibility for making equipment for the dairy industry, including milking machines.' Already by late 1988, '355 defence sector enterprises were reported to be engaged in making equipment for the food processing industry'.[52]

Such changes have occurred first within the militarized framework of the Soviet state and economy. However, 'There is little doubt that many reform-minded intellectuals regard the hypertrophied growth of the defence industry as a major factor in the country's present economic difficulties, and it is likely that this perception is now shared by Gorbachev and other political leaders.'[53] Recent developments suggest strongly, as Cooper argues, 'that the era of unquestioned priority for the armaments industry may now be coming to an end' – sixty years after Stalin first granted an overwhelming pre-eminence to military requirements in the Soviet economy.[54] Such a change in economic policy cannot but have profound social implications, and these are reinforced by the political changes which are taking place. The militarization of the Soviet state has been part of its authoritarian character. The process of democratization, with the questioning of hierarchical institutions and dogmas that it has brought about, has rapidly undermined the supremacy of military virtues in Soviet perceptions of citizenship and patriotism. Militarism is openly contested not only by minorities in the intelligentsia but by the national movements. The strength of 'socialist militarism' as a popular ideology, still seen by Mann (writing on the eve of the Gorbachev era) as a defining characteristic of Soviet society, is under unprecedented challenge.

In this sense, however important the continuing differences in the militarism of Eastern and Western industrial societies, common (and reciprocal) processes are at work. The decline of traditional militarism and mass armies, although by no means complete in the West, is now affecting the USSR and the more advanced countries of Eastern Europe. Just as the process is more developed in North America and north-western Europe than it is in southern Europe, so possibilities of demilitarization are more obvious in Hungary, Poland and Czechoslovakia than they are in

Bulgaria, Romania (where the revolution has partially reinforced the army's role) or Albania. This corresponds closely
with the divisions exposed in the USSR itself. To the northern
Europeans in the western USSR, identifying with economic modernization, democracy and Western culture, demilitarization is a
natural concomitant of change. In the industrially backward parts
of the USSR the pressures for demilitarization may be weaker,
and national conflicts may even give the military a heightened
role.

This pattern suggests that there is an association, albeit strongly
qualified by domestic and international politics, between industrial development and demilitarization. Classical militarism could
be seen as the product of the mix of statism, labour-extensive
mass production, and mechanized warfare, which has increasingly
been surpassed in the West, is now challenged in the East, but
remains powerful in the south. Demilitarization could be linked
to the changes which have brought about a decline of many kinds
of formal associations and ideologies and subordinated them to
consumer capitalism and mass culture. The decline of militarism
is akin to the decline of aggressive nationalism, traditional religion and mass labour movements, all of which were stronger in
earlier stages of industrial society. The transformation of militarism into armament culture is parallel to the way in which
nationalism and religion have been packaged within commercial
culture, most notably in the USA.

From this perspective, it is entirely predictable that traditional
militarism, like nationalism and traditional religion if not socialism, will be stronger in the south, which is only now undergoing
forms of industrialization. It is in Third World countries that
'total' wars have been fought since 1945, whether by conventional or guerrilla means; that armies have been increasing in
size; and that militaries most commonly exercise political power.
Here, surely, is the last refuge of traditional militarism.

## LIMITS OF THIRD WORLD MILITARISM

And yet even in the Third World context there is a formidable
challenge to the militarization thesis. As we have seen, Ross
(using a non-sociological definition of militarization) has documented how the military build-up of the 1960s and 1970s slowed
down in the 1980s. The only dimension on which, in his terms,

there has been further militarization is the spread of military regimes. Even this process has been regionalized: there has been a trend away from military regimes in Latin America, statistically overridden by an increase elsewhere, especially in Africa. Although military government is certainly an indicator of a particular sort of military influence over society, it is not necessarily associated with militarism, as we shall explain below.

At the centre of most accounts of 'militarization' is the arms transfer process, and this typically does not involve the growth of militarism in the host society. On the contrary, accounts of the arms trade often emphasize the disjunction between technologically advanced weapons systems and the cultures of importing societies. Luckham, for example, stresses that weapons come in 'culturally encoded packages'; Kaldor that armaments are part of 'Western industrial enclaves' in Third World countries, largely distinct from predominantly rural societies.[55]

Kaldor indeed goes further, to argue that high-technology Western weapons systems distort the economic development of Third World countries, imposing patterns of industrial development which have little relationship to the general development needs of societies. They assist the internationalisation of armament culture, but the most intensive, direct effects of this are limited to the military – industrial sectors themselves. The broader imagery of armament culture is diffused by film and television even to rural populations, but they experience little economic benefit from the concentration of limited national resources in highly expensive capital-intensive armaments projects – determined by competition in the global military order rather than by local economic needs. As we have seen in chapter 2, the balance of the economic effects of arms transfers is widely judged to be negative; the cultural effects are hardly less so.

To judge the extent of militarization by the effects of arms transfers is, however, extremely misleading. Although Third World militaries have increasingly sought to participate in a global military order by importing Western technology, they remain far less capital-intensive than Western or even Soviet armed forces. It is true that there are a number of data which suggest that the growth of armed forces is less significant than other forms of military build-up, that it has slowed down, and so on. As we have seen, Ross calculates that armies have grown in size at a lesser rate than increases in military expenditure (and therefore *a fortiori* of armaments); he also estimates that the number of armed forces per 1,000 people, in the Third World as a whole, has declined from 5.2 to 4.9 (from 1973 to 1983); and, as we have already quoted, that the rates of growth of armed forces have declined to virtually zero, i.e. there is overall stagnation.[56]

All this suggests that if there has been a process of societal militarization represented by the growth in armed forces, it has been checked. But despite these trends, the size of militaries remains far more important in the Third World than in the advanced industrial world, especially the West. Third World war-preparation, much more than that of East or West, is a hybrid of the capital-intensive (imported high-technology weapons systems) and labour-extensive (quantity of basically equipped men under arms). The history of modern Iran is the best illustration of this: as we have seen, in the 1970s the Shah aspired to make his state a regional 'sub-imperialism' by massive oil-financed imports of Western arms, which made Iran the best-equipped power in the region. And yet an essential ingredient of his ambitions was Iran's population, larger than any of the immediately neighbouring Arab states. The threat that this would be mobilized created fear in oil-richer Saudi Arabia and the Gulf because of their lack of comparable mobilizing capacity. When, following the overthrow of the Shah, Iraq sought to take advantage of the chaos in the Iranian state and armed forces, the Islamic regime's main resource was precisely what its neighbours had feared under the Shah. Khomeini poured hundreds of thousands of young Iranian men into the battlegrounds, where in places there was mass slaughter and trench warfare widely compared to the First World War. Alongside sophisticated modern weaponry, originally supplied by all the main arms-exporting states, were much more basic forces – poorly armed and trained masses of youth. Chemical warfare, itself a product of the first great trench stalemate, was a major means by which the less populous Iraqis checked the massive Iranian counter-advance.

Many recent wars, especially those between Third World states and between local states and insurgent forces, have involved less advanced technology and more basic military mobilization than the Iran–Iraq war. Classical total war, banished from the advanced world by nuclear weapons, is reproduced in these more limited contests. Limited by geography and weaponry, many wars are nevertheless total in their effects on the societies involved.

Militarization is as complete, and perhaps more so, in some of the more remote guerrilla struggles as in the larger conflicts of major states. Typically in guerrilla movements, the armed struggle can be sustained only by mobilization of and control over the population, with the military command as the centre of political authority.

National liberation movements have produced forms of Marxism–Leninism (now superseded everywhere in Europe) that equate military with political power, and introduce military command systems into social organization. But the militarization of insurgent societies is not confined to those which identify with left-wing ideologies, as cases such as those of UNITA in Angola and the Mujaheddin in Afghanistan demonstrate. A high degree of societal militarization is inherent in extensive guerrilla war.[57]

Although insurgent societies have their own special forms of militarization, states involved in civil war also tend towards highly militarized forms. Much depends on the size and centrality of the regions or provinces in which guerrilla struggles are located, and the success of insurgents in breaking down central state control. But states involved in serious internal battles inevitably tend towards a high degree of military control over society at large, and military-ideological mobilization of their populations. Right-wing El Salvador and the former left-wing Nicaragua, both faced with substantial guerrilla threats, each experienced serious militarization even if its political content and forms were very different.

Where internal contests coincide, as they often do, with external conflicts, militarization tends to be even more complete. The Kurdish struggle in war-torn Iran and Iraq; Ethiopia, where the civil wars in Eritrea and Tigre have intersected with war with Somalia; and the conjunction in Angola of the guerrilla war and the conflict with South Africa are all examples of the relationship of internal and external military struggles. Where, as if often the case, today's civil wars follow the earlier military triumph of a insurgent force, or a military coup or a war, the facility for direct military forms of power is likely to be greater.

The obvious is therefore true: militarism is strong in those Third World societies actually involved in wars. Economies are run for war purposes, societies are mobilized both to fight and to give support to armed struggle, and forms of state power take directly military forms. Militarism in the ideological sense, whether insurgent or state, revolutionary or counter-revolutionary, is a powerful force. Militarization in the sociological sense certainly occurs in these societies, although whether this can be said to be a general trend is much more doubtful. For as we have seen, it is difficult to sustain a case that the number or intensity of wars has unequivocally increased. For every society which today is rent by war and undergoing militarization, there is another in which a war begun ten or twenty years ago has eventually ended, or at least waned, and in which the trend is in the opposite direction.

The experience of militarism and total war in the Third World is not confined of course to guerrilla struggles. Major and prolonged inter-state wars, although not large in number, have led to the most important cases of militarization. The Vietnam war was not a total war for the USA, and produced no general militarization, but for Vietnam it was just such an experience. US military power threatened Vietnamese society, civilians as well as soldiers. Only by mobilizing the entire society at every level, including (for a relatively small country) a massive armed force, was Vietnam able to to counter the USA. The forms of mobilization varied because of the different conditions of the war: in the south, a guerrilla struggle, in the north a state mobilization. The outcome was not, however, a specifically military regime, or one which ruled directly my military means, but a party-state in which military power and ideology had a central role. (Here is a crucial difference with Kampuchea, where the Khmer Rouge came to power and ruled directly by military means, using their monopoly of force to terrorize society and carry out genocide.)

In the 1980s the Iran–Iraq war saw a similar development of total war, especially on the Iranian side, which used societal mobilization to overcome its initial military disadvantage. In revolutionary Iran everything became subordinated to the holy war; young men and boys had to be glad to die for their country and religion, women to send their husbands and sons for sacrifice on the front. Ultimately, in the 'war of the cities', missile attacks threatened civilians in the major centres of population as well as in border areas, although by comparison with the Second World War casualties from these attacks were light. Revolutionary Iran reproduced the original process of mass militarism in the experience of the French Revolution. Just as in France external attack on a popular revolution brought forth the first 'people's war', so in Iran the attack by Iraq aroused a revolutionary militarism.

It also reproduced the pattern of consolidation of a terroristic dictatorship through mass military struggle, if not the Napoleonic transformation of military leader into absolute ruler. Iran's revolutionary militarism gave a boost to Islamic militarism in other parts of the Muslim world, for example in the struggle of the Mujaheddin in Afghanistan, just as the militarization of the Russian Revolution paved the way for Communist revolutionary militarism in many other countries. And yet in the 1990s, Iran's civilian and increasingly secular leadership has moderated its Islamic and militarist excesses, while Islamic insurgency has been blocked in Afghanistan.

In Iraq the essentially secular nationalistic ideology of the Ba'ath has had a comparable role in creating mass militarism. An army of more than a million has been recruited from a population of 17 million, and the whole society has been mobilized behind Saddam Hussein's military ventures, first into Iran and later into Kuwait. In its conflict with the USA, Iraqi militarism became a component of a wider Arab nationalism, with considerable influence among the Palestinians and in Jordan. And yet the failure of this militarism in the Gulf war, with its appalling costs for Iraqi society, has brought it into question, in the Arab world at large as well as within Iraq.

These strongest cases of militarism in Third World countries are not the products of military regimes, but of societies with civilian governments, engaged in total wars – and mobilized by national political and religious ideologies. Militarism in the Third World today, just as in Europe, Japan and North America in the first part of this century, is not a product of military government. The 'high militarisms' of Iran and Iraq, moreover, are not typical of the Middle East as a whole, still less of other regions of the world. The Middle East is the world's most militarized region by far. On the most basic measure of military participation, the Middle East has more than double the global and Third World average of around five per thousand of population as members of armed forces. Other regions, taken as wholes, are close to this average (East Asia, Latin America), or below it (Africa, South Asia).[58]

Examination of the forms of military mobilization reveals stark regional differences in line with this distribution.[59] All Middle Eastern and North African states (Egypt, Libya, Tunisia, Algeria, Morocco) practise conscription, with the exceptions of the Lebanon (hardly a demilitarized enclave) and the small Gulf states of Bahrain, Oman, Qatar and the United Arab Emirates (whose professional armies receive Western, mainly British support). All the larger Latin American states also have the draft; countries not practising conscription are the lesser Central American and Caribbean states of the Bahamas, Barbados, Costa Rica, Dominican Republic, Guyana, Jamaica, Suriname, Trinidad and Tobago, and some even smaller islands. In East Asia, again, all major countries (China, the Koreas, Vietnam, Kampuchea, Laos, Thailand) have conscription, and maintain some of the largest armies outside the superpowers.

In South Asia, on the other hand, most major countries – with enormous, poor populations – manage to maintain substantial armies without general conscription. This is true both of the states of the Indian subcontinent (Burma apart) and of South East Asia (Malaysia and Indonesia; but both Singapore and the Philippines have the draft). In sub-Saharan Africa, moreover, although there are thirteen conscripting states, there are twenty-three non-conscripters. The former, apart from South Africa (for whites) are nine former French colonies, two former Portuguese (including Angola), and Zaire, although none of these maintains a very large army in global or even continental terms. The larger number of former British colonies, and more surprisingly the states in the Horn of Africa, do not conscript, although Nigeria and Ethiopia especially have large armed forces. The Ethiopian case has perhaps a symbolic interest: one of the world's poorest countries, it maintains an army of over 300,000, the same size as the armed forces of the UK, one of the world's richest and most powerful states, with three times Ethiopia's population.

Although, therefore, some non-conscripting states maintain mass armies, there is a close regional correlation between the ratio of the military to the general population and the prevalence of conscription. The extent of militarism in the Third World looks, in these terms, very uneven, although the relationship with the pattern of industrial development does not fit at first sight with the correlation of militarism and relative backwardness we observed in Europe. More developed Latin America, for example, is more obviously militarized than generally backward sub-Saharan Africa. This can perhaps be explained by a less one-dimensional approach. On a global scale, a three-tier model of states is perhaps most useful:

1   The richest and technologically most advanced Western states, together with a few of the richest and least populated Arab oil states, can afford to rely more on sophisticated weaponry than manpower. Those apart from the major continental conflicts do not need massive land armies. These are the states which dispense with or downgrade conscription and show considerable civilianization of armed forces, weakening of ideological militarism, etc. These states are also the centres of 'armament culture'.

2   Many of the most populous and/or poorest states, in South Asia and Africa, either can maintain mass armies without conscription or cannot afford significant armed forces at all. Traditional militarism exists, but often superimposed rather ineffectually on a massive, poverty-stricken civilian population concerned mainly with minimum subsistence.

3   The middle, and largest, group of states, chiefly in Eastern and Southern Europe, Latin America, the Middle East and East Asia, are those which are not so economically advanced or so detached from continental divisions that they can rely mainly on technology. They can afford both substantial weaponry (they include the major arms importers) and substantial armed forces (they maintain conscription). These are the countries in which traditional militarism flourishes most strongly, although its intensity varies hugely, largely according to the nature of regional or local conflicts, and the strength of national and religious ideologies.

Such a categorization, however, says little about trends. As we have seen, there has been some levelling off of increases in military expenditure in the 1980s. There is some argument, however, about whether increases in the size of armed forces have also slowed down. According to figures given by Sivard, those of the developed world taken as whole were roughly constant between 1960 and 1984 (at around 10 million armed personnel) but those of the developing world had almost doubled, from 8.4 million in 1960 to 16.5 million in 1984. The rate of increase, on her figures, has been maintained at approximately 3 per cent a year since 1960, with two or three years of exceptionally high increases in the late 1970s, but still a steady increase in the 1980s.

Certainly, there has been no dramatic reversal of the tendency towards increased size of militaries which characterized the 1960s and 1970s. Although nearly three-quarters of the increase in Third World armies is 'accounted for' by the increase in population (according to Sivard, a 71 per cent rise in population compared to a 96 per cent rise in armed forces), militaries are still growing faster than populations. Indeed, while in some years in the 1970s, military expenditure grew much faster than the size of armed forces, the 1980s slowdown in Third World military spending, which has cut arms imports, does not appear to have had a similar effect on military recruitment.[60]

This buoyancy in the size of armies reflects the low costs of soldiers in many Third World countries. Sivard gives the average military expenditure per soldier in 1983 at $55,000 in the developed world (a figure admittedly inflated by the massive weight of the US military machine), and less than $10,000 in the developing world. Even this average is increased by the high figures of some Middle Eastern states, so that in many individual countries expenditures are far lower – in Ethiopia, for example, less than $2,000, and even in India, little over $5,000.[61] These figures include, of course, the costs of such expensive weapons systems as are purchased, so that the marginal cost of a soldier must be considerably less, perhaps only hundreds of dollars per year in many countries.

If the maintenance of large armies is an index of militarization, the latter is not universally a reflection of warlike tendencies. Armies are maintained for some strictly military reasons – regional inter-state rivalries, internal rebellion and civil war – but often as means of political power. In 1986, according to Sivard, just over half (fifty-seven) of Third World states had military regimes (fifty-six had not). Of the military regimes, just over half again (twenty-nine) were in Africa, the rest distributed between Latin America (nine), the Far East (nine), the Middle East (six), South Asia (three), and Europe (one, Turkey).[62] Non-military regimes were more numerous in all regions except Africa, and South Asia where there was an equal number of military and non-military governments. Sivard also shows that, although there are certainly repressive non-military regimes, many more military than non-military governments commit extensive violence against citizens (torture, brutality, disappearances, political killings), and deny voting rights either completely or in part.[63] Although some of Sivard's categorizations are dubious (for example, her inclusion of selected southern European states in the Third World, which increases the proportion of non-military regimes; and of Iran as a military regime), the broad picture given by her data is illuminating.

The concentration of military regimes in Africa has been increasing: more African states have military governments now than ten or twenty years ago, while in Latin America and Asia the reverse is true. The relationship between 'militarized political power', as Sivard describes it, and the militarization of society is therefore appropriately studied in the African context. And yet an analysis by Luckham suggests that 'the distinctions between military and civilian governments appear increasingly superficial', since 'in the final analysis power in most African states (both under military and civilian government) is distributed and held on to by the control of the state security apparatus and organised military force'.[64] So military power is a central means by which the state apparatus controls society, and in this sense is militarized; but (according to Luckham) whether or not the military actually controls the regime is less relevant. Sivard has of course emphasized that the extent of repression is on average greater in military-ruled states; however, if Luckham is right such regimes may therefore be seen as one end of the spectrum of military–civilian power.

Luckham also presents evidence, however, which suggests a lack of correlation between militarization of political power, and militarization in the sense of a general influence of the military on society. Military regimes, he found, have actually been less likely to increase military expenditure than civilian regimes:[65]

> Nine civilian-ruled countries (53 per cent) had rapid increases in military spending in the 1970–80 period, compared with six with lower rates of military growth, and one ... which reduced its military expenditure. In contrast only five military-ruled countries (26 per cent) made major increases in their military expenditures, ten made smaller increases and four ... actually cut them back.

Of course, military spending is not in itself an indicator of societal militarization: but it is also true that there is no obvious correlation between military regimes and conscription in Africa, or between a particular level of increase in military spending and conscription.[66]

It may therefore be argued that 'there are few clear-cut relationships between army rule, military spending and development' – or, we may add, with militarization in a societal sense. Luckham argues that his evidence shows[67]

> a heavy concentration of military-dominated governments among that group of countries which has suffered low incomes, low GDP growth and low military growth since 1970. It would seem on this limited evidence that army rule, sluggish growth and stagnant military expenditure may all be symptoms of a broader crisis in the economies and state stystems of African countries, rather than any one of them being the principal determinant of the other.

Moreover, many military-dominated governments are in states which have a minimal military capability. Luckham identifies only seven African states, mostly in North Africa, with 'an all-round conventional military capability comparable to states outside the region'. Only two of these have military governments. A further seven to nine countries are seen as possessing 'a sub-regional military capability'; of these, four have military regimes. The remainder, among whom the majority of military regimes are found, include ten to twelve countries 'equipped with varying degrees of adequacy for defence against conventional attack' and others which 'maintain military establishments which can do no more than provide the regimes in power some protection from riots and threats to their internal security'. The latter account for around half of Africa's fifty-two states.

In Africa, therefore, there is little correlation between militarization of political power and other forms of militarization, for the simple reason that in most of the countries with military regimes there is little (in some, virtually no) capability to wage external war. The forms of militarization involved in the smaller, weaker and more backward African states comprise the control of the military over the state, and an (often limited) penetration of the military, as the strongest part of the state apparatus, into society.

State and societal militarization are not, however, one and the same thing: it is possible for a military regime to control society via a civilian apparatus, and arguably this is the most typical form of government in stable military regimes. As Luckham points out, 'military governments have "civilianised" themselves by co-opting politicians and civil servants or creating their own political support structures. More than half the military regimes in Africa have established their own political parties; and others ... have (at least in theory) established systems of popular consultation organised around people's committees.'[68] The military plays a greater direct role in social control where the state itself is weak, and in periods of crisis. Neither of these forms of military power, however, has much or often anything to do with warfare, except where political breakdown leads to civil war. Military regimes are not, typically, mobilizing their societies for war, either actually or potentially.

The African pattern is confirmed in an important respect by the Latin American experience. South and Central America have been, historically, regions in which the military has often dominated political power. The role of the military has been maintained until the 1980s and 1990s when a trend towards civilianization of regimes has increasingly prevailed. And yet, despite the past predominance of the military in many Latin American states, the continent has seen none of the major wars that have dominated other regions of the Third World. Despite a large number of rivalries and border disputes, there has been no major inter-state war between Latin American countries for more than half a century. Although South American states are increasingly well armed for such conflicts – and Brazil and Argentina have a nuclear capability – their powerful militaries have had to remain satisfied with a diet of local insurgency. The most serious recent conflicts in Latin America have been the civil war in El Salvador and the Contra attempt to overthrow the Sandinistas in Nicaragua. The only recent example of a major external war involving a Latin American state, the Falklands war, did (it is true) issue from the instability of the military regime in Argentina. But this rare example of a military regime leading to war and militarism is the exception which proves the rule: and the war, moreover, brought about the military's downfall.

The evidence seems, therefore, to suggest that military rule and militarism are very different and to a large degree unrelated. Military rule has become an increasingly typical form of government only in Africa, while military mobilization of society – including for major wars – has been far more widespread, mainly under civilian governments, in the Middle East and Asia. The amalgam of various military-related phenomena, which the proponents of the militarization thesis have sought to construct, is not a sustainable account of what is actually happening in the Third World. We can talk of the militarization of political power, and we can examine the cases where mass armies and ideological militarism are strong, but these are generally in different parts of the world.

The argument for global militarization was based, we have argued, on the escalation of the nuclear arms race in the early 1980s and the boom in arms transfers to the Third World in the late 1970s. It involved a conceptual confusion and a tendency to conflate various quite contradictory trends. In the late 1980s and early 1990s both the developments which gave the militarization thesis its plausibility have, fortunately, been undermined. We can see counter-processes of demilitarization in the advanced world, East and West, and we can see the military forms of power in some of the poorest countries as an index of their desperate economic situations rather than of societal militarization.

Militarism is strongest in the regional powers of the Third World that maintain mass armies and mobilize their peoples with nationalist and religious ideologies against neighbouring states. But even these states are forced to compete economically against one another and against the more advanced states, and may find it difficult to sustain the levels of military build-up which have developed over the last two decades. It would be rash to predict global pacification, as an alternative to global militarization. The geopolitical conditions for wars and mass military mobilization are still widespread. But global society is far from being militarized, and the peoples of the world are preoccupied mostly with economic and social concerns rather than the military ambitions of their rulers.

# Notes

1 Jacques van Doorn, 'The genesis of military and industrial organisation', in *The Soldier and Social Change* (London: Sage, 1973).
2 W. H. McNeill, *The Pursuit of Power: Technology, Armed Force*

*and Society since AD 1000* (Oxford: Blackwell, 1982), chap. 4, pp. 117–44.

3  Mary Kaldor, *The Baroque Arsenal* (London: Deutsch, 1982).

4  C. Wright Mills, *The Power Elite*, (New York: Oxford University Press, 1956).

5  Cynthia Enloe, *Does Khaki Become You? The Militarisation of Women's Lives* (London: Pluto, 1983).

6  E. P. Thompson, 'Notes on exterminism, the last stage of civilisation', in Thompson et al., *Exterminism and Cold War* (London: Verso, 1982).

7  Ibid., p. 22.

8  Andrew Ross, 'Dimensions of militarisation in the Third World', *Armed Forces and Society*, 13 (1987), p. 562.

9  Ibid., p. 564.

10  US Arms Control and Disarmament Agency figures, quoted ibid., table 1, p. 566.

11  Ibid., table 2, p. 568.

12  Ibid., table 3, p. 570.

13  Ibid., table 4, p. 571.

14  Ibid., pp. 572–3.

15  Kurt Lang, *Military Institutions and the Sociology of War* (London: Sage, 1973), p. 12.

16  Gwyn Harries-Jenkins and Charles C. Moscos, Jr, 'Armed forces and society', *Current Sociology*, 29, 3 (1981).

17  Jacques van Doorn, 'The military and the crisis of legitimacy', in Harries-Jenkins and van Doorn, eds, *The Military and the Problem of Legitimacy* (London: Sage, 1976), p. 17.

18  Ibid., p. 29.

19  Van Doorn, *The Soldier and Social Change*; Morris Janowitz, *The Professional Soldier* (Glencoe: Free Press, 1960); Janowitz, ed., *The New Military* (New York: Norton, 1969).

20  Van Doorn, 'The Military and the Crisis of Legitimacy', p. 29.

21  Morris Janowitz, 'Military institutions and citizenship in Western societies', in Harries-Jenkins and van Doorn, eds, *The Military and the Problem of Legitimacy*, p. 83.

22  Ibid., p. 90.

23  Giddens, *The Nation-State and Violence*, vol. 2 of *A Contemporary Critique of Historical Materialism* (Cambridge: Polity, 1985), and the discussion in Martin Shaw, 'War and the nation-state in social theorœy', in David Held and John B. Thompson, eds, *Social Theory of Modern Societies: Anthony Giddens and His Critics* (Cambridge: University Press, 1989), pp. 129–46.

24  Michael Mann, 'The roots and contradictions of modern militarism', *New Left Review*, 162, (1987), pp. 35–6.

25  For a critique, see Martin Shaw, *Dialectics of War: An Essay in the Social Theory of War and Peace* (London: Pluto, 1988), pp. 82–4.

26 Mann, 'Roots and contradictions', p. 36.
27 Ibid., p. 45.
28 Ibid., pp. 46–7.
29 Ibid., p. 48.
30 Ibid., pp. 48–9.
31 Ibid., p. 48.
32 John MacKenzie, *Propaganda and Empire: The Manipulation of British Public Opinion 1880–1960* (Manchester: University Press, 1984).
33 Robin Luckham, 'Of arms and culture', *Current Research on Peace and Violence*, VII, 1 (1984), pp. 2–3, emphasis in original. Luckham's male language may be deliberate rather than sexist, as he later attacks the 'world of war' as 'patriarchy incarnate'.
34 Ibid., p. 3, emphasis in original.
35 Ibid., p. 5.
36 Ibid., p. 8.
37 Ibid., p. 11.
38 Ibid., p. 13.
39 Ibid., p. 13.
40 Ibid., p. 16.
41 Ibid., p. 18.
42 Ibid., p. 22.
43 Ibid., p. 23.
44 Ibid., p. 31.
45 Ibid., p. 52.
46 Ibid., p. 46.
47 Peter Whittle, 'Conscientious objection to military service', *SIPRI Yearbook 1985*, chap. 18, tables 18.3, p. 625 and 18.4, p. 624.
48 Ibid., table 18.3, p. 625.
49 Michael Kidron and Dan Smith, *The War Atlas: Armed Conflict – Armed Peace* (London, Pan, 1983), table 27, p. 32.
50 Julian Cooper, 'Nuclear milking machines and perestroika', *Détente*, 14 (1989), p. 13.
51 Stephen Shenfield, 'Moscow's bitter harvest', *Marxism Today*, 33, 3 (March 1989), p. 7.
52 Cooper, 'Nuclear milking machines', pp. 12–13.
53 Ibid., p. 13.
54 Ibid.
55 Kaldor, *The Baroque Arsenal*, p. 110.
56 Ross, 'Dimensions of militarisation', pp. 568–9. Ross incorrectly gives these and other figures per 1,000 as percentages. If they were such, the figures would of course be 0.52 and 0.49.
57 On guerrilla struggle as a form of the militarization of socialism, see Martin Shaw, *Socialism and Militarism* (Nottingham: Spokesman, 1981).
58 Ross, 'Dimensions of militarisation', pp. 568–9.

59 Information on conscription derived from Whittle, 'Conscientious objection', tables 1 and 2, pp. 622–4.
60 Ruth Sivard, *World Military and Social Expenditures 1986* (Washington, DC: World Priorities, 1986) table I, p. 32.
61 Ibid., table III, pp. 36–9.
62 Ibid., p. 24, table headed 'Military control and repression in the Third World 1986'.
63 Ibid., chart 15, p. 25.
64 Luckham, 'Militarisation in Africa', *SIPRI Yearbook 1985*, chap. 9, p. 306.
65 Ibid.
66 This can be established by a comparison of Luckham, ibid., table 9.2, p. 298, and Whittle, 'Conscientious objection', table 18.1, pp. 622–3.
67 Luckham, ibid., pp. 306, 307.
68 Ibid., p. 323, n. 9.

# 4

# Militarism in Post-Military Society

If the militarization thesis is wrong, military institutions and values nevertheless remain of importance in increasingly demilitarized societies. We have seen that various general theses have been advanced about their roles: that the military is becoming civilianized (and consequently that there is a crisis of legitimacy in military institutions); that mass militarism is now of a 'spectator sport' variety; and that militarism as such is being replaced by an 'armament culture'. The wide-ranging overview of the previous chapter has attempted to look at these theses in comparative perspective, to point up unevenness in the trends identified, and to make important qualifications to them. It has identified contradictory processes of militarization and demilitarization, survivals and new growths of classical militarism as well as new forms and elements of decline. This survey has been inevitably almost as general and schematic, however, as most versions of the militarization thesis and the alternatives. It seems important to try to add some detail to the picture drawn.

In this chapter we shall look therefore at some of the principal dimensions of militarism in post-military society. In which particular ways does militarism continue to be important, in societies which are affected by demilitarization? How do military values affect societies, and how does social change affect professionalized armed forces, once the militarizing effects of conscription on society, and its civilianizing effects on the military, are removed? As post-military social relations extend to continental Europe, and even to the USSR and Eastern Europe, the experiences of the major 'offshore' states, the USA, Britain, the 'White Commonwealth' and Japan – all of which have ended mass military mobilization – are of general interest. They show something of the future prospects of European societies, as they finally deconstruct the infrastructure of mass militarism.

In one crucial respect, however, these experiences are limited as a general model. The demilitarization of the 'offshore' states has occurred within the framework of the Cold War – indeed under the stimulus of the nuclear arms race, which has promoted the substitution of high-technology weaponry for mass military participation. The societies that have been most advanced in the deconstruction of mass militarism have also been in the forefront of the Cold War. In this sense militarism has been sustained and renewed in these societies more than it will be in the societies of the post-Cold War era. Inevitably, by placing more detail on our picture of post-militarism, we risk giving an increasingly atypical account.

This problem is compounded by the fact that the social institutions, cultures and ideologies of militarism are highly nationally specific. Armed forces are core institutions of nation-states, and the military elements of cultures are important components of national cultures and political ideologies. The military and militarism are social and cultural forms of the competition between nation-states: inevitably, they accentuate differences between one national society and another. The effective abolition of military conflict among the states of the Western alliance has had only a limited effect in encouraging common patterns of militarism, or in reducing national differences.

COMPARATIVE ISSUES
IN WESTERN SOCIETIES

During almost half a century there has been no general war, and the wars that have been fought have not been in Europe or North America; the major Western powers have been welded together in an alliance which has suppressed the military rivalries between them; and there has been a common technologizing of military power. These three factors have worked towards a common pattern of decline in mass armies and mass militarism, affecting both societies and armed forces. And yet fundamental differences in military organization and culture, and their roles in societies, have remained between the major Western powers.

We have already seen the main structural difference, in the persistence of conscription in continental Europe, contrasting with its abandonment in the 'offshore' states. We have also referred to the differences resulting from the results of the Second World War, which have meant that in the defeated states, Germany and Japan, a far more thoroughgoing ideological demilitarization has occurred than in other societies. These differences qualify structural similarities: so that although Germany and France, for example, both retain mass conscript armies, they differ in other important respects. National military values, which have been both downgraded and democratized in Germany, retain their relatively unalloyed strength in France.

The variations of national militarisms, therefore, reflect important cultural differences and historical experiences of war, as well as structural differences arising from current military roles and forces. This can be seen in the American case: here a state which (the Civil War apart) had known only frontier wars and minor skirmishes with European powers, has been transformed in the twentieth century into a superpower. The American military has moved from historical marginality to centre stage. American society has become suffused with a great confidence in its military power, which Vietnam only temporarily damaged, and a vigorous patriotism without parallel in contemporary Europe. Americans revere 'the flag' and have the sort of pride in 'America', the European parallels of which have largely disappeared. The prestige of the military as an institution is correspondingly greater, too. And yet US public opinion, while easily manipulated into support for 'quick fix' military operations such as in Grenada and Panama, has been notoriously unwilling (after Vietnam) to stand for large 'body counts'. The anxieties of President Bush, as he prepared the American people for war against Iraq, are testimony to a considerable resistance to militarism in American culture. The ideological strength of American militarism is therefore qualified.

Structurally, moreover, the USA cannot seriously be described as a heavily militarized society, and not only because it has dispensed with the draft in favour of the all-volunteer force. Studies of the American military have emphasized its assimilation to civilian models of social organization – professionalism, managerialism, etc. Moscos, in a well-known thesis, has seen the USA as the model for the transition from an 'institutional' to an 'occupational' military.[1] The American military is a large volunteer force, competing for recruits with civilian occupations, and it has adjusted more than most to the demands for civilian-type conditions for its employees. It increasingly has to offer the satisfactions and rewards other jobs provide, not only in financial terms, but in opportunities for home ownership, family life, leisure, etc. The conflict in the demands of the military and family life have particularly drawn the attention of military sociologists: the military and the family, argues one recent writer, are both 'greedy institutions', demanding more of their members than most social institutions in industrial societies.[2] Although there is a new recognition that the military is 'more than just a job', it is still adapting to the requirements of occupationalism.

If the superpower military of the USA has had to change to survive in a post-military society, the transformation in the military context in European societies has been even more radical. The German military has experienced not only 'democratization', compared to its role in the imperial and National Socialist eras, but also the questioning of the basic military function, which is hardly an issue in the USA. Germany displays the most radical changes in military service of any European society. National service remains compulsory for young men, but they have the right (formerly subject to review, but since 1984 virtually without any official investigation of the individual case) to object to military service and to substitute *Zivildienst* (civilian service). The number of conscientious objectors has risen from 4,000 in 1964 to 77,000 in 1988. Over 90 per cent of objectors are actually drafted into civilian national service – most into forms of social work – so that the numbers in civilian service represent almost a third of the total conscripted. Opinion polls show considerable public acceptance of this extent of conscientious objection.[3]

To date, no other European society has such an extensive system of civilian national service, as an alternative to military conscription. The German situation is important, however, as the most developed model of a transitional stage between continental conscription and offshore post-militarism. As such, it is likely to attract increasing interest, in Eastern Europe and the USSR as well as in Western Europe. Ultimately, however, if the danger of war in Europe permanently recedes, European societies are likely to move beyond conscription altogether. Small professional military forces, suitable for global 'peace-keeping', are likely to become standard. Civilian service, which appears as an acceptable halfway house from compulsory military service, will probably diminish in attraction as the rationale for military conscription disappears.

In this context, the experience of Britain is likely to become of increasing general significance. The UK is the one major European state to have dispensed with conscription and mass civil defence: it has achieved a degree of practical military demobilization greater than that of any other major state. But this has been combined, paradoxically, with greater state military ambitions than most of its European counterparts. In this sense the British case represents a strong test case of the *survival* of militarism in a post-military society. In the discussion which follows, we shall make a detailed examination of the British case, as a society which combines structural demilitarization with continuing cultural, ideological and political forms of militarism. Finally, we shall look at the extent to which the British model may be relevant to the development of post-military society in continental Europe.

## MILITARISM AND NATIONAL MYTHS

One of the problems in seeing a given national situation as a model for general processes of change is that each society has its own historical legacy. It is necessary to define the historical character of British militarism by comparison with other European varieties. It may even be necessary to justify the use of the term 'British militarism', since it has been a widespread perception that even in the epoch of classical militarism, British society was not affected, and that when Britain was forced into war, it was war against militarism – the militarism of others. These are ideological judgements, but like most ideologies they contain elements of truth. British militarism, even at the height of empire, was a 'lower key' affair than many others. British society, like America, was not militarized in the same way or to the same extent as other major European states.

Even at the height of Britain's military power, in the nineteenth century, its army was small compared to those of its continental rivals: less than half the size of the French and German militaries on the eve of the South African war. It was 'axiomatic that only a very small percentage of the total male population had any experience of army life ... The resulting cultural and physical remoteness of the Victorian army was an important characteristic of its relationship with the parent society.' Not only was the army 'an unknown institution' to most of the public, but 'To many Victorians who lacked first-hand knowledge of military life, their army was an institution whose values differed from those of the population at large.' They 'mistrusted its apparently privileged position' and 'were critical of the life-style of the officers, where the daily routine seemed to reflect the social life of the country's upper classes at an earlier period of history'.[4]

One of the reasons for this was that Britain's armed forces were deployed primarily in maintaining its immense colonial empire; having defeated Napoleon at the beginning of the nineteenth century, it was a century before they were called upon to fight a European war. The army was subordinate to the navy, moreover, first in servicing imperial requirements, and then in the arms race of the quarter of a century before 1914. Naval expenditure leapt ahead of that of the army, increasing nearly five fold between 1884 and 1914, while the army's less than doubled.[5]

Elsewhere in Europe, by the 1890s, mass armies were seen as a central support of the state, 'teachers and guides, as well as defenders'.[6] Moreover, conscription was a near-universal fact, valued on the Continent as a 'pillar of the democratic state';[7] the English lack of universal military service was viewed, especially in Germany, as 'one of the shortcomings of English culture'.[8] In Britain, however, 'professionalism and a dedicated commitment to military life, like universal conscription, smacked too readily of a militaristic spirit which was totally foreign to the British way of life'.[9] A powerful navy and an amateurish army continued to work against mass military involvement. The functions of social discipline and promoting class collaboration, performed on the Continent by military service, were fulfilled in England – Kiernan suggests – by 'the ritual of sport'.[10]

Nevertheless, if there was in British (and not merely English) culture a resistance to the forms of continental militarism, a home-grown variety became important in the last decades of the nineteenth century. From the 1870s, MacKenzie points out, 'advertising, bric-a-brac and packaging all exploited royalty and imperialism, taking symbols of colonial adventures into every home'. In this 'spectacular theatre' of imperialism, the armed forces had a central role. Indeed, from earlier in the century, and before monarchy and empire became central themes, 'Military subjects had long been popular in spectacular theatrical presentations and in melodrama.' In the second half of the century, 'the army and its personnel rose in the public's esteem. Regiments became a source of local and civic pride, a vital part of national and local ceremonial and pageantry, particularly after the great expansion in the number of army bands took place.' Well before the First World War, 'Military sentiments and rhetoric spread into civilian life.'

Military Christianity developed, and just as the Churches played a greater part in army life, so 'The language of war entered into hymns, tracts and sermons.' Paramilitary organizations like the Salvation Army, Church Army and uniformed youth organizations followed. It was 'a short step to the dissemination of militarism in schools', with the proliferation of officer corps in public schools, and cadet corps and drilling in state schools as well. 'Military activities became an important source of recreation for the working classes, through the highly successful Volunteer forces, rifle clubs, ceremonial and drill units in factories', etc. 'In all these ways,' MacKenzie concludes, 'a very large proportion of the population came to have some connection with military and paramilitary organisations.' This practical involvement was reflected in a militarized popular culture, for example the 'patriotic music hall', in juvenile literature and the emerging popular press.[11]

This popular militarism, linked in large part to 'heroic' adventures in distant colonies, had a strong entertainment element. It was also closely linked to the cult of organized sport and athletics (which in this light appear more as variants of than substitutes for militarism). Whereas in most European countries mass militarism centred around the solid fact of conscription, in Britain there was a strong anticipation of Mann's modern 'spectator sport' form. And yet, unlike contemporary armament culture which is structurally divorced from mass military participation, the military culture of the turn of the century fed into a coming European war. Indeed, to a considerable extent this is precisely what it was designed to do. Working on the pervasive military ideology was an active propagandist element, in a variety of imperialist, pro-naval and pro-military organizations as well as in the press, advocating ever greater resources for the armed forces, and even conscription, in preparation for conflicts ahead.[12] Militarist traditions, like others – national, monarchical, imperial – were 'invented' with a special zeal in the period between 1870 and 1914, and Britain was no exception.[13]

If the 'spectator sport' element of popular militarism was prefigured in late nineteenth-century Britain, so was the 'deterrence–science' aspect. For Britain, first centre of industrial capitalism in the late eighteenth century, saw the first development of a technologically based military–industrial complex at the end of the nineteenth. As 'naval construction and the manufacture of the diverse kinds of machinery that went into warships became really big business,' McNeill recounts,' 'military [actually, naval] technology came to constitute the leading edge of British (and world) engineering and technical development'.[14] Military industry, with greater government intervention in the economy, grew apace in Britain, and was eventually replicated in other industrial states. The 'new naval version of command technology ... for thirty years, 1884–1914 ... grew like a cancer within the tissues of the world's market economy'.[15]

The resort to technological solutions for military problems, although obviously generalized to other industrial countries before, during and after the First World War, is seen as a peculiarly British preference by Edgerton.[16] The reliance on naval technology before 1914, and increasingly on aerial warfare between the two wars, reflected (he argues) a distinctive form of 'liberal militarism', continuing by different means the Victorian army's avoidance of mass military mobilization. In this perspective the institution of conscription during the First World War constitutes a brief departure from the general pattern of British militarism; the war mobilization of 1939–45 and the peacetime conscription of the 1950s a slightly longer detour. The insistence of British governments on developing their own atomic weapons, and the early adoption of the 'nuclear deterrent' as a defence posture replacing a conscript army, are for Edgerton all of a piece with this dominant tradition of technologically orientated liberal militarism.

It is easy to construct from this evidence the view, which chimes with much of the national ideology, that Britain has never known full-blooded militarism. The British tradition is centred on the navy – and in the last half-century, the air force – rather than a mass army. The British have traditionally been suspicious of their army, and have fought wars to resist the encroachments of more manifestly militarist nations. The British have never (apart from a decade and a half after 1945) known peacetime conscription. In France and Germany (and Japan before 1945) 'universal service became a truly national institution, an essential part of public life'. But for Britain (as for the USA), with its early-established nationhood and its technologically advanced naval tradition, conscription was – even in the late nineteenth century – 'too archaic'.[17]

The inadequacies of this view are that it fails to deal with the militarist component of the imperial ideology which saturated British culture around the turn of the century and reverberated through two world wars and into the 1950s; and even more that it treats as exceptional the periods of total war and their after-maths. Certainly, the process of war mobilization, especially in 1914–18, involved many deep departures from previous military traditions. The music-hall militarism of the turn of the century was hardly an adequate preparation for the shocks of total war, any more than the investment in the naval arms race could pay off in the trenches. Certainly, the war euphoria of 1914 gave way to weary disillusionment and, by the 1920s, to pacifism. Certainly, too, the approach to war in 1939 was more sombre, the content of the mobilizing ideology less imperialist and more democratic.

The experience of total war in 1914–18 nevertheless had profound effects in 1939–45, and not just on the state which was so much better prepared (and empowered) second time around. Despite the revival of *laissez-faire* and its counterpart in 'liberal militarism' between the wars, 1939–45 was to see a process of war mobilization that transformed British society. It is this largely 'new' militarism which is the historical basis of contemporary military culture in Britain. 'Liberal' (more accurately technological) militarism is at work in modern, nuclear Britain, but in the contradictory context bequeathed by the *mass* militarism of the Second World War.

This militarism is not often called by its name. Reactive, reluctant, anti-Fascist though it may have been, it was militarism in the sociological sense: there was a deep and extensive influence of military organization on society. Industry, politics and culture were transformed by the demands of war-making (a large historical literature now attends this process and debates the extent, but not the fact, of social change: it would be too much of a detour to go into this here). British war ideology was not of course straightforwardly militarist in the manner of the Prussian or Nazi glorification of all things military; it was in the nature of the ideologized world struggle that the differentiation must be sharp.

The British militarism of the Second World War nevertheless possessed its own ideology, a sometimes curious but effective fusion of social democracy and imperialism which has remained influential into recent times. In its political form it has been called 'Churchillism';[18] in its wider cultural diffusion it embraced King and Empire, home and family, the virtues of co-operation and planning, the necessities of greater equality and improved welfare in the society after the war. There was much that was not democratic – not least the form of military organization itself – about this British militarism of the Second World War and after. But the term 'democratic militarism' is useful to indicate the relationship of consent between state and society which (conscription and coercion notwithstanding) was at its heart. Britain as it emerged from the war can be described as having a 'military–democratic state', a particular form of warfare–welfare state in which a framework of social democratic reform was conditioned by the centralizing, even secretive needs of war mobilization in 1939–45 and Atlantic defence thereafter.[19]

That the democratic militarism of this period was largely a novel form, diverging from Britain's previous military traditions, made it more vulnerable once older military perspectives reasserted themselves, as they did from the late 1950s (when the UK was the first major state to abandon conscription). But the experience of the 1940s and 1950s, when mass military participation was normal, can hardly be treated simply as an exception to the general British pattern. For even if this was unusual, it was profoundly important to British society. For several generations, still alive and active today, national service – if not actual war experience – became a fundamental experience of the transition to adulthood. Its ending was a matter of defence practicality rather than any abrogation of the state's right to mobilize its citizens.

What has survived of the democratic militarism of the Second World War is what we can call the national military myth. War, the continuation of politics by violent means, reverberates powerfully on politics – and society. In most parts of Europe the experience of the Second World War has generated images and beliefs which still have a powerful role. British recollections of war are not those of injustice – such as those which have been revealed elsewhere in the last few years – but of threat and of common victory over it. Precisely because they rest on an experience of national participation in war, and on a successful outcome, they are a particularly potent source of myth.

The central tenets contributed by this myth are an ideology and imagery of totalitarian military threat, the belief that 'appeasing' such threats is wrong, and that military strength is the foundation of security. These concepts live on half a century later, constituting a sustaining myth of all British defence and military activity, and a central feature of the political culture. The comparison of the 'Soviet threat' with the Nazis has been at the heart of a wide defence consensus for most of the post-war period, and – when that consensus broke down in the 1980s – was successfully appropriated as a party doctrine by the Conservatives. The same analogy of threat from dictatorship was adapted to fit the Argentinian junta in 1982.

Memory of war, albeit increasingly past and distant, has therefore continued to play an important part in British politics and culture. The Argentinian mutation showed the flexibility of the national myth: and at the turn of the 1990s, as the 'Soviet threat' has self-destructed, there were already signs that the lessons of war ('be prepared') would be sustained in future by the more diffuse 'threats' of 'instability in Eastern Europe' (although precisely how such instability poses a military threat to British interests was not explained) and, more ominously, 'Islamic fundamentalism'. These attempts at a complex reconstruction of the 'threat' may not have succeeded, since they manifestly lacked the simplicity and superficial military plausibility of the Soviet bogey. But Saddam Hussein's invasion of Kuwait provided a ready fit with the need for a totalitarian 'threat', and in 1990 Margaret Thatcher chose the setting of a visit to post-Communist Czechoslovakia to link the 'appeasement' of Nazi Germany (for which she apologized to her Czech hosts) with the danger of appeasing Iraq.

New developments in international relations are therefore easily incorporated into the myth of the Second World War, which has had such a powerful influence in recent British politics. Two recent examples of the way this works are provided by the Falklands war of 1982 and the nuclear defence debate of the early and mid-1980s, leading to the general elections of 1983 and 1987. At the onset of the Falklands crisis, the intelligence débâcle that allowed the Argentinian junta to invade the islands provoked a violent parliamentary response. In the emergency debate of 3 April 1982 Labour leaders and Conservative backbenchers alike charged the government with 'betrayal' of the 1,800 British Falklanders, and challenged the government, in Michael Foot's words, 'to prove by deeds – they will never be able to do it by words – that they are not responsible for the betrayal and cannot be faced with that charge'.[20]

The language, as well as the situation in which a Labour minority combined with large parts of the Conservative majority to attack the government for inaction (if not appeasement), echoed the famous debate of May 1940 in which Parliament brought down the Chamberlain government for its ineffective prosecution of the Second World War. Thatcher, who could never play a Chamberlain, resolved to become her own Churchill. Consciously, in her own speeches and in those of her supporters – and increasingly as victory was assured – she was presented as the reincarnation of the great wartime leader. (I have argued elsewhere that Thatcher laid inappropriate claims to this mantle, since she opposed the patriotic side of Churchill's legacy to the social-democratic reformism to which, in 1939–45, it was inextricably linked.)[21]

Anthony Barnett argues, however, that 'Churchillism' was influential far beyond Thatcher and her immediate supporters – the speeches of Foot and other Labour leaders showed that they too shared this basically 'Second World War' approach to the Falklands issue.[22] The problem, for Labour, became that once it had legitimated the Task Force and ultimately the war in this way, it was difficult for it to argue for peace proposals or United Nations intervention, or to question particular aspects of the war. The Thatcher government was successful in polarizing public opinion, which in the early stages of the conflict was divided about the merits of actually using force or losing lives. Once fighting and killing took place, polls showed an increasing consolidation of support for the government and the war.[23]

Labour was marginalized by the ambiguity of its combining support for the Task Force with criticism of the actual use of force. Denis Healey and Neil Kinnock were both victims of this contradictory position in the 1983 election, when they attracted widespread criticism for attempting retrospectively to cast Thatcher in too bloodthirsty a light.[24] Despite the initial shock of the loss of life over these barely populated islands of which many British people had never heard, and despite the ultimate incongruity of the comparison between the Falklands and the Second World War, in the crisis the government was able to mobilize effectively the 'lessons' that 'appeasement' fails and that military strength is the only way to deal with 'dictators' who 'threaten the British way of life'.

A similar success was eventually achieved by the Thatcher government over nuclear weapons. Defence policy in general had been a matter of political consensus since the Second World War. After the controversy caused by the rise of the Campaign for Nuclear Disarmament (CND) in the late 1950s, it had played a minimal role in British politics. CND itself had peaked in 1960 and was eclipsed as a serious force by 1964. Nuclear weapons were not debated in Parliament between 1965 and 1980. The NATO decision (December 1979) to introduce cruise missiles into Western Europe, compounded by the Conservative government's announcement (1980) that it proposed to buy the American Trident nuclear system to replace Polaris as Britain's 'strategic deterrent', provoked a powerful and unexpected popular reaction. A new peace movement arose in Britain as it did simultaneously in a number of other Western European countries. The movement had obvious echoes in public opinion: polls quickly recorded majorities, which were to continue (with variation only in their size) over several years, against both cruise and Trident. The Churches, the trade unions and the Labour and Liberal parties were speedily influenced by the new anti-nuclear movement.[25]

So far, the British situation could have been compared with that in most Western European countries (except, significantly, France, where support for the national *force de frappe* remained widespread and that for the independent peace movement correspondingly weak). However, the defence debate in Britain, especially during the general elections, was very different from that elsewhere in Europe. In West Germany, the Netherlands and Belgium, for example, governments were forced to debate cruise missile deployment in great detail, to justify it as a 'dual track' decision (as both weapons modernization and a pressure for disarmament) and to delay deployment (the Dutch government was finally able to win Parliamentary support for deployment only in 1986, three years after cruise missiles were introduced into Britain). In the UK the government's response was very different: it sought to divert the debate from the specific issues of cruise missiles and Trident (on which opinion polls showed it was in a minority) to the most general level of whether Britain needed nuclear weapons in principle (on which polls showed consistently that a majority supported it).[26] The British debate started from the common European position; the government tried to force it into a more 'French' mould, even though the new missiles were of American, not national, origin.

In part it could be said that its opponents aided the Thatcher government in making this shift. Whereas the continental peace movements were mainly *ad hoc* coalitions formed to oppose cruise missiles, the British peace movement quickly consolidated under the banner of CND with its clear historic commitment to unilateral British nuclear disarmament. Nevertheless, the CND leadership understood, as their 'Nuclear Election' propaganda campaign of 1983 showed, that they needed to focus their efforts around cruise and Trident missiles if they were to win. That the government still succeeded in shifting the debate was in part due to the fact that when it came to elections, campaigning groups had little voice, compared to the parties who were directly competing for votes. (British election law emphasizes this by restricting legitimate expenditure to that which supports candidates, and broadcasting practice largely excludes non-party view.)[27] The peace movement had to rely on Labour, and to a lesser extent the Liberals, SDP and Nationalists, to make its case for it, in whole or in part.

Although the Labour party was formally 'unilateralist' and its leader, Foot, a long-term CND supporter, its parliamentary leadership as a whole were at best reluctant converts to a non-nuclear defence policy. Labour appeared hopelessly divided and confused over defence. Ironically, although the rejection of cruise and Trident missiles was an issue that genuinely united the Labour leadership and the party – and which had a wide resonance among Liberal–SDP and even Conservative voters – Labour failed to make these popular issues its campaigning points. Instead it fell back into defensive confusion over the basic 'unilateralist' issue, in the face of a much clearer, more direct Tory attack.

The Conservatives did more, however, than play to the weaknesses of their opponents; they capitalized on the same national myth which had served them so well in the Falklands war. You had to have nuclear weapons, they argued, to deter the 'Soviet threat'; as long as the USSR had nuclear weapons, Britain and NATO had to have theirs, and to modernize them as required. To do otherwise was to 'leave Britain defenceless'. By constant repetition of these very simple arguments – on a level which would have served no other European government so well – the Conservatives evaded, especially in the general elections, the more difficult questions about cruise and Trident as particular weapons systems. Polling data indicate their success, in moving defence to a priority election issue, and in swinging support their way: disapproval of unilateralism peaked during the election campaign, and polling on cruise missiles actually showed a majority in favour of their installation – a position which both previously and subsequently was rejected by consistent majorities.[28] Labour was seen overwhelmingly as having weaker policies on defence than the Conservatives. But, as Miller argues, this was not so much because Labour had a clear-cut defence policy which was rejected by the electors, but because it appeared to be hopelessly divided on the issue.[29]

In 1987 defence policies were not as important an issue in the political arena before the election as they had been in 1983, but all parties had learnt from the previous election the need for effective handling of the issue. Labour, after the failure of its confused disarmament policies in 1983, tried to anticipate attack by meeting the Conservatives on their own ground, with an approach which emphasized that Labour would protect Britain's conventional forces. The Tories, on the other hand, sought essentially to repeat their 1983 success, and were reinforced by the SDP–Liberal Alliance. The result was that 'defence operated as a "scare" in the 1987 campaign', frightening voters off Labour.[30] The salience of defence as a major talking point moved from 20 per cent on 18 May, early in the campaign, to 60 per cent on 29 May, in the run up to voting on 11 June; Labour's credibility on the issue fell accordingly.[31] This followed a concentrated Tory and Alliance attack with (unusually) support from the US President. A study of election leads on television news shows the following number one items on BBC bulletins: 'Owen, Thatcher attack Labour defence policy' (25 May); 'Conservatives, Alliance attack Labour on defence and extremism' (26 May); 'Kinnock reply on defence, Reagan backs Thatcher' (27 May); 'Thatcher rally: attacks Labour on defence' (28 May).[32]

The Conservative lead, which had been above 10 per cent in all polls taken before 14 May but below that figure in nearly all polls in the following two weeks, showed a new surge of leads over 10 per cent at the end of May (the election result was a lead of 12 per cent).[33] The evidence suggests that the defence assault was very important to the Conservatives' beating off Labour's attempt to undermine their lead in the campaign. Indeed defence became, largely as a result of the Tory and Alliance campaigns, the most prominent issue in television news coverage of the election, an importance it had not attained even in 1983.[34] Even if the economic prosperity of the majority of the population was the decisive underlying factor in the Conservatives' third successive election victory, defence played a crucial part in the mechanics of their success. (As a result of this, Labour turned in 1989 to acceptance of British nuclear weapons pending multilateral negotiations – ironically, just at the moment when change in Eastern Europe was about to alter the entire context of defence policy.)

The strength of the national defence myth revealed by these episodes is in inverse proportion to the actual involvement of the members of British society with military matters. The Second World War is still a benchmark, almost fifty years on, because it is the last major British experience of war. The simple arguments still work in British politics, not only due to this cultural conditioning, but because there is no need for most members of British society to engage closely with war. The 'threat' is general and abstract because there is no really concrete threat of invasion or bombardment. There is no border over which tanks can roll, and no one has been seriously able to envisage a maritime invasion of Britain, since by the time Soviet tanks reached the Channel, nuclear weapons would surely have been used. British perceptions of war have become 'all or nothing': a nuclear confrontation few believe they would survive. The government's civil defence policy, which protects the infrastructure of the state but

makes only the most feeble and implausible suggestions for pro-
tecting the population, has only reinforced this belief.[35]

The attitudes to defence issues revealed by polling data, and the
role of defence in elections, suggest that these are issues on which
people have strong underlying beliefs – which, if stirred, are
capable of influencing votes – but which have little practical
significance in their lives. This interpretation is supported by the
evidence of polls about the saliency of issues: even at the height of
the defence controversies of the early 1980s, it was rare for 20
per cent of those polled to rate defence issues as the most important; in the early stages of the Falklands conflict, far more people
still rated unemployment their most pressing political concern.
In general, unemployment, the health service, mortgages and (in
recent years) the poll tax have represented much bigger worries
for most people than defence. Even in 1983, when the Thatcher
government was widely seen as benefiting from the 'Falklands
factor', the evidence suggests that this was a background effect,
rather than a direct issue. Psephological research certainly suggests that economic concerns were the overriding issues in the
Conservative victory, then as subsequently.[36] What has not been
measured, perhaps, is the extent to which the war had helped
create the image of Conservative strength – and even more of
Labour weakness – which in turn influenced estimates of general
ability to manage the economy and other issues.

An equally interesting measure of the saliency of defence issues
is the response to questions about defence spending. In some ways
this is a more decisive indicator of public feeling than abstract
questions about the importance of defence, since it gauges support for resources – often in competition with other demands.
Two sorts of questions seem to have been asked. There are those
that ask directly about the level of defence spending, in which the
respondents' attention is drawn directly to defence but not to the
competition for resources. In the early 1980s, British opinion
polls tended to show majority support for existing levels of defence spending, with relatively small minorities favouring either
increases or cuts. (Older and more working-class respondents
tended more to favour increases, younger and more middle-class
respondents tended more to support cuts.)[37] On the other hand,
there are surveys which pose the comparative issue directly, such
as the British Social Attitudes surveys which over several years
have asked about people's priorities for increased spending. These

surveys have found tiny proportions of their samples volunteering defence as their first priority for increased spending: the figures have been as low as 4 per cent and even 2 per cent.[38]

## Nostalgia Militarism and Media Wars

In a post-military society, militarism takes a more ideological and cultural than a social-structural form. In part this new ideological-cultural form of militarism is based on the relatively universal 'armament culture', diffused primarily from the USA. On the other hand, however, it is highly nationally specific, relating to historical experiences of war and military traditions. National militarism has a general role in culture, which underpins the specifically political myths concerning war and defence. Nowhere is this role clearer than in Britain, where 'nostalgia militarism' takes many forms.

We have seen that although Britain prides itself on being a non-militaristic society, it shared (in the late nineteenth and early twentieth centuries) in the culture of classical militarism which was rife throughout Europe. This culture has institutional echoes even today, for example in the survival of the paramilitary youth organizations (Scouts, Boys' Brigades, etc.) created at the turn of the century, and the durability of some of the literature (again, especially boys' literature) produced in this period. Such institutions survive, however, only through adaptation to changing social conditions. The modernized Scouts (in 1990 they even abandoned traditional gender divisions by admitting girls, much to the consternation of the Guides) are a long way from Baden-Powell's original model.

In a study of public (i.e. private) schools – the educational base of the British elite – from 1900 to 1972, Otley concluded that 'it seems likely that school militarisation and militarism achieved a crescendo just before, and during, the First World War, and that thereafter it diminished in intensity, if only slowly'. By 1972 there were 'many signs of the decay of school militarisation and militarism': although cadet training was as common as in 1936, many contingents had become voluntary, it seemed likely that the impact of military ceremonial and commemorative activity was low, and 'the old leadership/service/sacrifice ethos has undoubtedly weakened – perhaps almost to vanishing point'. Most important, Otley argued, was that public schools had largely abandoned the traditions of preparing and supplying officers to the armed forces, so that only a minority of officers came from the public school sector.[39]

A number of institutions operate directly in the field of nostalgia militarism. Regimental and veterans' associations sustain the memories of the past among those once actively involved with wars, while national institutions such as Remembrance Day, and the sale of poppies to benefit those who have fought in wars, sustain these images in the wider population. Institutions such as the Royal British Legion, and the network of social clubs linked to it across Britain, provide a low-grade link with military values for large numbers of people, including those in working-class areas.

Many other institutions which aim to foster awareness of military culture have less overtly positive attitudes to war and the military. A new wave of military museums has opened in the 1980s, offering militarism as a component of the theme-park 'heritage' tourism that caters primarily for the domestic market – but which goes a long way to constituting Britain's international tourist appeal as well. Scattered across the land, in converted aircraft hangars and even Second World War prisoner-of-war camps, some of the military museums even offer local versions of the Imperial War Museum's 'Blitz experience', the centrepiece of its 1989 renovation:

> Sudden explosions seem to burst all around, thanks to the latest in soundaround electronics ... Then the rest of George's [the air-raid warden's] taped-over family piped up over the loudspeakers, jollying each other along and breaking into Roll Out the Barrel. Another shell exploded: this turned out to be the big one. The benches rocked forwards ... The all-clear sounded a bit too soon for comfort, I thought, hanging back to let others go first.
>
> We were led through the meticulously reconstructed rubble of a London street littered with gnarled railings and bits of wall. A kitsch lampshade poked out from between the ragged curtains of the remains of poor George's house.

> Hurried along, someone asked if they could stay a bit
> longer than the allotted seven minutes. 'Why?' asked the
> brisk PR. 'That's all there is. That *is* the Blitz.'[40]

The local (and especially regimental) museums do not all possess what has been described as the Imperial War Museum's
(IWM's) 'developed sense of its own liberal decorum'. But the
studied ambiguities of the IWM's attitude towards war not only
represent a benchmark for other museums; they say a good deal
about the nostalgic culture of militarism in Britain today.

> It takes seriously its commitment to pacifism, to the role
> of women in war, and to the Home Front. In short, it
> aims to be a war museum, not a military – still less a
> militaristic – one. This difference informs every aspect of
> the massive redesign, from the forthcoming and campaign
> to the new corporate logo. The IWM will strive to be-
> come 'part of you and your family's history'. Much less
> malleable than history, however, is the ambiguity of
> the museum's exhibits. A senior staff member calls it 'the
> biggest boy's bedroom in London'. Planes hang from the
> new glass-barrelled ceiling; tanks and missiles rise priapi-
> cally into the exhibition vault. To compensate, downstairs
> displays stress the cost of war, its social history and
> civilian experiences.[41]

This willingness to place military institutions and hardware in
an educational and even entertainment context extends to the
military itself. The armed forces all have developed educational
arms, which mount well-honed propaganda talks in thousands
of schools and colleges every year. Air displays, military tattoos
and naval regattas, at military bases throughout the country,
allow civilians to enjoy a 'day out' with the armed forces and
participate in the spectacles provided by military discipline and
hardware. A tattoo forms a popular element of the UK's most
important annual arts event, the Edinburgh Festival. At its highest
point, military spectacle becomes a central component of state
spectacle, as in the annual Trooping the Colour on the monarch's
official birthday and, more infrequently, in great state occasions
such as coronations and royal funerals.

Memories of war, especially of 1939–45, are cultivated by

every branch of the mass media. Old war films, brash American and cosy British, are still a staple of off-peak television. Popular nostalgia, gently self-deprecating in the true British wartime spirit, has lived on in highly popular television comedy series such as *Dad's Army* and *Allo! Allo!* The hold of wartime images on the imagination has been reinforced in recent years by the growing fascination with this other world, now half a century ago. Older generations relive their youth, young people engage with a reality far removed from anything they have experienced (or are likely to). The 1940s (and to a lesser extent the 1950s, the era of national service) underwent a distinct revival in the culture of the 1980s, making a prominent appearance in serious as well as popular literature and film.

The celebration of past wars may have contemporary political meanings, but it functions more as a component of a general consumer culture than of an active militarism. Film-making about the Second World War has undergone something of a revival – as witness Spielberg's *Empire of the Sun* and Puttnam's *Memphis Belle* (a British contribution to Hollywood). But this cinema has been increasingly displaced in popular culture – notably on the 'war' shelves of the video shops that have proliferated in the 1980s – by the cinema of Vietnam. British film culture is, at this level, little more than a component of the American-dominated mass culture that serves a largely uncritical diet of 'action' movies to an audience (chiefly young and male) which has no real knowledge of war. Some films are more sensitive than others, but as Bruce Robinson, screenwriter on *The Killing Fields*, has put it, 'when *The Killing Fields* came out everybody said, "Oh, *great*, an anti-war film," then six weeks later *Rambo* comes out and does three thousand times the business, and it's about this guy with these *huge* tits, killing the Vietnamese and winning the war. Which just reiterates from my point of view that film is nothing, film is entertainment.'[42]

Film may sometimes be more, but there is no doubt that entertainment is the overwhelming aim of war films. Even a Vietnam movie like *Full Metal Jacket* – which was marketed with a nuclear disarmament symbol on a soldier's helmet to indicate its critical pretensions – could be understood by the uncritical viewer as little more than 'war action' entertainment, since the film is at best ambivalent towards the near-orgy of killing in which it culminates. Essentially what the viewer gets from such a film depends a lot on his or her values and initial perceptions of war; the film itself typically gives one little idea of the basis from which one might criticize its violence.

It is important to ask how far in a nostalgic military culture the news media allow, and even encourage, viewers to appropriate real wars in an 'entertainment' mode at the time when they are actually being fought: or does their coverage have a serious political function? Conventional wisdom has it, of course, that television coverage encouraged American viewers to reject Vietnam, the first 'TV war'. Research has given little support to this view, and suggests that television reinforced attitudes rather than changed them: in the early stages of the war it may actually have helped to mobilize the support for the war, but when people were rejecting the war, coverage may have reinforced that rejection. Press coverage was often more critical than television, and the memorable 'negative' visual images of the war (the famous picture of a terrified, semi-naked girl running down a road, for example) were still photographs rather than television film. If television actually assisted the opposition to the war, it was due less to war coverage itself, than to coverage of massive anti-war demonstrations (the visual power of film of hundreds of thousands of people, rather than the verbal messages which accompanied them, helped to accelerate the momentum of the anti-war movement).[43]

For Britain, of course, the parallel is the Falklands war, and the British government clearly believed in the putative 'lessons of Vietnam' when it set out to restrict journalistic access to – and transmission from – the war zone. Television pictures of the fighting were, until the final stages, taking two or three weeks to return to the UK, and the government was able to exercise control over information almost unparalleled in modern warfare. Sections of the press, moreover, engaged in aggressively 'patriotic' propaganda campaigns, characterizing Argentinians as 'Argies' in the way that the Germans had been called 'Jerries' (and before that 'Huns'), culminating in the *Sun*'s notorious 'Gotcha!' headline on the sinking of the Argentine cruiser *Belgrano*. The government, with the active support of many of its backbenchers, encouraged this simplistic nationalism, and clearly believed that there was massive patriotic support for the war.[44]

Opinion polling shows that this was far from the case. Indeed, as a recent study of the audience reception and perception of Falklands war news coverage concludes, 'To an appreciable extent, it seems altogether that a large proportion of the British public hardly felt that Britain was at war with Argentina at all. The desire to transform a battle into a national struggle appears to have been missing.'[45] Morrison and Tumber's research shows that more than 20 per cent of *Sun* readers were dissatisfied with their paper's coverage of the conflict, and less than 70 per cent satisfied. Other 'patriotic' popular papers, such as the *Star* and the *Express*, also recorded higher levels of reader dissatisfaction than 'quality' conservative papers like *The Times* and the *Telegraph*, or even the *Mirror* (a target of the 'patriotic' lobby's rage because of its moderate and relatively even-handed coverage) and the liberal *Guardian* (much of whose coverage was critical of the war).[46] (The case of the *Guardian* is interesting: when it criticized the Suez campaign in 1956, it had lost readers; during the Falklands war, its critical stance gained them, although the research does show a small minority of readers 'very dissatisfied' with its policy.)

Most people relied for their information about the war principally on television news, rather than the press. This is largely because British television, unlike the press, has laid upon it the requirements of 'balance' and 'objectivity' in its coverage, and is widely perceived as more reliable. Academic research has nevertheless shown that news is 'constructed' by programme makers, and how despite the pursuit of objectivity and formal balance in coverage (e.g devoting equal time to both parties in an election, or both sides in an industrial dispute), the concepts and assumptions of programme-makers colour the presentation of information, not least in highly contentious areas such as war and defence policy. In the Falklands war, a Glasgow University Media Group study argues that[47]

> The broadcasters were not against censorship as such, but they did not wish the control to lie with outside agencies. They were afraid that their own credibility would be undermined if they were not 'seen' to be independent. Consequently, they were prepared to cut material themselves on grounds of 'taste' or what they saw as the 'public mood'.

The detailed research in the Glasgow study shows how television coverage of key incidents in the war tended to reinforce, rather than challenge, official definitions. One reason for this, it concedes, was that 'the official opposition was divided on its approach to the war, even though a substantial section of the population was against it. In the absence of a clear lead from the political apparatus, television was enable to feature anything like the public debate which existed.'[48] This is an important factor, perhaps understated in the overall presentation of the Glasgow group's case; in the light of Labour's role, some of the media coverage (in the 'quality' press as well as current affairs television, if not in mainsteam television news) begins to resemble a creditable display of intellectual and political independence. Morrison and Tumber are perhaps closer to a balanced view in seeing the struggle within journalism and broadcasting, and between journalists and those forces who wish to ensure a more homogeneous 'patriotic' coverage, as a genuine ideological battle reflecting a real external test of 'popular broadcasting culture' by the New Right.[49] Their study also has the advantage that it studies not just news output, but also the audience reception of this output.

These studies put contrasting constructions on the relationship of the broadcasters to public opinion. The Glasgow group point out that the broadcasting authorities tended to justify their relatively sympathetic relationship with the government's viewpoint by reference to 'public opinion'. They argue, however, that this too was a construct, not only of the pollsters but of the television journalists who reported it. 'We have here a situation', they conclude after a close examination of a number of 'public opinion' issues, 'in which television selectively informs people's attitudes, then selectively reports on what those attitudes are, and finally ... uses this version of public opinion to justify its own approach to reporting.'[50]

Morrison and Tumber, on the other hand, give more evidence to the conflict between broadcasters and government, and present new opinion survey evidence showing that there was a 'lack of general support for the attack' by the government on the the independence of the broadcasters, and that this depended 'on the ability of the public to dissociate the values of independent broadcasting with [sic] specific cultural groups and instead to hold them as valuable national values, the preserves of no one'.[51] In two different senses, however, these studies point to limits of militarization in British culture, as tested by the Falklands war. They agree that there was direct resistance to military definitions of reality; and Morrison and Tumber show support for independent broadcasting values against political demands for military definitions.

It is obviously important to ask how typical the Falklands war was in these respects: how wartime news coverage compares to general television coverage of issues related to international relations, defence and disarmament, and the military; and (more difficult to evaluate) how public reception of this coverage compares. Certainly these areas are marked out, as the Falklands conflict was, as politically sensitive in a way which is not true of most areas of domestic politics. Most instances of overt television censorship, by the broadcasting authorities or (as was increasingly the case under Thatcher) as a result of government intervention, have concerned programmes about Northern Ireland, nuclear weapons and the peace movement. A particularly notorious incident was the governing party's attempt, during Norman Tebbit's chairmanship, to attack the BBC's coverage of the US air raid (from bases in the UK) on Libya in 1986. In this sense the Falklands episode was both the most extreme case of a general pattern and also perhaps a stimulus to subsequent government actions in the media.

There is also evidence that the sorts of biases that existed in the Falklands coverage operate in other areas. The Glasgow group, in studies also reported in *War and Peace News*, locate much television coverage in the early 1980s within a 'propaganda war' waged against the USSR as part of the 'Second Cold War'. They look at television coverage of the Greenham Common women's peace camp, showing the subtle (and sometimes not so subtle) ways in which this was tilted against the peace campers.[52] At the same time they acknowledge a conflict among journalists about the way in which these issues are covered, and (writing in 1985) already detected 'a growing debate within news rooms and a commitment by some journalists to reporting news events in a way which does not reinforce the cold war'.[53]

It is arguable in any event that the Glasgow group's study, focused mainly on 1982–3 – which coincided with the Falklands war and the Conservative government's propaganda counteroffensive against the peace movement – may in some senses have been a 'worst case' study. In 1980–1 the peace movement not only held the political initiative but had the novelty value of a sudden outpouring of mass protest unexpected by state or media. A study of that period might well reveal that television coverage – although not free of the biases detected by the Glasgow study a year or so later – worked to fuel the rapidly growing momentum of opposition. Certainly it is important to stress that television does not operate in a one-dimensional way as the agent of government propaganda. It clearly responds to the political context, and contains within it the sort of debate which has been mentioned: a debate which has shifted quite drastically, not only in different phases of the 'Second Cold War', but also more recently in the era of Gorbachev and the 'end of the Cold War'.

Television news works not only in a political context, and within what Morrison and Tumber call 'popular broadcasting culture', but with the more slowly moving currents of popular ideas, beliefs and values that bear on war and peace, defence and disarmament, and the military, and the way these are represented within the general culture. Some of these cultural elements are, for strong historical reasons, nationalist, imperialist and militarist. An episode like the Falklands has been seen by Thompson as stirring a 'nationalist sediment which may cloud our political and cultural life'.[54] However, if the analogy is useful, the sediment will settle; arguably, it did so quite quickly, so that even in the 1983 election, although fought in the shadow of the Falklands, its legacy was almost entirely implicit.

Placing the militarist elements in British culture in perspective, we have to set against them the non- or even anti-militarism which, as we have seen, historians of the British army have stressed. And we must look at militarism in the context of the exceptionally market-based, secularized, consumer culture which has become dominant in Britain – especially England – since the 1950s. The decline of militarism could well be compared to the decline of organized religion and coherent class-based political cultures and ideologies, both of which have been marked features of British society in recent decades.

## THE MILITARY IN POST-MILITARY SOCIETY

The military, as an institution, exists ever more on the margins of post-military society. The paradox here is that although the armed forces may consume very large economic resources, and comprise extremely lethal means of violence, they constitute a smaller and often a more isolated section of the societies to which they belong. Even considered together with the social groups directly dependent on them, in military industry, this is still the case.

Britain is the strongest example of these trends in contemporary Europe. Considering that the UK, with its modest total population of around 60 million, contrives to be one of the world's major military powers and manufacturers of armaments (after the superpowers), the military sectors of British society are not large. Adding together the 300,000-plus armed forces personnel, the declining numbers (well below 200,000) of Ministry of Defence civilian staff, and rather more than 500,000 people directly or indirectly employed in defence work, a little more than a million workers (around 4 per cent of the total labour force) were accounted for by the military and defence industry sectors in the 1980s. If we count those in engaged in producing arms for sale to other states, this rose to 5 per cent.

Even in the period from 1979 to 1985, in which the Thatcher government increased British military expenditure by almost 30 per cent in real terms, the total numbers in these sectors fell (mainly because near-static numbers of military personnel and defence workers combined with a sharp reduction in numbers of civil servants).[55] The combination of a modest cutback in British defence spending and the contraction of world arms markets has since squeezed them still further: the late 1980s saw rationalization and large-scale lay-offs by arms manufacturers. As peace breaks out the defence cuts of the 1990s will only accelerate these trends: the reductions announced in 1990 will leave total armed forces of just over 250,000 and civilian employees of only 120,000.[56]

Although Britain's military sectors possess considerable international importance, both as armed forces and arms producers, they have therefore a limited role in British society. Military and economic weight is not reflected in social or political weight. Britain's reliance on technologically sophisticated professional armed forces and advanced science-based military industries means that the size of the workforces in both sectors is modest in relation to the resources they consume.

In some ways, of course, these sectors have a domestic political importance beyond the numbers they mobilize; but this is not because the armed forces, in particular, make a direct or open bid for political influence. With rare exceptions (such as at one or two points during the Falklands war) military leaders exert political leverage behind closed doors, and then only on matters related to the interests of the military itself. Defence industry interests are rather more overtly in the political arena, especially now as rationalization threatens employment; the concentrated nature of defence employment gives armaments workers considerable influence in a number of parliamentary constituencies (as we shall see below). But on the whole, the political significance of the military sectors is defined for them by government policies, and by the wider culture.

The British armed forces have probably been less directly exposed to a 'crisis of legitimacy' than their continental counterparts. The early transition to an all-professional force has insulated them, as in Victorian times, from the society of which they are a part. Unlike in the nineteenth century, however, the modern military has a general legitimacy as a result of the victorious conclusion of the Second World War. Here, of course, there is also a major difference between the British and most continental militaries. Although the British have never proclaimed the supremacy of military values in the manner of, for example, the Germans and Japanese, they have not suffered the thoroughgoing downgrading of them that has occurred in these countries as a result of defeat – and the association of militarism with genocide. Nor does the modern British military experience the incursion of civilian values that conscripts bring with them in the rest of Europe.

A professional military is far more able to control both its recruitment and its recruits, and on the whole the British military appears to have been successful in moulding successive generations of volunteers to its purposes. Basic military training has continued to emphasize the 'breaking in' of raw recruits, achieving their adaptation to military organization and culture. Although the informal military culture contains defensive mechanisms for ordinary soldiers,[57] it generates no demands for soldiers' unions or trade union representation (such as exist in the Netherlands and West Germany respectively). Issues of exemption from, alternatives to and conscientious objection to military service are of course completely lacking. The paradoxical combination of a professional military (avoiding mass participation) and a culture which generally legitimates the armed forces by reference to past victories (achieved by participation of a kind which no longer exists) is very effective in insulating the military from general social criticism.

British military culture has, of course, adapted greatly to the professionalization and technologization of armed force, just as earlier it adapted to masses of conscripts and the democratic ideology of the war against Fascism. Recruitment and training in all services have increasingly centred around the requirements of skill and expertise. Even the attributes of individual violence have become the specialized concern of increasingly high-profile units such as the SAS and Special Boat Services. In their officer recruitment, all the armed services constantly stress managerial skills. The most recent adaptation reveals the British armed forces, not surprisingly, as more effectively reconciled than those of many states to the needs of modern warfare. Surprisingly, then there are virtually no studies by military sociologists, comparable to many made in the USA and elsewhere in Western Europe, on the themes of the 'professionalization' and 'managerialization' of the military which were developed in the 1960s.[58]

There are strong formal continuities in British military traditions: this is not surprising given the absence of major defeats in living memory, or of any serious political intervention in military organization since 1945 (the ending of national service apart: and the effects of this were socially narrowing). Officer corps have not suffered the formal re-education of the military in defeated, revolutionized or less successful states, nor have the rank and file significantly alleviated the inequalities and deprivations of military life. Military ideology is based on traditions going back in some cases for centuries, emphasizing the differences between the main 'services' and indeed between particular branches and regiments within them.

The traditionalism of the armed forces is most continuously challenged by state defence policies themselves. Since the late 1950s these have contracted the numbers of military personnel and accentuated reliance on sophisticated – especially nuclear – technology. The balancing of commitments and weapons costs within a large but politically controlled budget has posed a constant threat to service traditions, making it necessary for the services repeatedly to justify their expenditures and establishments. In the early years of the Thatcher government there was a commitment to real annual rises in defence spending, including above-average increases in military pay; but even at this point the Navy (especially) saw its equipment, manpower and role threatened – largely by the overriding commitment to the renewal of the 'nuclear deterrent', which prevailed over the requirements of the conventional navy. Despite the long naval tradition, central to British imperial and military ideology, it was only the Falklands war which temporarily rescued the Navy from what its advocates saw as very 'damaging' cuts. The Falklands war was generally very useful to the armed forces in legitimating their claim to be effective military resources, in a way which no amount of impressive NATO exercises, or even counter-insurgency operations, could have hoped to achieve. It remains to be seen if the Gulf War will play a similar role in relegitimating the armed forces, just as the end of the Cold War had created an unprecedented crisis of military identity.

The British military has responded to the post-war shift of defence policies by emphasizing its professionalism and technological orientation, and its potential as an efficient fighting and deterrent force. If in some ways the technologization and professionalization of military force pose constant challenges to the military, in others they protect it from changes in the wider society. The experience of 1939–45, in which the British armed forces became mass organizations recruiting from across the social spectrum, has been put behind. The professional middle class and the organized labour movement, which supplied the critical elements for the political radicalization inside the military during the Second World War, have both ceased to be significant sources of manpower in the post-conscript armed forces.

Even during the period of peacetime conscription, indeed, the professional officer corps was able to re-establish its unquestioned supremacy over the more diffuse mass of conscripts. Subsequently, while officer recruitment has been on a more 'technocratic' and less socially exclusive basis than earlier in the century, this has been achieved by the adaptation of military traditions rather than by a direct ideological challenge to them. The social groups from which such a challenge might have come ceased to be coerced – and are no longer attracted – into military service.

The evidence of a recent study of elites in the British military system is that the growth of meritocracy, as a result of technocratization, has definite limits. Forty-nine per cent of Royal Military Academy (Sandhurst) cadets studied came from public school backgrounds – almost ten times the proportion of public school children in the total school population. Public school cadets were most highly concentrated in the elite arms, least present in the administrative and logistic arms. Cadets from the elite arms, such as the Household Cavalry, Cavalry, Foot Guards and Royal Green Jackets, come overwhelmingly not just from public schools, but from elite public schools. In the sample under study, a full 100 per cent of Household Cavalry cadets came from Head-masters' Conference schools, all but 13 per cent of them from elite schools. At the other extreme, only 4 per cent of cadets from the Corps of Royal Electrical and Mechanical Engineers, and 11 per cent of those from the Royal Army Ordnance Corps, came from a public school background.[59]

The same study looked at the recruitment of generals, showing the domination of these ranks by the 'teeth' arms, those in which elite educational backgrounds were most prominent. The arms in which public school recruits were fewest supplied virtually no generals. 'A comparison between generals and Sandhurst cadets for the various arms has shown', von Zugbach concludes, 'that there is a consistency in the educational/social background for the arms. There is clearly a cohesion of social background within the arms, with the background of cadets resembling that of generals.'[60]

The same author's study of officer selection in the army, examining the social background of candidates presenting themselves to Regular Commissions Boards, reinforces these conclusions. Forty per cent came to the Boards from public schools, compared to an 'output' of 49 per cent to the Royal Military Academy. The over-representation of 'the more privi-leged groups in society' is thus the result of self-selection, rein-forced by the army's own selection procedures. It reflects, von Zugbach suggests, the lack of information, contacts and a positive orientation to the army among pupils from state schools and 'lower' socio-economic groups.[61]

The only complicating twist to this picture of elite domination is the more detailed evidence of his analysis of success rates of Regular Commissions Board (RCB) candidates. Those from ser-vice backgrounds were more likely to succeed than those whose parents had civilian occupations; but sons of 'other ranks' were twice as successful as those of officers. Candidates from skilled manual (non-military) backgrounds also did well, compared to those from higher professional backgrounds; while those from lower professional backgrounds did worst. 'If there is a social bias at RCB,' von Zugbach concludes, 'it seems to be against day-school educated, lower-middle class candidates.'[62] The success of working-class candidates he ascribes to an active 'familial rejection', 'rejecting the value system of their parental home and alienating themselves from their family's way of life'. This, he believes, makes them more acceptable to the military selectors.[63]

The process and results of officer selection are at considerable variance, therefore, with the images of the professional, technical-managerial force in the army's recruitment publicity. Rank and file recruitment has also emphasized technical skills, offering recruits the chance to enhance their abilities, as well as seeking those with technical experience, but there is no comparable study of the social and educational background of 'other ranks'. Clearly, however, many recruits have come from the working class of traditional industrial areas in which trade unionism is strong. In the depressions of the 1970s and 1980s the armed forces have offered many young men employment not otherwise available.

Despite this pattern of recruitment, it seems generally to be understood and accepted that a job in the military excludes the right to collective organization and action. Recruits have acquiesced in the terms on which military service is offered. Again, we must surmise (although there is no research) that there is a strong element of self-selection: those for whom these terms are unacceptable often do not volunteer for the military. Those who discover, once inside the armed forces, that they find military ways difficult to handle, either utilize the opportunities military culture offers for expressing (but not generally resolving) dissatisfaction or they seek individual solutions, by 'buying themselves out' and in extreme cases by desertion. Although there is plenty of evidence of individual misery in service life, there is virtually no collective response by military personnel.

It is argued that this is partly a consequence of the way in which women are used and controlled by the military. Women as wives and prostitutes, nurses and social workers, pick up the bill, Enloe suggests, for the contradictions of military life. The British military, however, has hardly been as advanced in the (partial) 'militarization of women's lives' that she documents in the North American context. 'The British military establishment,' she notes, 'especially the army, has been wary of social workers and has generally kept the services which deal with military wives as peripheral as they have the wives themselves.[64]

Further evidence comes in a detailed study carried out in the mid-1980s by a sociologist with a Women's Royal Air Force background who is (as she describes herself) 'a military wife'. Ruth Jolly, as her title *Military Man, Family Man: Crown Property?* suggests, looks at the problem from the point of view of the 'military man who is also a family man', as much as from that of his wife or children. But in stressing 'the difficulties involved in sustaining a dual commitment to a military career and to the role of a husband or father', she deals from the other side with very much the same problems identified by Enloe in her more feminist and North American-based study: the isolation of military life and communities, the strain military life places on family relationships, and the informal, paternalistic ways in which the armed forces deal with the inevitable problems these cause for individuals, couples and families (servicemen, wives and children).[65]

The British armed forces, moreover, have been behind their North American counterparts in the recruitment of women: in the 1980s around 5 per cent of the total armed forces were female, compared to around 8 per cent in the USA and Canada.[66] Women in the women's services and nursing corps are kept rigidly (as they are in most other militaries) in non-combat roles in the 'rear'. The brief, albeit unintended military glory enjoyed by a small number of US women soldiers in Panama (1989) – the first occasion in which American women forces saw combat, although they were ineligible for the combat medals awarded to men – has so far eluded women in the British military. Although the proportion of non-combat to combat personnel has increased, most roles in the armed forces are still strictly gender-defined. The Gulf war, which saw an American woman soldier captured, left women in traditional support roles in the British forces.

There is little prospect of a radical change in this situation, not least because the pressure is already on the armed forces to civilianize support roles and so reduce levels of military staffing even further.[67] The most likely outcome of such rationalization is the maintainance of the overwhelming male dominance in the forces themselves, with women's supporting roles pushed even more into the civilian sphere. The inevitable cuts in military recruitment as a result of European détente are, moreover, hardly the most propitious circumstances for any radical opening up of new roles to women. Nevertheless, 1989–90 has seen interesting moves in the direction of sex equality: the Army announced that by posting women closer to the notional front line in the Rhine Army, an additional 10,000 jobs would be opened to them; the Royal Air Force decided to allow women to train as pilots, although still exempting them from 'direct combat' where possible; and, finally, the Navy agreed to allow Wrens (women sailors) on board warships, prompting speculation about a significant increase in the Women's Royal Navy Service.[68] It seems likely, however, in the circumstances, that these signals of a willingness in principle to accommodate greater sexual equality will have largely token importance.

The new reconsideration of the role of women does not, moreover, betoken any openness to sexual politics in a radical sense. The British armed services have not, in policy terms, carried out any evaluation of the issue of homosexuality, which is still simply repressed. The US Defense Department commissioned a study – *Non-Conforming Sexual Orientations and Military Suitability* – which concluded that there was no evidence that homosexuals were any more likely than heterosexuals to threaten the integrity of the services.[69] The Defense Department has so far been unable to accept this conclusion, and has not published the report. However, the issue of the rights of gays and lesbians is at least on the agenda in the USA, as it is (with greater official support) in the Netherlands, where the Defence Ministry has funded a Foundation for Homosexuality and the Armed Forces.[70] In Britain the issue has not even been recognized by the Ministry of Defence or the armed forces.

The social conservatism of the British military, compared to those of both North America and north-western Europe, is also reflected in its ethnic composition and racial policies. The small numbers of black military personnel have not made a distinctive impact on the UK armed forces, despite the rapid growth of black ethnic groups in British society over the last quarter of a century. Enloe points up the contrast between the predominance of nurses of Asian and West Indian origins in the National Health Service, and the white exclusiveness of the military nursing corps.[71] Until very recently, the Ministry of Defence and the armed forces were unwilling to admit the existence of a problem of racism in the military. As late as 1987 the Ministry of Defence was rejecting

the collection of data about ethnic origins of military personnel, as recommended by the House of Commons Defence Select
Committee.

Only recently has the revelation that ethnic minority recruitment amounted to just 1 per cent of the total in 1987–8
(compared with the 4 per cent of ethnic minorities in the general
population), forced the government to commission a report of
racism in the armed forces – not from social scientists but from
management consultants. The report, published in 1990, recognized the existence of racist stereotyping and language, and the
consultants, Peat Marwick McLintock – who interviewed 500
young people of Afro-Caribbean origin, and a control group of
500 whites – saw the services' poor image on racial issues as
the single most important reason for low application rates from
black minorities. They advocated a move from a policy of 'colour
blindness' to one of a positive approach to equal opportunities.
The Conservative government accepted most of the report's
recommendations, and adopted the goal of encouraging applications from black youth, but rejected proposals for special recruiting drives in inner cities and for concentrating black troops in
certain units.[72] The press had no difficulty, however, in identifying less positive responses to the report in the armed forces
themselves: 'Paras jump to dismiss "overstated" problem of pre-
judice', ran one headline; 'Calling recruits "Blackie" is not an
insult, says CO.'[73]

The belated recognition of gender and ethnic issues by the
armed forces partly reflects the increasing difficulty of maintaining what are seen as adequate levels of military personnel, once
the unemployment of the early and mid-1980s had ceased to act
as a recruiting sergeant. Another response has been the expansion
of the newly retitled 'Volunteer Reserve Forces', which include
the Territorial Army and the reserve arms of the other services.
The weakness of such forces – compared even to the reserves and
the National Guard in the USA – is another facet of the demilitarization of British society. The Conservative government has
committed itself, ideological as well as 'manpower' reasons, to
expanding the reserves.

The late 1980s have seen repeated press advertising campaigns,
constantly emphasizing the advantages Volunteer Reserve services
give their members in their civilian careers. One 1988 Territorial
Army advertisement expounds a theme common in officer recruitment:[74]

One thing separates top management from the rest.

The ability to make good decisions under intense pressure. Every day.

Handling such stress, both mental and physical, is just
one of the qualities you will gain during training as a
potential officer in the Territorial Army.

Another advertisement from the same year emphasizes the point:
Territorial Army officer training teaches you how to handle stress,
to think clearly and confidently under pressure, mental agility and
initiative, how to build loyalty and respect – 'And that's not just
crucial for us. You'll also find it a real advantage in your business
and private life.'[75]
By 1989 the Volunteer Reserve campaign was selling the same
advantages to ordinary recruits – including, interestingly, women:
one advertisement featured a dental assistant who in her spare
time is 'the first fully qualified female Port Diver in the Royal
Naval Reserve'. What the Volunteer Reserve has taught Wren
Karen McCurdy, apparently, is 'how to handle emergencies with
calm and confidence'. The advertisement also includes an appeal
to employers to give their workers time off for reserve activities –
so that they will reach high standards of self-discipline, initiative,
etc. 'in areas perhaps you wish you had time to teach employees
themselves'.[76] Another advertisement in the series also appeals to
women – as wives of potential reserve recruits: 'Does a weekend
on manoeuvres deserve a battle on the home front?' it asks.
'You've had to look after the children on your own. The garden
fence still hasn't been mended. Saturday night out with the girls
hasn't been quite the same as Saturday night out with your man.
In many ways, your weekend has probably been as tough as his.'
But the Volunteer Reserve still demands 'a little more understanding' for the man whose weekend manoeuvres are not only physically and psychologically demanding: 'The fact is, they are vital to
the nation's defences.'[77]
Advertising for the regular services has been somewhat less
socially aware, partly no doubt because it is aimed chiefly at very
young people (mainly young men) rather than those already in a
civilian career. It has often combined a technical and managerial
appeal – the skills open to the individual recruit – with a vaguely
idealistic appeal such as the advert for army officers which is

boldly headed 'PEACEMONGERS' and explains how 'big sticks' like a 62-ton battle tank with a computer-targeted gun, despatching rounds at four times the speed of sound, enables the Army 'to do some very useful soft talking all around the world', as part of United Nations peacekeeping forces, for example, as well as through NATO.[78] In 1990, however, due to recruitment problems, the Army launched its first television advertising campaign, emphasizing that a soldier's uniform is highly acceptable to a young man's peers – especially to members of the opposite sex.

The British armed forces project themselves as a 'post-modern' military. Their advertising agencies work unstintingly to portray them as managerial rather than regimental, deterrent-champions rather than war-fighters. As they adapt to a post-militarist world, however, they appear to be borrowing particular types of civilian expertise. They rely on advertising and management consultancy rather than on academic social science or even professional social work. Interestingly, despite small stirrings (a British Military Studies Group was established in 1989 with both military and academic participation),[79] there is still no real comparison with the much fuller military–academic co-operation which is the norm in the USA, where the Inter-University Seminar on Armed Forces and Society has long co-ordinated academic–armed forces involvement in military sociology, or in Germany where the Bundeswehr maintains its own Social Scientific Institute in Munich.

Academic studies of the British military have given little credence, moreover, to this 'post-modern' imagery. The British military, concludes Cathy Downes, remains 'institutional' rather than 'occupational':[80] it has not radically adapted the structures and ideologies inherited from the nineteenth and early twentieth centuries. Harries-Jenkins sees the regimental tradition as a source of cohesion in the army;[81] but it remains to be seen if the system can survive the radical reductions likely in the 1990s, which will again push the military to modify its traditions in rationalizing its forces.

If the armed forces in a post-military society remain institutionally and socially conservative, they are also politically restricted. In Britain a century or more of global hegemony failed to elevate the military – even the Navy – to the centre of the power system. The nuclear 'deterrent' has been an important token for the political elite as a whole, but it was conferred little additional importance on the armed forces. For them it has represented as much a threat to their more traditional roles and force structures as an opportunity for greater power.

The armed forces have certainly consolidated a certain power in the period since 1945: they have been tenacious of their budget allocations and weapons programmes, and only rarely have governments, still less Parliament, made serious inroads into them. Hartley shows that real defence spending remained nearly constant for thirty years between 1948 and 1979: the contraction of manpower from 850,000 to 315,000 was balanced by a quadrupling of expenditure per head of service personnel; reductions in defence spending (such as those in the late 1960s) were gradually recovered by annual increments in succeeding years – 'the number of annual increases greatly exceeded the number of cuts'.[82] Another study of the Ministry of Defence budgeting process concludes that it is led by long-term costings, i.e. it is still basically an 'input-biased system'. Real 'output budgeting' based on actual military effectiveness, which would enable greater political control or legislative accountability, does not operate; 'output budgeting techniques are used for presentational purposes' but do not really describe the budgeting process.[83] The 'inputs' are filtered within the Ministry of Defence, but they originate in the demands of the services themselves.

The military's influence in matters related to its own interests or sphere of action is therefore considerable. Obviously, the forces' inputs influence defence policy – although the major increases in defence spending such as the Korean war and Second Cold War rearmaments were due to external factors, as is the post-Cold War disarmament of the 1990s. Equally, it is obvious that the military has political clout in time of war: forces leaders such as Chief of the Defence Staff, Admiral Lewin, had a major influence on the conduct of the Falklands war. Indeed, Lewin was briefly canvassed as a possible Defence Secretary following the war – which would have represented a radical raising of the military's political profile – although Thatcher preferred Michael Heseltine's propagandist skills in order to defeat the peace movement. This seems to have been a unique moment: nine years on, the thought of a military leader being translated into the government seems as improbable as it would have before 1982.

The military also has a history of 'intervention' in British society: but it has been intervention at the behest of the political authority, rather than substituting for it, as has occurred else-where. The military has rarely, in the twentieth century, taken a directly political role – even, for example, playing no serious part in the general strike of 1926. This 'rarity of military aid to the Civil power in Britain', argues Jeffery, 'stems from two main causes: the comparative lack of violence in British political life and the success of the police alone in maintaining public order'.[84] The main form of military 'intervention' has therefore been as substitute labour in industrial disputes: a role the military played in at least thirty disputes between 1945 and 1983, with increasing frequency in the 1970s (although somewhat less often in the 1980s). This trend was directly related to the general pattern of industrial militancy, especially in public services.[85] However, although the deployment of the armed forces as strike-breakers has provoked some trade union opposition, they have hardly been used in a military-policing role, and so there has been no major direct confrontation between soldiers and workers. Workers have not been killed by the military in Britain since before the First World War.

The distinction between military policing functions is highly developed in Britain, and thoroughly internalized in the ideology of the military. 'It would,' writes Sir Edwin Bramall, a former Chief of the General Staff, in a rare exposition of the armed forces' view of their public order role,[86]

> in a society like ours, be totally inappropriate to use them
> in a main public order role, unless disorder was occurring
> on such a scale that the police could not cope and our
> whole parliamentary system was threatened or a minor-
> ity, by violent means and armed force, was attempting to
> challenge the very authority of Government with view to
> changing and overthrowing it.

The military remains a 'last resort' agency in the internal defence of the state. The fact that there was no overt involvement of the army in the 1984–5 miners' strike, the single most important public order crisis of the last few decades, is testimony – on one level – to the successful differentiation of functions between the police and the military. This distinction was maintained, however, by the paramilitarization that was very much in evidence in the arming, equipping and deployment of the police during the strike.

The differentiation of police and military roles threatened to break down during the industrial and political crises of the 1970s, in which the issue of a 'third force' (between police and army) to deal with public order became a live one. Such forces exist in many other countries (CRS in France, National Guard in the USA, Interior Ministry troops in the USSR) but had never been created in Britain. During the 1990s the rapid aiming of the police and the creation of special patrol groups (SPGs) in most forces led to speculation about the possibility of a fully fledged riot police.[87] In the event, the opposition to the SPGs, and their counter-productive role in the Brixton and Toxteth riots of 1981, led instead to a more pragmatic and lower-profile approach to political policing. This could be seen in the miners' strike, during which a nationally organized and at times brutally paramilitaristic police nevertheless operated within a formal structure of unified local forces – without specialized paramilitary wings.

The Army's detachment from a public order role in Britain contrasts starkly, as Bramall admits, with the way in which it has carried out this role in many colonial and neo-colonial situations since 1945. The British Army has increasingly specialized in counter-insurgency, and since 1969 has fought the longest and most demanding such campaign of recent European history within the UK itself – in Northern Ireland. There were many on the British left in the 1970s who predicted the transfer of the Army's Irish skills to the mainland of Great Britain. Frank Kitson's *Low-Intensity Operations*,[88] which summarized military thinking on counter-insurgency, was widely greeted as a manual for suppressing domestic insurrection. In the event, while the military experience in Northern Ireland provided some lessons for the British police, both government and the military itself have eschewed any comparison between the role of the armed forces in Northern Ireland and Britain. Quite clearly, although Northern Ireland remains part of the UK state, there is no correspondence of state and society: the society, culture and politics of Ulster and Ireland are quite distinct from those of Britain. The different roles of the military reflect this reality.

The effects of the military and military industry on society, as on politics, are limited and localized. The direct beneficiaries of defence expenditure are not evenly spread across British society. Unlike the USA, where the 'military–industrial complex' is virtually omni-present, there is no general 'pork-barrel' effect of defence in British politics. Military numbers have radically contracted over the last few decades, and military industry has become increasingly specialized, high-technology based and employing smaller numbers. As we have seen, the overall size of the military sector is not large, considering its international importance. Defence has, however, a regional and local political significance which arises from the uneven distribution of military bases and armaments industries.

The concentration of the military in the south of England is well known: Heseltine, when Secretary of State for Defence, identified this as a problem, and was reported in 1985 to be trying to impose a wide-ranging relocation programme on his ministry and the armed forces.[89] Little came of this initiative and military establishments are still overwhelmingly concentrated south of a line from the Wash to the Severn. Military industry is similarly concentrated: according to Southwood, in 1985 seven out of ten county or regional councils with the highest concentration of defence industry sites were in the South East or South West regions; seven out of twelve towns having five or more defence sites in or around their boundaries were in these regions.[90] There are also, however, important concentrations in the North and Scotland, as a study of aerospace by Lovering shows: two of the largest aerospace centres, with a high proportion of local employment in the industry, are Derby and Preston. Overall the most important centre, however, is Bristol, and the most important region the South West, especially its northern sub-region.[91]

The location of military industry may be politically significant in two main ways. On the one hand, workers in the military sector have tended to be better paid than comparable workers elsewhere. Military employment, Lovering suggests, created 'islands of prosperity' in the depressed Britain of the early 1980s. These islands were largely concentrated, however, in the South, which has suffered far less generally from the recessions of recent decades. Arms workers could therefore be seen as a group who would be less likely to be economically dissatisfied than other manufacturing workers. To the extent that they are concentrated in relatively prosperous regions, therefore, they may contribute to the general affluence and economic satisfaction levels in these regions. It is interesting to note a correlation between the regions in which defence employment is most concentrated (South West, South East), and those in which the highest swings to the Conservatives occurred consistently in general elections right through from 1970 to 1987.[92] Clearly, the regional variation in military employment is not a sufficiently strong factor to explain this deep, long-term trend in British voting behaviour, but it is a component of the deepening regional economic inequalities which, as a whole, have been a major factor in political change.

There may, however, be a sharper political significance to the geographical distribution of the military section. As defence has become a more salient and controversial field of politics, and as the Conservatives have been more successful in claiming that they are 'pro-defence' and that Labour is 'anti-' (the latter part of the claim being reinforced by the centre parties), it would not be surprising if seats containing significant numbers of military workers had swung more strongly to the Conservatives than other seats. There is certainly impressionistic evidence that this has occurred: for example, it was widely believed that the traditionally Labour town of Barrow-in-Furness – in which the Trident nuclear submarines are being built – which became Conservative in 1983 on a swing of 11.7 per cent (considerably higher than the swing in any neighbouring Cumbrian seat), did so because of the defence issue.[93]

Despite the increase in opinion poll data about defence in the 1980s, most polls, as Crewe has observed, 'disclose the answers of all respondents, and not of sub-groups'.[94] To the extent that 'sub-groups' are reported, the electorate is broken down by conventional class, age and sex categories, which reveal modest differences, at best, in attitudes to defence. Thus, as Crewe summarizes, men are consistently but marginally more 'hard-line' on defence; there are no general generational differences in attitudes; and 'to know individuals' social classes tells one next to nothing about their attitudes on defence matters'. Nevertheless, Crewe finds that working-class voters are both 'more unilateralist and more expansionist in their attitude to nuclear weapons', and argues that this pattern 'hints at the existence of bipolar working class opinion, divided between traditional Labour loyalists adopting their party line on cruise missiles, Polaris and defence spending generally and a "tough-minded patriotic" working class (many of them Conservative voters) with hard-line views on the need to mantain, or, if necessary, enhance Britain's nuclear capacity'.[95]

It may be that, just as party affiliation has been found still to correlate with class – once one defines class more precisely – so defence attitudes will correlate with social groupings, once these are specified more closely. As Crewe points out, data suggest that educational level has a definite relationship to defence attitudes, with more educated respondents being most radically anti-nuclear.[96] It would be interesting to research the extent to which specific interest groups – for example the military itself, arms workers and, by contrast, workers in sectors like education and health which compete with the military for public spending – can be found to have specific attitudes to defence. There has been no research into military sector opinion, but some comparable 'specialist' effects on voting behaviour have been reported. Surveys of teachers have shown Conservative support falling from 44 to 24 per cent between 1983 and 1987 (a period during which Conservative support in the electorate as a whole was constant).[97] This must almost certainly be related to Conservative cuts in education spending, which had made them appear 'anti-education'. It is clearly plausible to suggest that Conservative increases in defence spending, and the nuclear defence debate in which they were seen as 'pro-' and Labour as 'anti-defence', would have produced a similar effect in favour of the Conservatives among military voters and workers in defence-dependent industries.

Just as militarily formed values may carry over into voting behaviour, they may be introduced into society in a number of different ways. Military attitudes and methods are carried into daily life by ex-military personnel. Retired high-ranking officers are no doubt to be found in boardrooms, middle-ranking officers in management, and skilled other ranks in trades for which military experience fits them. Whether or not they obtain the benefits, in civilian employment, of their military training (as promised by the recruitment advertising) – or whether they actually carry over habits produced by military discipline into civilian careers – is difficult to say, since there appears to be have been little or no research in this area.

There is, however, some evidence of military personnel cashing in on their training in the controlled use of violence. A considerable number of the members of special forces, such as the SAS, join security and 'VIP protection' firms on retirement: according to one report, 'insiders say more than 40 per cent join private protection companies when they leave'. 'Having to share their industry with people they regard as crooks and villains is a source of considerable irritation to many special forces veterans', according to the same report.[98] And small numbers of ex-military men are clearly involved in less reputable activities – as mercenaries, for example with the UNITA forces in Angola. At the margins, the military's supply of specialists in violence meets a demand in this dubious corner of the private labour market.

Equally at odds with the benign image of the military commonly portrayed by the nostalgia industry is the role that military training plays in individual violence by ex-members of the armed forces. Again, this is a little-researched area, but there have been a number of cases in which reports of killings, rapes and other attacks have suggested that the nature of the violence owed something to the perpetrator's military background. One multiple rapist, according to a press report, 'reconnoitred his victims' flats and always broke in while the women were out. He would then lie in wait for them to return when he applied the strong-arm tactics he had learned in the Parachute Regiment of the Territorial Army.'[99] During the police search prior to his arrest, it had been assumed that the rapist had received military training. How common such cases are is difficult to estimate, and they do not, of course, demonstrate that military training makes a man violent. What they draw our attention to is the possibility that certain sorts of person may be attracted to the violent side of military life, and may find some uses or meanings in military training which, in some cases, they apply with destructive effects in society.

A separate but related issue is the brutalizing nature of some aspects of military life. Many accounts have been given (in the British case, see the recent study by Hockey)[100] of the way in which military units 'break in' their recruits in order to make them submissive instruments. Although one function of such initiation rituals is to make soldiers capable of controlled aggression in battle, there is considerable evidence of an ongoing brutalization of military life in general. Military organizations have traditionally been highly authoritarian, lesser ranks being at the risk of arbitrary actions by, or with the sanction of, those placed in authority over them. The British armed forces are, in this respect, highly traditional: the democratization of the military which has occurred in different ways in other north-west European countries (such as the Netherlands, West Germany and Sweden) has largely passed Britain by. Cases regularly surface of bullying and violence by officers, but governments have been reluctant to introduce any independent mechanism for complaints, arguing, for example, that this would 'undermine the authority ... of the chain of command, and would thus strike at the root of the Army's organization'.[101] As Tatchell has pointed out, there is a contradiction here between the nature of military organization and the democratic ethos 'which they are supposed to be defending'.[102]

The social conservatism of the British military, comparable with the traditional authoritarianism of its other total institutions (prisons spring immediately to mind), includes therefore the acceptance of a certain amount of unofficial brutality and violence. How far, and in what ways, this violence within the armed forces is both a product of and contributes to a wider culture of violence is difficult to estimate. Many traditional male subcultures in British society, from working-class family to public school, involve violent or despotic behaviour, which may simply be reproduced within the armed forces. At the same time, the nature of military institutions, particularly in Britain, may encourage or reinforce this behaviour in certain contexts. This may then be reproduced by military personnel in their relationships outside the armed forces, in family life and in the wider community.

This issue is only one dimension of a broader problem: the extent to which military modes, and the resort to war in particular, are cultural models of violence which are taken up in other contexts. In Britain, like the USA but unlike most other European societies, the example of the armed forces in action, usually against colonial peoples easily assimilated into racial or national chauvinism, has been present throughout most of the period since 1945. For the most part these episodes seem to have acted as a low-level stimulant to deep-rooted undercurrents of the national culture, but with the Falklands war, aggressive British nationalism (especially English nationalism: the Welsh in particular had a different relationship to the war) was 'born again'. Thatcher's claim that she had put the 'Great' back into Great Britain certainly struck a chord with a section of the population, and there is no doubt that the orgy of 'Argy-bashing' in some popular papers, even if it repelled some of their readers (as we have seen the poll evidence indicates) was nevertheless lapped up by many others.

How far has this had lasting effects on British society and culture? Young, particularly less educated working-class men, who make up a significant part of the readership of the *Sun* and the *Star*, may be regarded as particularly receptive to these ideas. There are clear affinities, for example, between the superficial patriotism which surfaced in the Falklands war and the aggressive nationalism of some groups of 'football supporters' who follow the England team on European tours. The connection is made by the 'fans' themselves: a reporter quotes a young man complaining in 1988 that 'a while back you was supposed to be patriotic; with the Falklands and all that. But they don't wanna know now it's football.' The connection is also made by extreme right-wing groups like the National Front and the British Movement, who infiltrate football crowds and whose slogans, incongruously echoing both Nazism and Britain's Second World War victory over Germany, contribute to the 'St George brutalism' of those who bring violence in the wake of the national team.

It is difficult, however, to attribute this violence simply or directly to the influence of the Falklands, or of militaristic ideas in general. As the same report concludes, 'English football has the most violent fans because it has provided an environment that suits them, one characterised by the ignorance, chauvinism and decay that have become a definitive part of English life.'[103] Militarism, however stimulated by the Falklands, provides images which are effective only when they cohere with others, in a sub-culture drenched with racism, machismo and alcohol.

Such manifestations of military values have only limited impact on society at large. Other measurable influences are even more specific to areas of direct military presence. A few towns (such as Aldershot, 'home of the British Army')[104] have been largely dominated by one or other of the armed services, but such cases are generally smaller communities. Several kinds of issue can arise which have strong local resonance.

Land is appropriated by the armed forces, often on the pretext of wartime emergency, which is then denied for ever to local communities. Greenham Common, in the 1980s a site of radical protest against cruise missiles, is in the 1990s the subject of a conservative rural dispute, led by former Master of the Rolls Lord Denning, over 'common rights' abrogated by the military presence. Burghfield, where British nuclear weapons are made (and another 1980s protest target), is now the scene of a local conflict over radiation and child cancer.[105] Holcombe Moor, near Manchester, is the focus of another dispute: the Ministry of Defence wishes to expand the Army's training area because of the return of troops from Germany and the expansion of the reserve forces.[106]

Other such disputes centre around the effects of military activity: the situation in the Clyde estuary, where Royal Navy and US Navy submarines were suspected of catching the nets of trawlers, causing loss of life by fishermen, led to concessions by the government in 1990. More widespread are the complaints about low-flying aircraft causing noise, disturbance and danger (from crashes), especially in rural areas.[107] Such incidents, while they may generate significant local resistance to the military, sometimes over long periods, often occur in areas in which the local economy depends significantly on military employment and trade, which may reduce their impact. They are also ineffectual in generating a widespread cultural or political resistance to militarism, because they are isolated, generally in rural areas, and because they involve contesting only the side-effects of military activity.

## POST-MILITARISM IN EUROPE

As continental European societies move further in the post-military direction, their experiences will not replicate those of Britain, but the same survivals of militarism will be found in one form or another. Each society has developed its own national militarism, and while many have longer histories than Britain of mass military participation through conscription, few in the future will have the stimuli from the Cold War and ex-colonial situations which have kept the British military active since 1945. In this sense, although national military traditions may have been more historically pervasive, there is less to maintain them (especially in Western Europe) now that the Cold War is over. Most European states, indeed, have experienced a fundamental loss of independent military role during the Cold War period.

In most societies the national myths deriving from wartime experience are less capable of actively sustaining militarism. The legacies of occupation and defeat, and even of resistance, are rather different from those of victory. Only in France is there a real parallel with the British case, and the Gaullist inheritance maintains a case for national defence which unites all major political forces. (Only in France, of course, has there been a potential for nuclear status and independent military action similar to that of Britain.) The national myths of the new Germany are, in contrast, decidedly anti-militarist, as negative lessons have been learnt from the Nazi experience. In countries such as the USSR and Yugoslavia, the myths of victorious wartime struggle, which have legitimated the state and the military for four decades, are now fiercely contested by alternative (and hitherto suppressed) myths of national oppression among minority peoples – myths that often (in the Baltic states, for instance) draw upon different versions of the same Second World War experience.

The scope for nostalgia militarism is therefore rather more limited in most European societies. The legacy of the Second World War is still an enormously important cultural and political fact in virtually all societies. National identities are heavily bound up with wartime experiences, and the element of historical memory is universally powerful – as has become very apparent at the end of the Cold War. National feelings are, however, in most cases, strengthened by histories of subordination rather than (as in the British case) of military triumph over the threat of oppression. The heroic, militarily victorious myths of many Central and Eastern European peoples hark back to the very distant past, even to the late Middle Ages. The recent, especially Second World War, experiences are most commonly those of national defeat, occupation and oppression. Nationalism is stronger, precisely because of that, but nationalism is not automatically militaristic. The smaller states, societies and minority communities of Eastern Europe, in common with those of the West, will need to find non-militarist ways of expressing national identity. Historic militarism will undoubtedly be cultivated, but more often as a support for political than military nationalism.

The scope for participation in 'media wars' is likewise limited. Media warfare operates primarily in societies whose states are actually involved in wars. Media coverage of war, and its reception, in societies which are marginal to the actual conflict are typically very different. Western European media coverage of American wars and military interventions, from Vietnam to Central America, or of the British in the Falklands, has sharply

contrasted with that in the combatant states. Even the Gulf operation, although involving token forces from many states, remained
primarily American. Many European states which sent forces
were not seriously committed in the war – Belgium had even
made clear in principle its refusal to be involved[108] – and there
were very significant differences in media coverage and social
attitudes, as I discuss below (chapter 6). Although, clearly, multinational European forces may be involved in future 'peacekeeping' ventures, the relationship to war and the military through the
media, which is important in Britain and the USA, is not likely to
be so strongly reproduced.

As European states move in the direction of smaller, more
professional armed forces – with surviving but declining forms
of conscription – they will face the problems of such militaries
which we have highlighted in the British case. European militaries
– except the Soviet – are likely to have even fewer active military
functions, confined effectively to the symbolic and (in some cases)
internal security roles, with some contributions to international
peacekeeping. The problems of institutional atrophy and social
conservatism, which are apparent in Britain's all-professional
forces, are likely to be magnified. However, the fact that conscription will be both functionally and socially contested means that
the development of largely or wholly professional forces will take
place as the result of a debate, in which continental European
societies have at least the possibility of learning the lessons of the
offshore states which have already taken this course. The weaker
cultural supports for militarism mean that the running down
of its structural foundations may, in the post-Cold War period,
allow the development of a form of post-military society which
more radically transcends militarism.

## Notes

1 Charles C. Moscos and F. R. Wood, eds, *The Military: More than
Just a Job?* (London, Pergamon-Brassey, 1988).
2 Mady Wechsler, 'The army and the family as greedy institutions', in
ibid.

3 Jürgen Kuhlmann, 'National service policy and programs: the case of West Germany', unpublished paper (Munich: Sozialwissen-shchaftliches Institut der Bundeswehr, 1990), passim.

4 Gwyn Harries-Jenkins, *The Army in Victorian Society* (London: Routledge & Kegan Paul, 1977), p. 5.

5 W. H. McNeill, *The Pursuit of Power: Technology, Armed Force and Society since AD 1000* (Oxford: Blackwell, 1982), p. 287.

6 Victor Kiernan, 'Conscription and society in Europe before the war of 1914–18', in M. R. D. Foot, ed., *War and Society* (London: Elek, 1973), p. 143.

7 H. Gollwitzer, quoted with qualifications by ibid., p. 142.

8 H. von Treitschke, quoted by ibid., p. 151.

9 Harries-Jenkins, *The Army in Victorian Society*, pp. 6–7.

10 Kiernan, 'Conscription and society', p. 146.

11 MacKenzie, *Propaganda and Empire: The Manipulation of British Public Opinion 1880–1960* (Manchester: University Press, 1984), pp. 5–6.

12 Ibid., chap. 6, esp. pp. 148–58.

13 Eric Hobsbawm, 'Mass-producing traditions: Europe 1870–1914', in Hobsbawm and Terence Ranger, eds, *The Invention of Tradition* (Cambridge: University Press, 1983), pp. 263–307.

14 McNeill, *The Pursuit of Power*, p. 285.

15 Ibid., p. 280.

16 David Edgerton, 'The British state: neither militant nor industrial?' and 'The state, war and technical innovation in Britain', unpublished papers (University of Manchester: Centre for the History of Science, Technology and Medicine).

17 Kiernan, 'Conscription and society', p. 146.

18 Anthony Barnett, *Iron Britannia* (London: Allison & Busby, 1982).

19 Martin Shaw, 'The rise and fall of the military–democratic state: Britain 1940–85', in Creighton and Shaw, eds, *The Sociology of War and Peace* (London: Macmillan, 1987), pp. 148–50.

20 Quoted in Lawrence Freedman, *Britain and the Falklands War* (Oxford: Blackwell, 1988), p. 85.

21 Shaw, 'Rise and fall', p. 143.

22 Barnett, *Iron Britannia*.

23 A useful analysis of polling data is given in Freedman, *Britain and the Falklands War*, pp. 92–104; see p. 99 for attitudes to loss of life.

24 Ibid., p. 101.

25 Peter Bird, 'Britain', in Walter Kaltefleiter and Robert L. Pfalzgraff, eds, *The Peace Movements in Western Europe and the United States* (London: Croom Helm, 1985).

26 For polling evidence, see Ivor Crewe, 'Britain: two and a half cheers for the Atlantic alliance', in Gregory Flynn and Hans Rattinger,

eds, *The Public and Atlantic Defense* (London: Croom Helm, 1985), pp. 11–68.

27  Richard Taylor, 'CND and the 1983 election', in Ivor Crewe and Martin Harrop, eds, *Political Communications: The General Election Campaign of 1983* (Cambridge: University Press, 1986), pp. 205–16.

28  The polling data compiled by Crewe, 'Britain: two and a half cheers', is updated by Taylor, ibid., p. 211.

29  William L. Miller, *There was no Alternative – The British General Election of 1983* (Glasgow: Strathclyde Papers on Government and Politics, No. 19, 1984), p. 25.

30  William L. Miller et al., *How Voters Change: The 1987 British Election Campaign in Perspective* (Oxford: Clarendon Press, 1990), p. 184.

31  David Butler and Dennis Kavanagh, *The British General Election of 1987* (London: Macmillan, 1988), p. 134.

32  Ibid., p. 147.

33  Ibid., table 6.1, p. 125.

34  Ibid., table 7.1, p. 141.

35  For a full account of civil defence in Britain, see Duncan Campbell, *War Plan UK* (London: Burnett Books, 1982).

36  See the discussion in Freedman, *Britain and the Falklands War*, pp. 100–4.

37  Marplan poll, January 1983, cited in tables 2.26 and 2.27 by Crewe, 'Britain: two and a half cheers', pp. 54–7.

38  Roger Jowell, Sharon Witherspoon and Lindsay Brook, eds, *British Social Attitudes: the 1986 Report*, table 7.2, 'First priority for extra government spending'. In three national sample surveys, 4 per cent (1983) and 2 per cent (1984 and 1985) of respondents volunteered defence as their first priority, compared, for example, to 37–51 per cent who named health.

39  C. B. Otley, 'Militarism and militarisation in the public schools, 1900–1972', *British Journal of Sociology*, 29, 3 (September 1978), pp. 334–5.

40  Judy Rumbold, 'All the fun of the fear', *Guardian* (29 June 1989), p. 19. Terence Wise's *A Guide to Military Museums*, 6th edn (Doncaster: Athena Books, 1988) lists well over 200 regiments and branches of the armed forces which are represented by their own museums, and over 60 other museums with a military interest.

41  Editorial, 'Out of battle', *New Statesman and Society* (30 June 1989), p. 5.

42  Bruce Robinson, quoted by Andrew Yule, 'Shooting script', *Guardian* (4 November 1988), p. 25.

43  Michael Mandelbaum, 'Vietnam: the television war', *Daedalus*, III, 4 (Fall 1987), pp. 157–69; see also Daniel Hallin, *The 'Uncensored*

War': The Media and Vietnam (New York: Oxford University Press, 1986).

44 For a description of government policy and press coverage see Robert Harris, *Gotcha! The Government, the Media and the Falklands War* (London: Faber, 1983).

45 David E. Morrison and Howard Tumber, *Journalists at War: The Dynamics of News Reporting during the Falklands Conflict* (London: Sage 1988), p. 342.

46 Ibid., table 12.3, p. 292.

47 Glasgow University Media Group, *War and Peace News* (Milton Keynes: Open University Press, 1985), p. 12

48 Ibid., p. 15.

49 Morrison and Tumber, *Journalists at War*, p. 344.

50 Glasgow University Media Group, *War and Peace News*, p. 143.

51 Morrison and Tumber, *Journalists at War*.

52 Glasgow University Media Group, *War and Peace News*, chap. 6, 'Breaching the peace at Greenham Common', pp. 196–214.

53 Ibid., p. 195.

54 E. P. Thompson, 'The war of Thatcher's face', in *Zero Option* (London: Merlin, 1982), p. 195.

55 See the analysis in Shaw, *Dialectics of War: An Essay in the Social Theory of War and Peace* (London: Pluto, 1988), p. 138, n. 37, based on Peter Southwood, *The UK Defence Industry* (Bradford Peace Research Report, No. 8, 1985), tables 3 and 4, pp. 20 and 24.

56 House of Commons statement by Tom King, Minister of Defence, 25 July 1990, reported *Guardian* (26 July 1990), p. 1.

57 John Hockey, *Squaddies: Portrait of a Sub-Culture* (Exeter: University Press, 1986).

58 See for example, Morris Janowitz, ed., *The New Military* (New York: Norton, 1969).

59 R. L. von Zugbach, 'Elites and the British military system', in *Forum 9* (Munich: Sozialwissenschaftliches Institut der Bundeswehr, 1990), table iii, p. 164. See also his *Power and Prestige in the British Military System* (Aldershot: Gower, 1988).

60 Von Zugbach, 'Elites', p. 174.

61 Von Zugbach, 'Class and officer selection in the British Army', in *Forum 9* (Munich: Sozialwissenschaftliches Institut der Bundeswehr, 1990), pp. 183–4.

62 Ibid., p. 184.

63 Ibid., p. 189.

64 Cynthia Enloe, *Does Khaki Become You? The Militarisation of Women's Lives* (London: Pluto, 1983), p. 63.

65 Ruth Jolly, *Military Man. Family Man: Crown Property?* (London: Brasseys, 1987).

66 Enloe, *Does Khaki Become You?*, pp. 127–30.
67 Ministry of Defence, *Control and Use of Manpower: Report by the Comptroller and Auditor-General* (London: HMSO, 1989).
68 David Fairhall, 'Wrens to serve at sea in warships', *Guardian* (6 February 1990).
69 US Department of Defense study, prepared by Professor Theodore Sarbin, University of California, unpublished; report in *Guardian* (23 October 1989).
70 Marion Anderson-Boers, 'Making the army gay', *IUS Newsletter*, 8 (October 1990).
71 Enloe, *Does Khaki Become You?*, p. 102.
72 Susan Tirbutt, *Guardian* (24 January 1990).
73 Andrew Cuff, *Guardian* (24 January 1990).
74 *Guardian* (Spring 1988).
75 *Guardian* (31 October 1988).
76 *Guardian* (3 October 1989).
77 *Guardian* (18 September 1989).
78 *Guardian* (15 November 1989).
79 British Military Studies Group, *The Armed Forces into the '90s: Personnel Problems and the Future of the Military Contract* (London: Brasseys, 1990). The secretary of the British Military Studies Group is Christopher Dandeker, Department of War Studies, Kings College, London.
80 Cathy Downes, 'Great Britain'.
81 Gwyn Harries-Jenkins, 'Cohesion and morale in the military: the regimental system', *Forum 9* (Munich: Sozialwissenschaftliches Institut der Bundeswehr, 1990), pp. 117–51.
82 Keith Hartley, 'Defence with less money? The British experience', in Gwyn Harries-Jenkins, ed., *The Armed Forces and Welfare Societies: Challenges in the 1980s* (London: Macmillan/IISS, 1982), pp. 12–13.
83 Stephen Kirby and Andrew Cox, 'Defence budgeting and accountability in Britain and America: executive innovation and legislative response', in Martin Shaw, ed., *War, State and Society* (London: Macmillan, 1984), p. 254.
84 Keith Jeffery, 'Military aid to the civil power in the United Kingdom – an historical perspective', in Peter J. Rowe and Christopher J. Whelan, eds, *Military Intervention in Democratic Societies* (London: Croom Helm, 1985), pp. 52–72.
85 Christopher J. Whelan, 'Armed forces, industrial disputes and the law in Great Britain', in Rowe and Whelan, ibid., pp. 110–12.
86 Sir Edwin Bramall, 'The place of the British Army in public order', in Rowe and Whelan, ibid., p. 69.
87 Background paper, 'Policing the eighties: the iron fist', *State Research*, 3, 19 (Aug.–Sept. 1980), pp. 146–68, esp. p. 153.

88  Frank Kitson, *Low-Intensity Operations* (London: Faber, 1971).
89  John Witherow and Philp Beresford, 'Northward Ho! says Heseltine', *Sunday Times* (27 October 1985), p. 5.
90  Peter Southwood, *The UK Defence Industry* (Bradford: University of Bradford School of Peace Studies, Peace Research Report No. 8, 1985).
91  John Lovering, 'Islands of prosperity: the spatial impact of high-technology defence industry in Britain', in Michael J. Breheny, ed., *Defence Expenditure and Regional Development* (London: Mansell, 1988), table 2, p. 38.
92  Butler and Kavanagh, *The British General Election of 1987*, table A2.9, p. 330.
93  Figures in David Butler and Dennis Kavanagh, *The British General Election of 1983* (London: Macmillan, 1984), p. 307.
94  Crewe, 'Britain: two and a half cheers', p. 14.
95  Ibid., pp. 48–53.
96  Ibid., p. 53.
97  MORI poll cited in Butler and Kavanagh, *The British General Election of 1987*, pp. 130–1.
98  Dean Nelson, 'Danger: security men at work', *New Statesman and Society* (30 September 1988), p. 23.
99  Paul Keel, 'Burglar who turned to rape as area became gentrified', *Guardian* (14 April 1989), p. 3.
100 Hockey, *Squaddies*, chap. 1.
101 Roger Freeman MP, Armed Forces Minister, quoted by Patrick Wintour, '"Dossier of brutality" in Army', *Guardian* (3 December 1987).
102 Peter Tatchell, 'Why can't the armed forces enjoy the sort of democracy which they are supposed to be defending?', *Tribune* (17 July 1987), p. 6.
103 Dave Hill, 'Blighty's bulldogs', *New Stateman and Society* (17 June 1987), p. 15.
104 Peter Dietz, 'Aldershot: home of the British Army', in *Garrison: Ten British Military Towns* (London: Brasseys, 1986); Peter Holt, 'The local community: Aldershot – a case study', in John Sweetman, ed., *Sword and Mace* (London: Brasseys, 1986).
105 Paul Brown, 'Riddle of radiation divides Burghfield', *Guardian* (23 June 1989), p. 2.
106 Tom Sharratt, 'Villagers braced for fight against MoD moor plans', *Guardian* (7 March 1988).
107 (Anon) 'Low-flying: a breach of the peace', *Campaign*, ii–iii, supplement to *Sanity* (June 1990); Rachel Cullen, 'NATO: living in the flightpath', *CND News* (spring 1989), pp. 8–9.
108 David Fairhall, 'Belgium rejects UK plea for Gulf ammunition', *Guardian* (3 January 1991), p. 1.

# 5

# Post-Military Citizenship

The collapse of the Stalinist system, and with it of the Cold War division of Europe, has highlighted the possibility of an entirely new relationship between the military sphere and society. Initially, this will be largely confined to the advanced industrial north, but it will have – indeed is already having – ramifications on a global scale. In general terms, this possibility, indeed opportunity (for it is by no means certain and will require conscious action to realize it), is that of a much more radical demilitarization of society than has occurred so far in the 'nuclear age'. As demilitarization develops, there will be profound consequences for the relationships of individuals and social groups to the state, and for our conceptions of citizenship.

The USSR and Eastern Europe were the last bastions of classical militarism in the northern industrial world. The end of Stalinism is also the end of 'socialist militarism', and has brought with it a major upheaval in the military institutions of all the former Warsaw Pact countries, and in their relationships with society. But these changes are not just the results of a transformation of political system. Military institutions never reflect only the political system of a society: they are at the intersection between this system and the international system of states. It is because the collapse of Stalinism has been simultaneously the collapse of the Cold War that the challenge to military institutions and ideology has been so strong.

It is for this reason, too, that the challenge is not confined to the East. The disintegration of Stalinism as a political system is, for the West, the disintegration of 'the Soviet threat' as a military reality and, even more, as its own political ideology. It poses the most fundamental problems for the ideological militarisms of the West, especially in those societies like the USA and Britain which have undergone the greatest degree of *de facto* demilitarization. The challenge is apparent in the debates about troop levels, weapons systems and military expenditure which preoccupy political leaders in all Western states. It is also present, however, if less obviously, in the questions about the duration and status of conscription which are surfacing in Western European countries, and in the culture of a new united Europe which is taking root in most continental societies – even if it is slower to affect its offshore islands.

The political transformation of the USSR and Eastern Europe is raising the questions of democracy, social justice and national self-determination in new forms. The end of the Cold War raises the prospect of a new European – and inter-superpower – security order based on political, economic and even military co-operation, rather than confrontational military blocs. The institutions developing from the Conference on Security and Co-operation in Europe may be more important, in the long term, than those of NATO – whose *alter ego*, the Warsaw Pact, will have been wound up. The development of the European Community is simultaneously raising the prospect of supranational citizenship as a pratical possibility as well as an idealistic hope. In all these debates the role of military service in citizenship, the great institutional legacy of European militarism, is brought into question. The aim of this concluding chapter, in surveying the new debate about the military in European societies, is to clarify what citizenship could mean in the post-military society of the future, and to look at the prospects and problems of its realization.

## DEMILITARIZATION IN EUROPE

The upheaval in the role of the military began in the USSR with Gorbachev's accession to power. There is no doubt that a driving force of the reform programme was his recognition of 'the militarization of our economy that swallowed countless billions of roubles which could have been spent on improving people's living standards' as a fundamental evil of the old system.[1]

Gorbachev's policies have led, directly and indirectly, to a major crisis in the role of the Soviet armed forces. Manpower has been massively cut through unilateral decrees, multilateral negotiations in the CFE (conventional forces in Europe) talks, and the withdrawals forced by newly independent Hungary and Czechoslovakia and reunified Germany. The USSR is publicly committed to bringing back all its troops from abroad (estimated by the USSR itself at over 600,000 at the end of 1989) by the end of the century.[2] They may well be back sooner. These reductions have had profound international effects, undermining the Cold War and enlarging the space for democracy in Eastern Europe, but they have also had a major impact inside the USSR. Not all the effects have been positive – the rapid withdrawal of troops from Eastern Europe has created acute housing problems at military bases in the USSR, and rapid demobilization without alternative employment has created disillusionment among soldiers and ex-soldiers (including officers).[3] But the military shake-up has forced a discussion on the role of the armed forces that would have been inconceivable even in the mid-1980s.

At the higher and middle levels of the military, especially, there are those who feel threatened by change, and who identify with the conservative neo-Stalinist wing of the Communist party and with Russian nationalism. For many officers, the loss of Eastern Europe, 'the retreat of socialism', is also a loss of role for the military. The integrity of the military is also threatened by the national revolts within the USSR, and – although the deployment of the army to crush protest has hastened the decline in its legitimacy – there are certainly those within the officer corps who see the reassertion of the old system as the only way to restore their authority. Correspondingly, an appeal to military interests has been a major platform of conservative forces in the party.

Other officers, however, have been in the vanguard of calls for reform. Shield, a radical union to defend the rights of military personnel, was formed in 1989, and includes serving officers who sit in the Soviet Parliament. (It is at present inconceivable that such an organization could exist in the UK or the USA; only in one or two smaller NATO countries, such as the Netherlands, have soldiers organized or spoken out in this way.) Shield calls for the abolition of the system of political commissars, a gradual

reduction of conscription and an eventual all-professional army –
'a new type of army . . . democratized and humanized . . . free of
bureaucracy, protectionism and nepotism, as well as of barrack-
room bullying'.[4]

Reform of the military has been a part of the programme of
radical reformers, since the first elections to the Soviet Parliament
in 1989. This appeal has been taken up at high levels: Boris
Yeltsin, President of the Russian Federation, for example, has
'advocated a gradual move to a professional army and the provision, in the meantime, of alternative service for conscripts with
conscientious or religious objections'. At the same time, he has
'made a big play for military support by saying their poor housing
conditions and pension rights must be improved immediately,
especially with the switch to a professional army'.[5]

It is far from certain that the USSR will move to a professional,
all-volunteer force. Similar ideas are being raised, however, at a
high level in Czechoslovakia, with President Vaclav Havel's call,
following Civic Forum's victory in the 1990 elections, for 'dramatic reductions in our army, a shortening of military service, its
abolition and the adoption of the principle of a small but high
quality professional army'.[6] The implementation of these ideas
will depend of course on the development of a new European
security regime, as well as on domestic politics. What is remarkable is that proposals for a wholly different kind of army are now
part of serious political debate in countries which for four decades have been part of an entrenched 'socialist militarism'. It is
even more remarkable, when one considers that the debate in the
USSR and Czechoslovakia is actually in advance of that in Western Europe, where at the beginning of the 1990s there was still no
mainstream challenge to the very principle of conscription.

The challenge to militarism which has developed in the East has
been a fundamental component of the democratic national revolutions. This was for three reasons: because military institutions (notably Soviet forces in Eastern Europe and the minority
republics of the USSR) had been agencies of national and international repression; because the Warsaw Pact was seen in Eastern
Europe as a structure of subordination; and because the priority
of military expenditure was seen, inside the USSR especially, as a
block to social progress.

The Eastern European revolutions reflected, therefore, a recognition by some leading participants of the need for a non-

militarist politics. Czechoslovakia's 'velvet revolution' was based on the principles of non-violence and dialogue; many of the leading activists of Civic Forum had participated, as supporters of the Charter 77 human rights movement, in dialogue with Western peace movements earlier in the 1980s.[7] East Germany's New Forum, and the other opposition groups that initiated the revolution of November 1989, contained many who had been active in unofficial peace movements earlier in the decade. A pacifist priest, Rainer Eppelmann, became Minister of Defence and Disarmanent in the short-lived coalition government which managed the transition to a united Germany in 1990.[8] The democratic revolution sheltered at first under the same umbrella of the Protestant churches which, earlier, had protected the peace movement. In Hungary too, peace movements had been the first independent organizations to be tolerated in the 1980s, and their members were prominent, particularly in the Free Democrats, which emerged as the main opposition party in the 1990 elections.[9]

The peacefulness of the 1989 revolutions reflected more, however, than the good intentions of the unofficial reformers. As the development of the East German revolution showed, and the 1990 elections there (as in Hungary) dramatically confirmed, such forces could be easily marginalized by new parties of the moderate right. (The Czechoslovak experience, in which the activists of Civic Forum triumphed, was clearly the – probably temporary – exception.) Much more important still was the fact that the Communist regimes recognized the inevitability of their fall when confronted with massive opposition. Clearly deprived by Gorbachev of Soviet military backing, they rejected the option of bloody repression. In both East Germany and Czechoslovakia, however, this was a nearer thing than the widespread impression of a peaceful transition would suggest; the Stalinist leader, Erich Honecker, was only just prevented from using military might in Leipzig, and his counterpart in Prague, Milos Jakes, advocated the same solution.[10] The Romanian case, in which the regime resisted bloodily, stands out as the exception; it might have been otherwise.

Nevertheless, the peacefulness of the transition has been very important to the subsequent development of democratization and demilitarization in Eastern Europe. Romania again demonstrates this negatively: since its revolution could succeed only through popular violence and the support of the armed forces, violent confrontation and military intervention remained the norm in the first year after the revolution. Elsewhere, by contrast, not only has the post-revolutionary transition been remarkably peaceful, but demilitarization has been a general trend. Although Western politicians, seeking a substitute for the 'Soviet threat', have often conjured up 'instability' in Eastern Europe, the new governments, even in such potentially difficult cases as between Hungary and Romania, have sought peaceful means of resolving differences. The Czechoslovak government, especially, has been active in advocating a new all-European security system, based on the Conference on Security and Co-operation in Europe, which would guarantee all existing borders and prevent new military conflicts.[11]

The main dangers of instability, leading to military intervention with possible international repercussions, have been in the national conflicts within the USSR itself. In Tbilisi, Georgia, in 1989 the Soviet army mowed down unarmed demonstrators; attempts to bring those responsible to account continue. In Azerbaijan the regime had the pretext of inter-communal violence for its bloody repression of a national movement. In Lithuania the demonstrative use of military force combined with economic sanctions has partly succeeded in containing the independence movement. Clearly the Soviet regime prefers non-military means of containment, both for domestic reasons and to avoid the international repercussions of military repression. How far it will manage to maintain this policy remains to be seen. It is of major significance that in situations like Azerbaijan the military has been the only institution on which the state could rely to enforce its control. 'This circumstance', as Shenfield has argued, 'sets definite limits on demilitarisation.'[12]

Whether national movements themselves can be seen as forces for demilitarization is a crucial issue. Memories of aggressive nationalisms, and of national revolts which ignite larger conflicts, are too powerful to be dismissed out of hand. Pessimistic interpretations of the new situation invariably invoke the spectre of a return to pre-1914 Europe: all the old national conflicts suppressed by Stalinism and the Cold War have not only re-emerged, it is often argued, but could too easily lead again to war.

It is clear that there are tensions inside the smaller nationalities between the desire to assert national autonomy, including military independence, and the realities of power. There were attempts in Lithuania, following its declaration of independence early in 1990, to raise a national self-defence force. But since it was apparent that this force had no military function in the face of the vastly more powerful Soviet forces, and that its political significance was provocative and hence counter-productive, it failed to become established. This experience reflects the situation of national minorities throughout the USSR (and Yugoslavia), and was repeated in Moldova (and Croatia) in 1991; there is little future for them in a military challenge to established power. To a large extent it reflects the position of small nations in Eastern Europe as well: surrounded by much larger and more powerful states, they can hope to prosper only through a international regime which guarantees their independence or autonomy, not through military strength. This is a powerful lesson of the last century which is well appreciated in some of the newly invigorated capitals, but probably not in all.

In this situation the smaller nationalities can offer more effective opposition to established militaries and militarisms through political means than by attempting military efforts of their own. The newly independent Eastern European countries are asserting their political and military autonomy from the USSR by winding up the Warsaw Pact. As for military substance, they may follow Havel's advice and engage in radical cutbacks and restructuring of their smaller but genuinely national forces. Likewise, the Soviet republics may insist on the 'nationalization' of the present Red Army – breaking it up into national territorial units – as part of a new Union treaty. The actions of Lithuania and Armenia in 'suspending' the call-up of young men to the Soviet armed forces, and of the Ukraine in asserting its right to raise its own army, are steps in this direction. But if a full territorialization were achieved, it would be of largely political rather than military importance, giving additional substance to the autonomy of the republics within a Soviet Federation. Despite – or because of – the vigour of national conflicts such as that between Armenia and Azerbaijan, it is hardly conceivable that any Soviet government will ever permit the republics to obtain full military autonomy to the point where their forces could be used in inter-republican war. The reawakening of national identities in the former Soviet empire has certainly revived the symbolic importance of warrior patriotism; but there are likely to be severe limits in practice to the realization of these ideals.

These limits to any new 'national militarisms' are likely to be reinforced both by concessions by the Soviet state and by pressures within society. It is clear that the Soviet state can survive only by transforming itself into a federation which permits genuine autonomy to all its republics, and probably independence to some. Only with some such settlement of national demands is it likely that solutions to the socio-economic and political problems of the USSR will be successfully implemented. There is thus a considerable degree of common interest, in the longer term at least, between the republics' demands for national self-determination and the centre's programme of restructuring. The most serious danger appears not so much as Balkanization as 'Lebanonization': the development of communal strife within as much as between republics.[13]

If a Soviet state survives the transition from Stalinism, it is likely to be as federation accommodating diverse nationalisms and so inhibiting military confrontations between them. It is, of course, possible that the opposite will happen: that national and ethnic demands and rivalries, together with the economic and political contradictions, will lead to civil war and break up the USSR; or that the threat of this will lead to military intervention. (A similarly pessimistic scenario can be devised for Yugoslavia.) These possibilities cannot be excluded, and both could lead, in the short term, to a significant remilitarization of society. In the longer term, however, the growth of international co-operation, the need for economic transfers from the West, and pressures from within society would all work against any reconstruction of militarism, whether at the national (republican) level or by a military-dominated central state.

One of the most remarkable features of the Soviet crisis has been, indeed, the growth of popular anti-militarism. This is partly the result of disillusionment with the war in Afghanistan; returning *Afgantsi* and their families helped to create in the later 1980s a widespread sense of the futility of the conflict, later legitimized by Gorbachev's own attacks on his predecessors' policies.[14] More recently, the combination of détente and *glasnost* has exposed a great deal of disillusionment with the armed forces in general, and military service in particular, especially among young people. The poor conditions in which conscripts serve, and the prevalence of bullying, have been widely complained of.

Resistance to conscription has been growing, notably in some of the minority republics: the widely publicized refusal of military service in Lithuania, a critical issue between that republic and the central state, it the tip of a much larger iceberg. Reports speak of a 'huge wave of draft-dodging and anti-army activity which has been developing throughout the Soviet Union'. Young Russians and their parents fear that they will be drafted into ethnic conflicts in the Caucasus, and resent the boredom and bullying of army life; young men from the minority republics resent conscription into a 'foreign' army. 'In all three Baltic republics, as well as Georgia, a movement called Geneva-49 is telling young men called up to return their call-up papers. The movement relies on the 1949 Geneva convention which bans conscription to an "occupying army".'[15] Resistance to conscription has also surfaced in Romania, the one Eastern European country where the army has found a major post-revolutionary role: 'no military service for any student' was a demand of the Bucharest students in the earliest days of the 1989 revolution.[16]

The evidence is that, despite the symbolically important attempts of the military to seize draft resisters in Lithuania, many young men are getting away with refusing the call-up. Authorities and courts in the minority republics tacitly, or even openly, encourage resistance. High-ranking military figures repeatedly fume against the draft resisters and their protectors; the Central Committee of the Communist Party has even called on the media to reinstate the romantic myths of the Soviet soldier. This issue is an explosive component of the military reaction to disarmament and *perestroika*; it is clearly conceivable that some sections of the military might attempt to use military power in an attempt to restore what they can of the old order and the old militarism. Even if such a reaction occurred, however, it is difficult to see it succeeding without an appalling conflict throughout the USSR, and it is even more difficult to believe that, in the long run, the powerful momentum for change – including demilitarization – could be totally blocked. The most the military could achieve is to postpone the day of reckoning.

In the short term the pressures for reform from the top and from society are most likely to result in revisions of the system of conscription, rather than its abolition. The USSR and the Eastern European countries have had the longest terms of military service of all European militaries, and an almost complete lack of alternatives to military service. The cuts in troop numbers will inevitably lead to reductions in the length of military service; the anti-conscription movement will most probably lead to provision of alternatives. In the Eastern European countries, of course, the collapse of Stalinism has already produced drastic changes. In East Germany an announcement of alternatives to military service was one of the first decisions of the interim regime after Honecker was overthrown; it was rapidly followed by the near-collapse of the *Volksarmee*, as East Germans saw little point in continuing service in an army which was about to disappear. Cuts in conscription are under wide consideration: Poland, for example, cut its term from twenty-four to eighteen months in 1990.

All over Eastern Europe, the Stalinist militarist propaganda which permeated schools, universities and society at large is rapidly disappearing. In the USSR itself, where Communism has stronger roots, its future is also contested: the debate over whether to maintain Party commissars in the armed forces, or to depoliticize them, represents an issue which has wider significance for the role of the military in society.

In Western Europe the debate about the role of the military is generally more leisured, a response to the Soviet and Eastern European developments, and to disarmament, rather than a product of profound social and political turmoil within society. It is in Germany, of course, that change has been most dramatic: even before the East German revolution and the prospect of reunification, the Federal Republic was profoundly affected by the movement towards disarmament and the easing of tension. The West German government opposed the modernization of NATO's battlefield nuclear weapons, as advocated by the USA and the UK; and it had cancelled a planned increase in military service from fifteen to eighteen months. By 1990, after the revolution, it was considering reducing the term to twelve months, the period to which it had been reduced in East Germany. By the same summer it had been agreed as a price of unification that the German army would have only 370,000 soldiers (instead of a combined 660,000 in the former separate states in 1989). This, the ruling Christian Democrats' general secretary rationalized, was because 'our people rightly expect that in a period when confrontation is being replaced by co-operation, there should be fewer charges on the defence account – therefore, a smaller army, shorter period of military service, fewer exercises and less money spent on defence.'[17]

Germany is clearly experiencing a more profound demilitarization than other Western European countries. The end of the Cold War removed the threat of instantaneous destruction of Germany, as well (of course) as leading to reunification. The West Germans looked forward to peaceful economic hegemony over Eastern Europe. Most Western states are reducing military force and expenditure levels, and those with forces in Germany have announced withdrawals. In the USA the Pentagon's strategic review envisages 25 per cent cuts in budgets and manpower over a five year period. More than a hundred European bases are to be closed, mostly in Germany. In the UK, despite official caution, reductions in military expenditure have eventually been announced. In the Netherlands wide-ranging cuts were announced in 1990: the Defence Minister argued, however, that 'personnel cuts would not lead to the eventual abolition of conscription'.[18]

In other Western countries, however, a debate about conscription is beginning. Michel Rocard, French Prime Minister, insisted in 1989 'that France must seize on the easing of East–West relations to run down its huge conscript-based army and "rationalize" military spending to favour basic education and professional training'.[19] A reduction in military service from twelve to ten months was announced in 1990. In Spain the abolition of military service has surfaced as an issue: 'a principal complaint of young men is surrendering a year of their lives to military service for wages of 950 pesetas (£5.15) per month. A government poll conducted in 1986 found that only 12 per cent of recruits felt that the *mili* – as it is popularly known – was useful and necessary. More than half of Spaniards support the idea of a professional army.' All opposition parties – including the conservative People's Party – offered cuts in military service in the 1989 election, both the Centre and United Left parties broaching the issue of abolition. An army colonel who advocated a professional army suffered house arrest, as conscription is clearly as important to the army's value system (it 'has a value which transcends defence considerations') in post-Francoist Spain as in post-Stalinist USSR. But the momentum for change, here as in the East, is considerable.[20]

Across Europe, therefore, 'from the Atlantic to the Urals', pressures for demilitarization are building up. Cuts in military expenditure and troop reductions do not necessarily imply abolishing compulsory military service, or challenging the value of the military as an institution. But traditional militarism, already frayed in the West, is under renewed challenge. 'Socialist militarism' is rapidly being deconstructed in post-Communist Eastern Europe, and is under strong popular democratic pressure in the USSR itself. The purpose of military service, the last major institutional residue of classical militarism in the West, is being brought into question. It is possible to see the outlines of a genuinely post-militarist society emerging in Europe.

CONSCRIPTION AND CITIZENSHIP

The idea of citizenship, as the way in which the individual's relationship to the state is defined, has developed over the two centuries since the French Revolution. It has been very much in evidence in recent discourse: many have seen the revolutions of 1989 as successful reclamation by the peoples of Eastern Europe of the rights and duties of genuine citizenship. No longer mere subjects of an authoritarian state, they now have the chance to act as responsible citizens, participating individually and collectively in a democratic polity. The duties of citizens to the state will be defined no longer in terms of blind obedience, but as conditional on the accountability of the state to a democracy.

Recent debate has not been exclusive to Eastern Europe: a new concern with citizenship has been apparent in some Western societies. In the German Federal Republic the consolidation of a democratic polity has involved, from the 1950s, the creation of new relationships between civil rights and military duties. The provisions for non-military alternatives ot conscription have been fuller than in any other country; in recent years they have been further liberalized, and in the 1980s, as we have seen, about a third of young men of military age were opting for the non-military form of national service, the *Zivildienst*.[21]

In the USA a debate on national service has developed, in which a persuasive case for a voluntary scheme of non-military national service has been made by military sociologist Charles Moscos.[22] The lobby for national service, which claims the ear of possible Democratic presidential contenders, argues for a scheme that will develop civic values and participation, especially among young people, in a society which has moved beyond 'the draft'.

Whether such a scheme can really gather widespread political support is debatable, however.

In Britain, where the call for a form of national service is not on the mainstream political agenda, a rather different debate on citizenship developed on the centre-left under the Thatcher government. The British debate about citizenship has traditionally focused on the extension of rights from the narrowly political to the social and economic. Recent concern has reflected alarm, first, that the post-war extension of citizens' rights in the 'welfare state' is being threatened; and, second, that the political freedoms of the British are inadequately protected by their 'unwritten constitution' and unreformed electoral system.

The British debate has been limited in that it has rarely grappled with the military dimension of citizenship. This is largely because Britain has known only relatively short periods of conscription, and the right of the state to demand military service – although conceded in practice – has not been fully incorporated into the understanding of citizenship. Recent debate has parochially assumed that this issue, because it no longer pertains directly to Britain, no longer needs to be addressed. And yet the echoes of conscription linger on in British society, raised periodically in the demand for some form of national (even if non-military) service and in the recently advanced concept of 'active citizenship'. These represent the continuing importance of the idea that the state must demand duties of citizens in return for the rights they enjoy.

In other European societies this side of citizenship is a much more concrete question, for, as we have seen, states everywhere continue to demand military service of their young men. In the politically united European Community of the future, the issue of military service as an element of citizenship will have to be faced. In many countries this will involve a challenge to long-established traditions.

For a century or more conscription has been viewed, in most European states, as an essential part of citizenship. The origins of modern conscription lie in the French Revolution, when the revolutionary state introduced the *levée en masse* of 1793, followed by the general Law of Conscription of 1798, under which all unmarried Frenchmen between the ages of eighteen and twenty-five were made liable to service, although in practice only a minority served. Universal conscription in the modern form, in which all young men (with whatever exceptions) underwent a period of military training and then remained liable to recall until they reached middle age, was first introduced by Prussia in the nineteenth century. By the last quarter of the century, this system was universal among the great states of continental Europe: Italy, Russia and Austro-Hungary as well as France and Germany. Conscription came to be seen, as we have already noted, as one of the 'pillars of the democratic state': a foundation of social order, a school of political socialization, an essential bond between citizen and state.

The inadequacies of conscription, as an ingredient of citizenship, are quite evident with the benefit of twentieth-century experience. Conscription has proved as effective a tool of the authoritarian and totalitarian as it has of the democratic state. And even in the 'democracies', as Kiernan points out of the late nineteenth century, 'within armies anything democratic was firmly ruled out'.[23] The picture has not changed so dramatically even in the late twentieth century: few conscript armies allow their recruits many rights, although some Western European armies, such as the Dutch (with their soldiers' organizations) and the German (with largely token trade union organization), are more democratic than most. Even these militaries, however, are hardly 'democratic' institutions: hierarchy remains their essential principle. Whatever 'democratic' political education is given within a military context is in a fundamental sense negated by the way in which military organizations actually operate.

Various solutions were offered to this problem by classical socialist and anarchist thought, centring on the concept of the 'democratic army' (or, more commonly, workers' or peoples' militia) with officers elected by the soldiers themselves, and other measures to break down the hierarchical model. 'Militias were to be set up', says Deutscher, summarizing Jean Jaurès, 'on the basis of productive units, factories and village communities; the militiamen were to receive their training locally and were to continue to live and work as normal citizens, devoting themselves part-time and intermittently to the art and craft of war.'[24] (This type of organization was an early casualty of Bolshevik centralization, when Trotsky, as founder of the Red Army, seemed 'to be burning all that he had worshipped and worshipping all that he had burned'.[25] Centralization returned with a vengeance in the successful prosecution of the civil war.)

Although the purists would argue that democratic militias have never been fully tested (for example, they were supplanted by a centralized Republican army in the Spanish Civil War, again at Stalinist insistence), their military potential is at the very best unproven. They have continued to have their devotees – in Britain the ex-Communist Tom Wintringham advocated turning the Home Guard into a democratic militia during 1939–45, and this was seen by Tatchell as a possible model for 'democratic defence' in the 1980s.[26] The Swiss army (also untested in modern war) is in fact probably closest to realizing these ideas. It is doubtful, however, that they really have a relevance today. The whole problematic of 'democratizing warfare' is the wrong one for a period in which warfare itself is ceasing to be a viable option in relations between European states (if not so fully in other regions of the world).

A good instance of this problem is the issue of women's participation in the military. A central defect of conscription as a facet of citizenship is that it has applied almost always only to men. To be fully democratized, it would have first to be extended to the majority of women who are now excluded from a military role, and these women would have to be allowed to participate in the military on an equal basis with men. There are few armed forces of any kind in which anything approaching such equal participation occurs, and one side of the feminist debate about the military is precisely the demand for equality in this as in all other spheres. One does not have to go to the other extreme in the feminist debate, to claim a uniquely caring, maternal-pacifist role for women, to see the problem of this perspective.[27] A democratization of conscript armed forces to include women would amount to a massive militarization of one half of society. It is much more relevant to think of the exclusion of the majority of women from the military as positive sign of the limits of militarization, and to look at how these limits can be pushed further into the world of men. A genuinely sex-equal citizenship will be post-military, not military.

## The Nation-State and Post-Military Society

An even more fundamental problem with thinking about citizenship in terms of conscription is that this continues the identification of the citizen with the nation-state. This identification is in one sense realistic: nations remain central 'imagined communities'[28] for nearly all human beings, states remain for the most part (if however imperfectly) nation-states, and it is still difficult to conceive of citizenship very concretely outside this context. Part of the current ferment, moreover, is the reclamation not just of citizenship but of nationhood — by the peoples of Eastern Europe, the nations of the USSR, and minorities in many of the multi- or imperfectly national states of the south (not to mention the West).

This resurgence of nationalism is, however, only part of the general movement, coexisting with (and indeed understandable only as part of) a profound internationalization. The breaking up of the Soviet empire goes hand in hand with the breaking down of Cold War division: nationalism with Europeanism, indeed globalism. The realities of economics, politics, culture and communications – not to mention warfare – dictate that small (or even large) nation-states cannot be 'islands unto themselves'. Co-operation is an ineluctable reality. At the point where the triumph of the nation-state appears complete, it also merges with an enormous movement toward European and global solutions.

However much, therefore, the revival of nationalism points towards classical nineteenth-century concepts of the nation-in-arms, its citizens mobilized against historic rivals – and even if this becomes a reality on some of the eastern margins of Europe – this is an essentially anachronistic concept. The fragmentation of the backward East of the continent is matched by the unification of the advanced West – and it is not difficult to see which is likely to prove the stronger development in the medium and longer terms.

The nation-state lives, to be sure, within the European Community, but it is partly and increasingly transcended by Community structures. The citizen of a Community state is also a citizen of the Community, and this membership has a growing meaning for individuals and societies. Not only does the individual's citizenship of his or her nation-state have no military significance in relation to the other member states, but his or her citizenship of the Community equally lacks a military meaning in relation to states outside it. In this sense it may turn out to be of no little historical significance that the European Community was established as an economic community distinct from NATO. Even if, with political union, the Community develops a 'security role', it

is difficult to see this involving the same sort of military nationalism that has been associated with the existing nation-states.

A crucial issue is whether this concrete supranational, non-
military extension of citizenship within the Community can be
linked to the widespread aspiration for wider European, indeed
global citizenship which exists both within and beyond the Community. The collapse of the Berlin Wall opened up the vision of a
united Europe based on peace, democracy and economic co-
operation, linked in a new friendship with both North America
and the USSR. However much this vision has been dimmed by
subsequent economic divisions, many, especially young people,
in Eastern and Western Europe aspire to be citizens of such a
Europe as well as of their own nations; or of their nations as
members of such a Europe. Whether these aspirations can begin
to be realized depends on the extent to which leaders of the main
European states, especially in the Community and NATO, as well
as of the superpowers, are willing and able to take the steps
necessary to secure a new international order. If they do,
citizenship will quite clearly come to be defined, in the twenty-
first century, in terms of the individual's relationship to transnational institutions as well as to the nation. This in turn has
profound implications for the military dimension of citizenship.

Although in the short term the end of the Cold War is far more
likely to bring about the reform than the abolition of conscription
in most European countries, the development of a stable, secure
pan-European order must bring the institution into fundamental
question within a matter of years. Despite all we know about
cultural lag, the tradition of military service would be unlikely to
withstand the dual pressure of cost-cutting and efficiency from the
top, and the demand from below for an end to coercion. Once the
shape of a new European order had clearly emerged, and consolidation was taking effect, the rationale for continuing to take a
large proportion of young men, against their will, to learn and
prepare to fight would disappear.

A shift of attention to 'out of area threats' and global policing
would still not provide the justification for the scale of forces any
meaningful measure of conscription would produce. It will be
seen on all sides as more rational to maintain much smaller,
professional forces for such purposes. Eventually they may be
organized not merely on an alliance or European Community
basis, but on a pattern which cuts across the former East–West

divide and so consolidates in military organization the politcial, economic and cultural unification of Europe and the northern industrialized world. In global terms such a transformation of military (as well as political) institutions in Europe and the north could lead to a transformation of world order. Northern co-operation could give a new substance to the United Nations and other international institutions and lead eventually towards a new global settlement. The hesitant north–south international co-operation on environmental issues at the beginning of the 1990s could, if developed much more strongly, prove the commencement of this process. In this way, the development of increasingly non-military European citizenship could give some meaning to what, at the moment, is still a very remote ideal of global citizenship.

In the societies of the future, then, in Europe and possibly also the world, citizenship will be increasingly divorced from military participation. The military will become, as it is increasingly in the industralized countries off the Europe land-mass, a specialized institution apart from the mass of the population. Citizens will join armed forces as a specialized job, not as a duty of citizenship. Democratic control over the military will be achieved not by universal military participation – which has never, in any case, guaranteed such control – but by greater democratic accountability of the military to parliamentary institutions, as well as specific measures of democracy within the armed forces. These might include opening up all positions to women and men alike, introducing rights of free speech, political organization and trade union representation, and other measures to convert the military into a social institution more like others.

## A NEW WORLD ORDER?

Post-military societies are becoming realities, and with them the demand for post-military citizenship will grow. Moscos has recently outlined the prospect of a 'warless society' (by contrast with the 'war deterrence society' of the Cold War era, and the 'war readiness society' of the era of mass militarism). In such a society armed forces would increasingly be based on reserves, civilian and military national service for young people would be combined in a single scheme, and the dominant type of military professional would be the 'soldier–scholar', reflecting the military's acceptance of disarmament and 'mission substitution' (the replacement of war-fighting and even deterrence by symbolic and peace-keeping functions).[29] This professedly schematic picture, however questionable in detail (for example, national service might indeed disappear rather than be civilianized), is an interesting sketch of the possible future of post-military society. To write of a 'warless society', however, assumes radical further changes, and minimizes the major contradictions in these developments: in the inter-state context in which societies become demilitarized, and in the social relations and culture of demilitarizing societies themselves.

The most fundamental problem, as we stressed in the first and second chapters, is that although social changes underlie the present transformation of the global military situation, there is nothing automatic about the connections between social change in general and changing military relations between states. Societal demilitarization is only partly a product of secular changes in the economics, social organization and culture of militaries, as well as of wider social changes such as the extension of commodity culture and consumerism. Above all, demilitarization depends on the context of inter-state relations. These, as we have seen in the East European revolutions of 1989, interact with social movements more than most international relations theorists (and even some social theorists) have allowed. But without the post-Cold War changes in international relations, the optimistic scenario for post-military citizenship painted above would have little credibility. And even the transformation of East–West relations which has occurred does not remove some major institutional obstacles to demilitarization, which are located in the inter-state system.

Increasingly demilitarized societies exist, it needs to be emphasized, in what is still a highly militarized world of nation-states. States, in coming to new understandings about major issues in Europe, abandon neither their fundamental conceptions of their own 'national' self-interest nor their capacity to mobilize these in military terms. While the rhetoric proclaims a brave new world, states move only partly and cautiously from their previous positions. While political positions and strategic deployments may change, nation-states still compete to maintain their relative advantages over one another. Disarmament removes relatively few, and often old and outmoded, nuclear weapons. The industrialized world. But the quality of societal demilitarization may be crucially limited, not least because this sort of use of military force reinforces the crudest among all the cultural stereotypes which legitimate the military.

Whether or not this occurs depends, first, on the development of international security relations which permanently link former rivals in new relationships of co-operation. The *de facto* dissolution of the Warsaw Pact in 1989–90 removed one pole of the former antagonistic structure of East–West relations, although a reformed USSR could, at some point in the future, once again become a major military factor (it still has large resources at its disposal). It is not yet clear how far the NATO countries will go towards formal, structural consolidation of new security structures as alternatives to the old alliances. Western states have enormous levers, economic even more than political or military, with which to ensure that the restructuring of Europe takes place on terms acceptable to them. There will certainly be dilemmas, in which choices have to be made between policies most immediately favourable to Western or national interests and those which support the weaker Eastern European and Soviet nations in the interests of longer-term stability and integration. It is far from guaranteed that far-sighted policies will continue to be followed, as this will go against a long history of narrower conceptions of self-interest.

Much will obviously depend, in this context, on political, economic and social developments within the USSR and the former East European countries. A deepening of the Soviet crisis to the point at which a reactionary politics becomes clearly dominant would be the most dangerous single event, likely to push the West back into narrower conceptions of its own interests. At the time of writing, the outcome of the conflict between such forces and the democrats is still unclear. The acute economic crises in both the USSR and the former Eastern Europe states may demand more from the Western states than short-term economic interests may allow, if they are not to damage the process of international reform.

A new world order, with long-term political stability between states, the general avoidance of war, reductions in armaments and demilitarization, depends in any case on far more than a European settlement. Many of the trends in the south have been, as we have seen, towards fragmentation: a greater number of rival states, divided within by competing nationalisms which cut across international conflicts, their conflicts fuelled by uneven economic growth and by trade and alliances with the northern powers. There may have been trends for fewer wars and for a slowing down in arms supply, but numerous regional conflicts retain the capability to produce major wars with global significance. Iraq alone has already intitiated two such conflicts: the Iran–Iraq war of the 1980s, and the Gulf war of 1991.

In the longer run, therefore, a new world order will depend on how the new détente of the industrialized north is extended to the south. A combination of the economic expansionism from the newly industrializing countries, the crises of poverty and starvation in the poorest regions, and environmental challenges to both north and south, may compel greater attempts to globalize what at the present time is primarily a northern, European-centred restructuring of the international order. The imitative effects of the Eastern European democratic revolutions in a number of Third World authoritarian states – in the pro-Western one-party states of Africa and Asia, and the former military regimes of Latin America as well as in Communist countries – may also assist this process of globalization. The settlement of the Palestinian problem, the abolition of apartheid in South Africa and the removal of the Stalinist regime in China are examples of changes which would, if accomplished through peaceful transitions to democratic states, be of particular importance to this process. If, on the other hand, such transitions are not managed peacefully, they could have disastrous results for international stability.

In the medium term, however, it is probable that large parts of the south will continue to produce the political instability at a national and international level which will lead to wars; and that the north's response will increasingly be one of military 'policing'. It is entirely possible that in the twenty-first century, new military powers, some of them nuclear-armed, will emerge from rapidly expanding states of the south. It is difficult not to see the south, and the north's policies towards it, as a crucial limit to a new international order. Northern demilitarization may proceed apace, for the sorts of forces required for regional policing in the Third World will be both smaller and less nuclear-armed than those needed for East–West war in Europe. Even the Gulf war has not produced a remobilization sufficient to reverse the massive reductions in military forces under way throughout the industrialized world. But the quality of societal demilitarization may be crucially limited, not least because this sort of use of military force reinforces the crudest among all the cultural stereotypes which legitimate the military.

## THE TWO FACES OF POST-MILITARY SOCIETY

Societies *are* moving, however unevenly, in a post-military direction. Post-militarism, as much as post-industrialism and post-modernism, is a defining characteristic of the end of the twentieth century. But just as post-industrialism does not abolish industry, or post-modernism modernity, so post-militarism, while it transforms the military and militarism, does not remove them from central positions in the social structure. Rather, military and militarism are constantly transformed, and the question of their future roles becomes an ever more open issue on the agenda of twenty-first-century society.

Post-military society presents us, at the moment of transition from the Cold War era, with two faces. One is that of the relatively smaller – but still absolutely very large – armed forces, professionalized and technologized, with unprecedented destructive power. The classical mass army is being replaced, and the structural basis of military participation (conscription) is becoming attenuated – and will ultimately be abolished – in most advanced states, East as well as West. The culture and ideology of militarism is being adapted to a technologically determined 'armament' element in mass consumer culture.

The other face of post-military society is the large and growing space for non-militarized life which has been opened up. The nuclear age has allowed a great expansion of economy and culture, in which individuals and social groups have gained strong interests independent of the nation-state. High-technology war-preparation has reduced the military demands the state makes on society. Young men have been able to escape the fear of an early death on the battlefield, which blighted earlier generations. Improvements in health and living standards have enabled individuals to look forward to long and peaceful lives, as the norm rather than the exception. The prosperity of the post-war West has greatly enhanced the area of individual freedom for its citizens, and both are regarded with awe by many in the East and the south.

The 'revolution of rising expectations' has become permanent, and is accelerating. On the one hand, this contributes to international tensions, but on the other there is much awareness that improvements in living standards depend on continuing international co-operation – on peace rather than war. Within modern society there are great cultural resources for peace, which have been strengthened at the expense of military culture. These are mobilized periodically – for example in the transnational peace movements of the early 1980s – and increasingly seem capable of contributing to more peaceful international relations between states. As economies and cultures become transnational, and nation-states increasingly operate within a context of global social relations, the social interests in peace are increasingly able to make themselves felt in the international system. As Rosenau suggests, the division between sub-national and international politics is largely transcended in the development of the turbulent world of 'post-international' politics.[30]

Within the increasing flux of the world political system, however much societal developments influence international events, nation-states nevertheless remain powerful structures. The peaceful potential of post-military society will be realized only in so far as it is reflected in new ways of structuring and managing international relations between states. If states' relationships remain anarchic, and new global institutions and processes do not become strong enough to inhibit war-preparation, a peaceful world will remain a frustrated aspiration of most members of world society.

In the first half of the twenty-first century it is probable that nation-state rivalries will remain strong, even in the north but certainly in the south. This will bring with it the danger of lethal wars which in turn feed back into a residual militarism and armament culture. The ever increasing sophistication of weaponry, conventional as well as nuclear, could still result – despite the apparent removal of the threat of US–Soviet nuclear war – in wars so destructive as to alter radically the course of history, rendering hopes of peace illusory.

Post-military society, as we know it today, is not therefore in itself a *peaceful* society. Post-militarism brings with it only the possibility of peace, in the sense of the absence of war. Post-military social relationships are outgrowths of the specialization of weaponry in the nuclear arms race – of the ironic subversion of militarism by war-preparation itself. There is no sense, therefore, in which post-militarism is automatically pacific. History grants us 'progress', not in the form of inevitability, but in the form of possibility. The development of a post-military society gives us the opportunity for peace: the opportunity to fashion global political and military relationships in ways that reflect the growing transnationalism of economic, social and cultural relations.

Post-military society can, therefore, be a stage in the development towards a more peaceful world – or to a new and more lethal stage of warfare. The two faces of post-militarism are two directions in which states and societies can go. As recently as the Second Cold War, it seemed that the arms race was about to enter a new and possibly terminal upward spiral. It is good to reflect that the political forces which could undermine it were to be found within the advanced industrial societies of East and West. The implosion of the Soviet empire and with it of the Cold War system has greatly strengthened the development of post-militarism – and the possibilities of peaceful relationships in the north. But the fragility of the new peace has been graphically demonstrated in the Gulf: the willingness of the USA to go to war constrasts starkly with the sustained war-avoidance of the Cold War itself.

The two sides of post-militarism may not, of course, be complete opposites. Just as the nuclear arms race has been the context in which post-militarism originally developed, so the use of military force by the US-led coalition in the Gulf may act as a deterrent in future situations. But it is more probable that it will exacerbate political tensions and provide the incentive for further rearmament by states in the south, thus increasing the long-term likelihood of further wars. It would create stronger grounds for hope if the great powers were insistent on avoiding war in such a crisis: the 'war to end wars' is by now very difficult to believe in.

Military force will inevitably have a role in the creation of a more peaceful world order – even the most perfect global institutions would, in the foreseeable future, require a considerable policing or peace-keeping capacity. But the transition to a peaceful world depends on the progressive weakening of military institutions in favour of political mechanisms for resolving international disputes. This will not occur simply as a result of developments between nation-states themselves: it requires the active intervention of the members of societies, as individuals and in organized groups. The non-military side of post-military societies needs to be expressed in a variety of activities to assist states in creating a peaceful framework for international relations.

Just as the citizen formerly owed a military duty to the state, the active side of post-military citizenship can be defined in terms of the citizen's duty towards peace. In this sense the idea of giving a different, non-military meaning to the duties of citizenship, to an 'active citizenship', is not to be dismissed. However, instead of creating 'volunteer armies' to tackle social problems, taking on the responsibility abdicated by the state, 'active citizens' should be concerned with positively extending the demilitarization the end of the Cold War has begun, with entrenching the civil rights and democracy that exist all too precariously in the West as well as the East, with undertaking responsibility for tackling global inequality and environmental crisis, and with transforming our culture so that a demilitarized, democratic society can exist within it. Active citizens will be brought into confrontation with nation-states whose institutions will too often continue to operate in terms of military, national, inegalitarian and ecologically irresponsible definitions of reality.

The creation of a peaceful society is therefore far more than a task for 'peace movements'. Such movements, as they existed in the first half of the 1980s, were the products of the special conjuncture of the Second Cold War, in which the arms race actively threatened to lead to war between the superpowers, with devastating consequences for European peoples. Even though this threat potentially affected all members of society, only minorities drawn (research tells us) largely from the educated middle class were actively involved in nuclear disarmament movements.[31] The lack of visible, concrete mediations between nuclear weapons and people's daily lives was an important factor in limiting active support for peace movements; the issues seemed, for the most part, abstract and remote, although opinion polls showed a good deal of passive support.

The peace movements no longer exist in their 1980s forms. Those of the West have become more compact organizational shells, not without influence, but no longer movements of mass mobilization; those of the East fed into the mass democratic movements of 1989 but have, in large part, lost their specific identities. New movements and organizations have come into existence at the beginning of the 1990s, concerned with the problems of military demobilization and de-occupation, together with the rights of soldiers and conscripts. This time, reversing the direction, the movements are arising from the East first, because the problems of military–society relationships are far more acute there. But, as we have argued, the general nature of the problems implies that there will be responses in Western countries over the coming years.

To achieve a genuinely peaceful society will necessitate, however, more from 'active citizens' than to question these specific institutions. Just as the peoples of Eastern Europe had to make the historic breakthrough which destroyed the Berlin Wall and with it the remnants of the Cold War, so the peoples of Europe, East and West, and of North America, will need to remain active in order to reinforce the movement of their states and the superpowers towards a new international order. There may be no new 'peace movement', but a more complex pattern of citizens' movements, political parties and environmental campaigns all working in similar directions.

Beyond specific political tasks, culture will remain the last refuge of militarism. A fully post-military citizenship will be achieved only when the ideas, values and concepts of military culture, which permeate society at the deepest levels, have been genuinely domesticated. Military traditions are a powerful residue, which the 'nostalgia industry' only partly neutralizes. Armament culture has spread rapidly, and indeed is likely to make new inroads into Eastern Europe with the incorporation into Western consumer culture and 'the market'. At an even deeper level, the insinuation of military terms into the language of non-military life, which is remarkable in contemporary English, is likely to permeate other languages even more than it has already done, through the same processes of marketization.[32]

Of the cultural limits to militarism, gender is perhaps the most crucial. Warfare has been defined in most societies as a male prerogative, and warlikeness as an attribute of masculinity. Femininity, on the other hand, has been associated with peace – but also with passivity. Female warriors have been seen as exceptions to their sex.[33] A profound transformation of these cultural stereotypes is under way in Western societies, leading to a questioning of both male aggression and militarism by men, and equally of female passivity by women. As a consequence of this, women are increasingly to be found in armed forces, as we have seen, and the argument is made for women's equal participation in the military as a concomitant of full citizenship for women.[34] Women should certainly have equal rights to participate in armed forces, and this would undoubtedly assist in the deconstruction of military culture both within the armed forces and in the wider society. If this were the only or main consequence of the change in relations between the sexes, however, this would be a profoundly limiting result. It would be regressive at a time of general demilitarization, to seek to militarize women as a whole through military service. On the contrary, the peaceful values associated with women, when generalized from the narrow role-context of motherhood, constitute a resource for the construction of a post-military culture by both sexes, and ultimately a foundation for a more peaceful world.

The importance of defining values is that they help us to give a positive content to peace. It is not enough that we have a post-military society, in which military culture and institutions are less dominant, or even that we define the goal of abolishing war. We need to understand how a world society would be organized, in which war was no longer a means of resolving disputes. Such a society, a peaceful society, would be based on several main principles. First, it would clearly be a society in which nation-states had surrendered a fundamental core of their authority to trans-national institutions which would resolve disputes by non-military means. Second, it would be a society in which global economic interdependence had been recognized as imposing obligations on all to ensure the welfare of others – in particular to overcome the dire poverty and structural inequality that divides north from south. And third, it would be a society in which there were common values, of care and respect for other human beings, and a shared conception of our role in the world, which were beginning to transcend the divisions of culture, religion and ideology.

To spell out such goals is inevitably to seem utopian: they are a long way from where we are now. And yet after the 'century of total war' it is remarkable that we are living in the post-military society which is now developing the northern hemisphere. It is not unrealistic to hope that, in the twenty-first century, the contradictions of this post-militarism will lead towards the creation of a more genuinely peaceful human society. What is certain, however, is that this goal will be achieved only by great efforts, not only by those who control nation-states but also by their citizens.

# Notes

1 Mikhail Gorbachev, quoted *Guardian* (3 July 1990), p. 1.
2 'Soviet Union has 627,000 troops abroad, minister says', *Guardian* (16 December 1989).
3 Paddy Ashdown MP, 'What do you do with redundant soldiers?', *Guardian* (28 November 1989).
4 Extracts from the programme of Shield are given by Jonathan Steele, 'Red Army has a bad attack of the blues', *Guardian* (23 October 1989), p. 8.
5 Jonathan Steele, profile of Yeltsin, *Guardian* (18 June 1990), p. 17.
6 Vaclav Havel, quoted *Guardian* (30 June 1990), p. 8.
7 Havel, interview, in Jan Kavan and Zdena Tomin, eds, *Voices from Prague: Czechoslovakia. Human Rights and the Peace Movement* (London: Merlin/European Nuclear Disarmament, 1982), pp. 42–3.
8 Stephen Brown, profile of Eppelmann, *Sanity* (June 1990), p. 21.
9 For accounts of the peace movements in the early 1980s, see John Sandford, *The Sword and the Ploughshare: Autonomous Peace Initiatives in East Germany* and Ferenc Köszegi and E. P. Thompson, *The New Hungarian Peace Movement* (London: Merlin/European Nuclear Disarmament, 1983 and n.d.).
10 John Gittings, 'Peaceable Prague contrasts with Tiananmen turmoil', *Guardian* (15 December 1989), p. 11.
11 See for example Havel's speech at the Parliamentary Assembly of the Council of Europe, Strasbourg, 10 May 1990, in *East European Reporter*, 4, 2 (Spring/Summer 1990), pp. 65–6, and other documents in the same issue.
12 Stephen Shenfield, 'Moscow's bitter harvest', *Marxism Today*, 33, 3 (March 1989), p. 7.
13 Boris Kagarlistky, *Farewell Perestroika: A Soviet Chronicle* (London: Verso, 1990), p. 170.
14 Jim Riordan, 'Return of the Afgantsi', *Détente*, 12 (1988), pp. 13–16.
15 Jonathan Steele, 'Soviet teenagers warned against draft-dodging', *Guardian* (28 March 1990).

16 Ed Vulliamy, 'Students of the revolution press home their demands', *Guardian* (29 December 1989).
17 Volker Rühe, quoted in David Gow, 'Bonn announces cuts in troops as tension eases', *Guardian* (30 March 1990).
18 Peter Spinks, 'Dutch plan huge defence cuts', *Guardian* (26 May 1990).
19 Paul Webster, 'French Defence Minister threatens to resign', *Guardian* (26 May 1989).
20 John Hooper, 'Spanish wooed by pledge to cut army service', *Guardian* (21 October 1989).
21 Jürgen Kuhlmann, 'National service policy and programs: the case of West Germany', unpublished paper (Munich: Sozialwissenschaftliches Institut der Bundeswehr, 1990).
22 Charles C. Moscos, *A Case for Civic Service* (New York: Council for National Service, 1988).
23 Victor Kiernan, 'Conscription and society in Europe before the war of 1914–18', in M. R. D. Foot, ed., War and Society (London: Elek, 1973), p. 142.
24 Isaac Deutscher (discussing Jean Jaurès), *The Prophet Armed: Trotsky 1879–1921* (New York: Vintage, n.d.), p. 477.
25 Ibid., p. 406.
26 Peter Tatchell, *Domocratic Defence* (London: Heretic Books, 1985).
27 A good comparative discussion of women's role is to be found in Sharon Macdonald, Pat Holden and Shirley Ardener, eds, *Images of Women in Peace and War: Cross-Cultural and Historical Perspectives* (London: Macmillan, 1987).
28 The term is Benedict Anderson's, *Imagined Communities: Reflections on the Origin and Spread of Nationalism* (London: Verso, 1983).
29 Charles C. Moscos, 'Armed forces in a warless society', unpublished paper presented to the British Military Studies Group (1990).
30 James N. Rosenau, *Turbulence in World Politics* (Princeton: University Press, 1990).
31 See Kaltefleiter and Pfalzgraff, eds, *The Peace Movements in Europe and the United States* (London: Croom Helm, 1985), and Creighton and Shaw, eds, *The Sociology of War and Peace* (London: Macmillan, 1987), part III, 'The sociology of peace movements'.
32 See the discussion in Martin Shaw, 'Strategy and social process: lessons from strategic studies', *Sociology*, 16, 4 (August 1990).
33 Sharon Macdonald, 'Drawing the lines: gender, peace and war: an introduction', in Macdonald, Holden and Ardener, eds, *Images of Women in Peace and War*, pp. 1–23.
34 See for example M. W. Segal, 'The argument for female combatants', in N. L. Goldman, ed., *Female Soldiers: Combatants or Non-Combatants?* (London: Greenwood, 1982), pp. 267–90.

# 6

# POSTSCRIPT: THE GULF WAR AND POST-MILITARY SOCIETY

The Gulf war of January–February 1991[1] has in its time sharpened, as all major wars do, the definitions of war, peace and militarism. The experiences of this war cast new light on all the main issues of this book. As we argued above, 'War-preparation and militarism are vastly different in a situation of actual war, compared to a non-war situation.'[2] The lack of a major war of global significance in recent decades – the worst recent war, that between Iran and Iraq, although longer and bloodier, was in contrast a regional conflict – means that the impact of the Gulf war has been all the more striking. The timing of the war, barely a year after the fall of the Berlin Wall, means that it will have particular significance in shaping the 'post-Cold War' international and social orders. Its ideological effect has been dramatic, as the US-led coalition's victory first generated extraordinary euphoria about the possibilities of the precise use of military power, and then quickly turned sour as the human tragedy of the unsuccessful rebellions inside Iraq unfolded on the world's television screens. There is no doubt that it will continue to make waves long after this comment is written.

The Gulf war was based upon the unity of the northern industrial world against a recalcitrant southern state. In this sense it both demonstrated the significance of the end of the Cold War and confirmed that the growth of military power in the south is a crucial limit to the 'peaceful' international order which 1989 had seemed to presage. At the same time, of course, the war showed the extent to which the 'new' international order reproduced, indeed accentuated, old realities. The subordination not only of the other Western states, but even of the USSR, and the impotence of social movements (in contrast to 1989), all confirmed the USA as even more dominant than it had been in the Cold War years.

The war seemed to confirm old realities in an even more fundamental sense. The decisive role of military power in resolving international disputes, compared to political and diplomatic instruments, appeared to have been underlined. War seemed to have been inevitable; but in an almost unique sense it was the result of a political choice by the US President. Although the military initiative had been taken by Iraq, the unparalleled effectiveness of international economic sanctions had created another option, short of war, for the states ranged against Iraq. The preference for resolving the crisis by military action (if Iraq did not back down) was arrived at by the USA as a result of the logic of the troop deployment in Saudi Arabia, initially undertaken for defensive reasons. Although it appeared to have been spectacularly vindicated by the initial success of Desert Storm (the coalition offensive against Iraq), this choice looks more problematic in the light of its aftermath.

As the scale of the suffering of the Iraqi Kurds and Shi'as has become apparent, it can be argued that the real choice was between reliance on sanctions to weaken the Iraqi regime, and all-out military destruction of that regime. The actual policy of the USA – involving the military liberation of Kuwait but military non-intervention in Iraq beyond what was necessary for this limited goal – appears to have fallen between two stools, with appalling consequences for the people of Iraq. The resulting political fall-out shows definite limits to the role of military power, even at the moment of its greatest success.

This paradox reflects the basic inequality of the war, between the most advanced military powers and a well-armed but, in comparison, fundamentally backward middle-ranking state. Unlike in Vietnam, where the USA's adversaries were able to compensate for an even greater inequality by unconventional warfare, this was a conventional contest – and an overwhelming rout. Saddam Hussein's evident hope that he could impose enough casualties on the USA to turn its public opinion against the war was not realized: figures of seventy-nine American and twenty-three British dead, against tens or even hundreds of thousands of Iraqis, had little impact except to reinforce the self-congratulation of the victors. With a deep and dismal irony, however, the Western public's presumed aversion to death and suffering, skilfully contained during the coalition offensive, has returned to haunt its leaders in the tragedy of Kurdistan, requiring rapid political action to limit its damage.

Looked at in the historical perspective of this book, this reflects a meshing of two very different realities. In many parts of the Middle East the age of total war lives on in aggressive nationalisms sustained by rival nation-states, between which only minimal trust exists. Saddam Hussein was the most plausible reincarnation of Hitler yet (if still falling short) because the situation in the region matched, in some respects, the historical experiences of Europe before 1945. The extreme inequalities of industrialization, exaggerated by oil, and resistance to despotism, fired a classical revolutionary movement in Iran. Saddam's Iraq had tried to profit from the weakening of Iran's military power in the 1979 revolution, and launched the attack which began an eight-year war, precipitating the growth of revolutionary militarism in Iraq. The Gulf crisis, after all, was but an after-effect of this war, as Saddam sought to overcome his desperate financial crisis by raising the price of oil and plundering a rich but smaller neighbour. The Gulf war, in turn, has engendered not the pan-Arab nationalism which was widely heralded, but the revolutionary disintegration of Iraq which was the predictable consequence of that state's inevitable defeat. There are definite parallels with the relations of Germany to its revolutionary neighbour in Russia after 1917, but also crucial differences: not least of which is that Iraq is only a middle-ranking state, against which the great powers had many levers.

Western powers and societies bring to this situation very different political, social and moral standards as well as a superior military technology. What we are witnessing in the aftermath of the Gulf war is the complexity of the Western moral and political engagement with Middle Eastern realities, in contrast with the brutal simplicity of the military 'fix' perpetrated at the beginning of 1991. The difficulties of Western responses – resulting not so much from cultural differences, as from wholly different experiences of violence – are becoming much more apparent in the aftermath than they were during the war itself. This is not to say, however, that such difficulties were not present then, only that they were more effectively managed.

## VIOLENCE AND POST-MILITARY SOCIETY

The situation in the Middle East represents a baleful interaction of modern and pre-modern social forms. States disposing of vast oil revenues and commanding large, well-equipped armed forces are nevertheless not, in most cases, stable nation-states. Violence is endemic in both intra- and inter-state relationships which lack widespread legitimacy.

The rise of the modern nation-state, as Giddens has argued, is based on a resolution of this problem, at least at the level of the society. Violence is 'extruded', not just from economic relationships as Marx believed, but from the relationships of nation-state and society. States dominate societies through extensive surveillance, rather than through military force, which becomes specialized in the outward-pointing function of inter-state warfare.[3] Even if this argument should be qualified, to point out that total war itself has been a major context of social and political violence,[4] it is nevertheless of central importance. The pacification of societies – notably in North America and Western Europe – accentuated the contradiction between the illegitimacy of violence within societies (even, for example in the abandonment of the death penalty, by states themselves) and the legitimacy of ever greater violence between states in war.

This contradiction has been partly controlled in the nuclear age by the fact that military violence, while approaching the theoretical limit of absolute war, has nevertheless remained theoretical. Increasingly, not only societies but also inter-state relations have been pacified – first within the West, then *de facto* between East and West, and now more and more within a unified northern industrial world. In the process, the potential violence of war became highly abstract. In this situation the actual use of violence is a radical departure from what is accepted as normal by most members of these societies: this was the effect of the Gulf war.

This war, far more than anything else we have seen since 1945, was the Third World War made real, in a *Third World* war. The technology and forces – short of nuclear weapons – which the

USA and its allies had prepared for use against the USSR were shipped, courtesy of the end of the Cold War, out of Europe and into the Middle East, and turned against Iraq's inferior version of Soviet weaponry and forces. Having neutralized Iraq's air force, the US-led coalition systematically bombarded Iraq's armed forces and its political, economic and social infrastructure, if not its civilian population as such. The Iraqi forces in their bunkers and fox-holes suffered a far more efficient, one-sided, high-technology version of the slaughter of the trenches in the First World War. Iraqi civilians suffered 'collateral damage' in new forms, which also reflected the weapons revolution that gave us 'flexible response'.

The numbers of civilians killed by bombing were modest by recent historical standards; the Gulf war appeared at first to have reversed the twentieth-century trend for more civilians than sol-diers to die in wars. They experienced, however, the deliberate and systematic destruction of the means of life – electricity, water supply, sewage – which caused many more lives to be lost. 'The bombing was called surgical,' an American civilian doctor stated, 'but we're calling it neurosurgical: with extraordinary accuracy the allied bombs took the brain out of the country's ability to survive.' Or as his colleague put it: 'Bomb now, die later. You don't kill people, you just cause the system to collapse.'[5] In the context of the attendant political breakdown, finally, they were fatally encouraged to rebel against the Saddam regime. The death toll of Kurdish men, women and children, from cold, disease and hunger as well as the violence of the Iraqi army, has meant that this war has been no exception to the general law of civilian casualties.

The Iraqi, like the Kuwaiti, people, therefore, cannot but have a great deal of understanding of the nature of modern war and its social effects. The peoples of Western societies, on the other hand, have been insulated from the immediate reality and direct threat of violence (marginal and sporadic terrorist incidents apart). Nevertheless, the lives of people in these societies have been linked by a whole set of abstract relationships to the violence of the war. As Giddens argues, the transformation of relationships of time and space in modern society means the involvement of people in distant risks and dangers, and a well-distributed aware-ness of these. 'Disembedding mechanisms' in social relations have, he argues, 'provided large areas of security', but 'the new array of risks which have thereby been brought into being are truly formidable.' The circumstances in which we live today have a 'menacing appearance'.[6] In the Gulf war many people who were not directly threatened nevertheless felt themselves to be living with the dangerous situation developing thousands of miles away.

Abstract relationships and personal involvement are not, of course, opposed but interrelated.[7] Some people in Western societies were living with this tension in a much more personal way than others. American reports headlined the problem of the 'home alone' children of dual-career military families, where both parents were in the Gulf.[8] A survey of a random sample of a local population, carried out during the war by the present author and Roy Carr-Hill in a northern English city, found 13 per cent of respondents who claimed to to be 'worried about family or friends in the Gulf'. Of these, 56 per cent claimed that a member of their family (in over half of the cases, a child or teenager) had been 'adversely affected by the violence of the war', compared to 21 per cent in the sample as a whole.

Much larger numbers of those who had no such personal involvement also claimed to be 'worried about the violence of the war in general' (32 per cent) than 'felt good because of allied or British successes' (12 per cent). On the other hand, 39 per cent claimed not to have been personally affected by the war. Women, especially older women, and readers of 'quality' newspapers were particularly likely to say they were 'worried'.[9] This research was carried out during the war itself, and our questions framed at the beginning of the war: we were therefore unable to ask about events in the war in detail (although this is the aim of a post-war follow-up survey).[10] The responses we obtained, moreover, depended on the information available to respondents at the time. This in turn depended on the coverage of the mass media of communication.

The mass media were the major instrument in the process of mediating violence to distant populations, not just in Western societies but throughout the world. Much commentary has emphasized, rightly, the manipulation of the media by governments and the military, and of viewers and readers by the media.[11] There is no doubt that most media in most Western countries presented a highly sanitized version of events and rarely asked the awkward questions. The political and military authorities had five months in which to plan the control of information. The putative 'lessons of Vietnam' – however challenged by academic research[12] – as refined by the (from the military point of view) more positive experiences of the Falklands, Grenada and Panama, inspired an efficient media campaign. This faltered only when confronted with rare unexpected failure: the bombing of the civilian bunker, believed to be a military communications centre, on 13 February, stands out in this respect. It was at such points that significant parts of the media, even in the USA and the UK, departed in their coverage from the smooth track which the military had provided for them.[13] Otherwise, there were relatively few attempts to break out of the military stranglehold. There was, for example, extraordinarily little speculation about the numbers of Iraqi military casualties until the war was over; then US and UK military sources began to divulge their horrific estimates of anything from 40,000 to 200,000 killed. Similarly, very few dead bodies – the shrouded remains of the Baghdad bunker victims together with a few Israeli victims were probably the only exceptions – appeared on any television screens or in any newspapers until the war was practically over.

Coverage of the early phase of the war emphasized its high-technology efficiency: American fighter pilots' descriptions – 'exactly like the movies', 'Baghdad was lit up like a Christmas tree. It was tremendous!', 'It was kinda neat'[14] – were broadcast across the globe. Television news frequently matched this description of a BBC bulletin: 'a very muscular and loyalist affair, straight out of Biggles: our top guns on bridge-busting, Israeli jets zapping Palestinians around Sidon, the B–52s lumbering into Fairford and an almost black and blank screen from Baghdad courtesy of CNN'.[15] Even the land war, with its instant success, was widely presented in a glamorous light, at least until the extent of the carnage was revealed. The image of a local evening paper advertising 'Land War: Sunday Colour Special', sandwiched between billboards for a 'Big Fight Sensation' and 'City Match Report', evokes the sporting metaphor for war.[16] 'Saddam voodoo dolls' were quickly marketed in the USA;[17] cutaway diagrams of Challenger battle tanks and F–15E fighters covered the centrefold of the children's supplement to a British 'quality' paper.[18]

If ever there was a vindication of the 'armament culture' and 'spectator sport' concepts of militarism, this was it. However, as we have noted, these theories concentrate on the production of images of armaments and war, rather than the consumption of them by the members of societies.[19] Moreover, it is unclear that these approaches have the same validity for wartime as for peacetime militarism. They were tested in the research referred to above, in which we asked our respondents to say which of a number of statements best described the allied air attacks, and why they watched television coverage of the war. Only tiny minorities of around 5 per cent of the sample identifed with the description 'like video or computer games', or admitted to finding the war 'fascinating' or 'exciting'. Those who acknowledged the latter were almost exclusively younger men, notably those with some military connection but no personal involvement with the war, and readers of sensational pro-war papers. Far larger numbers of people – especially women – were 'worried', as we have seen, either about family or friends in the war, or generally about the violence of the war.[20] This evidence suggests that, despite the similarities of form between the air attacks and armament elements in popular culture, most people are aware of the differences between films and games and the real thing.

What is less clear is whether, when people expressed anxiety about violence, they were responding to the violence actually being carried out, chiefly by coalition forces against Iraqis. They may have been expressing instead their own more diffuse vulnerability to the threat of violence implicit in a novel and unknown situation. Our research showed highly differentiated levels of concern for the various nationalities involved in the conflict. We asked our respondents whether they were 'very concerned', 'concerned' or 'not concerned' about loss of life among a number of groups; only just over 20 per cent were very concerned about life in all groups. Well over 87 per cent were very concerned about British service personnel, yet only 36 per cent professed such concern for Iraqi civilians and 22 per cent for Iraqi service personnel. More people were *not* concerned about Iraqi soldiers. Women were markedly more humanitarian than men, and 'quality' newspaper readers more than tabloid readers.[21]

There was certainly little intimation, in much of the reporting, of the real violence involved in the attacks. Video film of missiles approaching their targets was released – but not the film of the horrified face of an Iraqi lorry driver a split second away from death.[22] The campaign was systematically presented as an attack on things – weapons, transporters, bridges, buildings – but not on people.

I happened to read Arno Mayer's account of *Cristallnacht* at this point in the war: 'By portraying the pogrom of November 9/10, 1938, as the "night of broken glass",' he argues, 'Nazi propagandists meant to fix attention on this material damage. They went out of their way to stress that Jews were neither looted nor physically harmed.'[23] I do not wish to compare the politics of the Gulf coalition to the Nazis in any way, but the propaganda methods were strikingly similar in their denial of the violence actually being perpetrated on human beings. There is some evidence that this account was widely accepted, at least in Britain: we found, in our survey, that 80 per cent identified with a description of the air attacks as 'precise strikes against strategic targets with minimum civilian casualties'; only 8 per cent saw them as 'intensive bombing with unacceptable civilian casualties'.[24]

A further element of denial was the refusal, or transfer, of responsibility by leaders and media. Western political leaders claimed that it was Saddam Hussein who had chosen war – which of course he had – denying the element of choice that lay with them, and which laid responsibility on them, too, for the results of the war. When American planes bombed the bunker in Baghdad in which several hundred civilians were killed, there were many attempts to blame Saddam Hussein for this grisly mistake, arguing either that he should not have placed civilians in a place which also had a military function, or more extremely that he had deliberately placed civilians there so as to make political capital out of their deaths. One British newspaper headlined this story 'Victims of Saddam', denying the responsibility of those who had actually launched the missiles which killed the people in the bunker.[25] Less than a week later, the IRA bombed Victoria station in London, killing one person, and issued a statement blaming the police for this death because they failed to clear the area. The police responded with a statement that the IRA's attempt to abdicate responsibility for the killing which they caused 'almost beggars belief'.[26] No one noticed the irony.

The issue of responsibility for killing and death was to emerge with a vengeance, however, as a result of the Kurdish crisis. President Bush, who had called for the overthrow of Saddam

Hussein, found himself being blamed for the slaughter of Shi'a and Kurdish rebels by the Iraqi army. Initial attempts to distance the West from this situation, by treating it as an internal Iraqi affair, foundered when it became clear that over a million refugees were facing appalling hardships, and many of them death, in the mountains between Iraq, Turkey and Iran. British Prime Minister John Major, whose first reaction had been to say that 'I don't recall asking the Kurds to mount this particular uprising',[27] was forced within a week to propose Western intervention to protect the victims of Iraqi repression.

The denial of responsibility for killing and death was part of a more fundamental denial of these realities, which was carried to extraordinary lengths in some of the initial responses of decision-makers in Western societies. British reactions were particularly extreme, including the notorious banning by the BBC of sixty-seven popular songs, including many whose comment on war or death was oblique or non-existent, and comedies like *Allo! Allo!* and even *Monty Python*.[28] The Victoria and Albert Museum banned an exhibition, 'The Art of Death', which included tomb-stones, mourning fans and funeral loaves. The denial of death, the organizer commented, was a 'peculiarly 20th century attitude'.[29]

The control of information in most coalition countries was designed to secure a 'black-out on human costs', as an account of US censorship puts it.[30] In addition, censorship had specific political purposes: as in the banning of pro-Saddam magazines, videos and songs in France,[31] of reporting about the role of the Incirlik US air base on Turkish television,[32] and the dampening down of pro-Iraqi feeling in the Arab countries which were part of the US-led coalition.[33] In Iraq, of course, the control of information was complete, conspiring with Western accounts to minimize the appalling death toll to its forces, while exploiting civilian casualties for both domestic and international propaganda.

There is also evidence of denial among the coalition troops inflicting death and destruction on the Iraqi forces and cities. The 'gung ho' celebration of 'action' reported in the early days of the war was, of course, in its own way just such a response. In the aftermath of the massacre on the Kuwait to Basra road which concluded the war, however, there was 'little pride' when US soldiers talked about the previous week's war: 'more a horror at the one-sidedness of it all'.[34]

At leadership level, there was a central ambiguity in General Colin Powell's declaration, one week into the war, that:[35]

> The Iraqi army is for the most part just sitting there, waiting to be attacked, and attacked it will be. First we are going to cut it off. Then we are going to kill it. As we get into the process of cutting it off we will also step up the process of killing it by going after his stockpiles, ammunition, food, stripping away their gun air defence, using air attacks.

The context suggests that General Powell was referring chiefly to the destruction of the Iraqi forces' ability to fight, but the repeated use of 'kill' indicates another meaning, which is contained in the first: the killing of the human beings who make up the Iraqi military force. Subsequent evidence suggests that this meaning was also intended. Every single Iraqi vehicle, down to the smallest, even if it was deviating from the main convoy, and every soldier among the forces retreating from Kuwait, was systematically destroyed at Mutla Ridge.[36] When British Air Vice-Marshal Tony Mason asserted that the bombing offensive was 'the most humane method of preparing for the expulsion of Iraqi ground forces from Kuwait', he appears to have meant that it saved coalition troops' lives and did not directly target Iraqi civilians; he can hardly have meant that it was humane to the Iraqi forces. Nevertheless, he hoped by his argument to contribute to a 'reduction in political and psychological collateral damage'.[37]

These problems of the legitimacy of killing are not new: they have been with us at least since the classical militarist glorification of war was confronted with the reality of the slaughter in the trenches, three-quarters of a century ago. In more recent times they were hugely reinforced by the experience of Vietnam, in which the global revulsion at the suffering of the Vietnamese merged with middle America's horror at its own 'body count'. Mass media can be the instruments of doubt, but the military belief that all you have do is to control the media is naive and doomed to failure. The doubt reflects the dilemmas of culture and power in post-military society; and in any case, as the Gulf war has shown, although you can control most of the media most of the time, you cannot control all of them all of the time.

## Post-Military Societies at War

The contrast between the classically militarized Iraqi society, in which even old men and early teenagers were drawn into military service and military ideology pervaded everyday life, and the post-military societies of the West was sharp – and lay behind the contrasting attitudes to killing and death. Nevertheless, other differences were also evident: between Iraq and the rich Gulf states, which depended on Western arms and Western troops rather than indigenous mobilization for their defence; and in the varying forms of militarism in Western states.

The contradictions between different processes of change in the militarism of industrial societies, which were central to much of our discussion in the second half of the book, have been of critical importance in the Gulf war. The chief 'offshore' states (the USA and the UK), which combine structural demilitarization with culturally and ideologically strong militarism, were able to mobilize strongly and effectively for war, with overwhelming popular support after the fighting started (the interpretation of 'public opinion' is, however, a complex matter, which is discussed further below). The continental European states, on the other hand, which have residual structural militarism but weak ideological militarism, were more inhibited from action and manifested much more contradictory public attitudes.

The maintenance of conscription was actually a barrier to direct participation in the conflict, as governments anticipated the resistance to mobilizing conscripts for fighting. In Germany – where the constitution was interpreted as a barrier to military involvement – many nevertheless reacted strongly to the possibility that conscripts would be mobilized for war. Almost a thousand active soldiers, including sixty-three at two bases deploying missile systems to Turkey for the war, together with 9,000 reservists and 11,000 young men liable to conscription, registered as conscientious objectors in January 1991[38] (a 54 per cent increase on the previous year's already high level of conscientious objection).[39] Even in Britain, where there was no prospect of a reintroduction of conscription, there was a slight moral panic about conscription among young people at the start of the war.[40]

The role of national experiences and national myths of war was strongly evident, in different reactions between countries within each of these two categories. Before the war there was a clear difference between the USA and the UK in the level of political debate about the war. In the USA, under the influence of Vietnam, there was a vigorous debate: Congress and public opinion were both fairly evenly divided between supporters and opponents of war, right up to its outbreak. In the UK, by contrast, where recent experiences of war have all been successful, observers commented on the 'lack of debate and sluggish reaction to the Gulf crisis'[41] – although (curiously rare) opinion polls showed almost half of British respondents, too, reluctant to envisage military action.[42] A principal reason, of course, was the Labour leadership's low profile, as it calculated that criticism of the drive towards war would cost it electoral support, as it appeared to have done during and after the Falklands war.

In continental European countries, support for military action before the war actually began was substantially weaker than in the USA and the UK. A German poll on the eve of war found that 79 per cent of civilians and 71 per cent of soldiers thought there should be no war; only 11 per cent were prepared to back military action. Similar figures were recorded in Spain, where a majority supported a call for Spanish ships to return home, and Italy, where most respondents advocated a supportive, not an interventionist, role for the Italian force. Sixty per cent of Belgians supported their government's non-participation in the conflict. In France a large majority supported the government's last-minute efforts to keep the peace, and half of all respondents believed that the USA had not done all it could to secure peace.[43]

Once the attacks on Iraq had begun, opinion changed radically in many countries. Even in Germany polls produced 70 per cent majorities endorsing the war, and there was a current on the German intellectual left which, identifying Saddam Hussein with Hitler, felt it its duty to rally to the war.[44] On the other hand, Germany maintained a strong opposition current, with the largest demonstrations against the war. The divided response to the war was widely seen as a reflection of the country's 'identity crisis'.[45]

In Italy, on the other hand, opposition to the war was much more widely maintained, fuelled by an unprecedented alliance of the Communist party and Pope, whose denunciation of the war was uncompromising and carried many Italian Catholics with it. (According to our survey, in Britain in contrast the Pope's stand had little resonance among ordinary Catholics.)[46] In France the commitment to the war (French ground troops as well as air and naval forces were involved) strained the ruling Socialist party's unity, with the resignation of the Defence Minister, Jean-Pierre Chevenement. In France, too, more than anywhere else in Europe, the war created tensions both among Arab immigrants and between them and the majority,[47] although there was also conflict involving the Muslim community in Britain.[48]

In the USA and the UK, in contrast, the solidification of public opinion behind the war, according to headline poll findings, appeared far more complete than in continental Europe. American popular support for the war was more explicit, in displays of flags, rallies and parades, than was the case in Britain. British opinion polls found record majorities for the war (consistently 80 per cent or more, even higher than in the USA), but a national paper could claim with some justice that 'Britain has gone to war the way a mature democracy should when it has to fight. No gung-ho jingoism. No histrionic gestures or speeches. No euphoria about easy victory. No war fever, despite the over-whelming support for waging war.'[49] The traditional British denial of militarist ideology – which we have seen in liberal–technological militarism, the understated militarism of the Second World War and the detachment of nostalgia militarism – was once more to the fore.

Attempts by popular papers to reproduce the superficial militarism of the Falklands were widely judged unsuccessful: 'The mood on the streets – as evidenced by the absence of paper flags [distributed by Murdoch's *Sun*] – doesn't match the mood of the tabloids.'[50] Nevertheless, our survey showed that attitudes to the war were more strongly differentiated by newspaper readership than by any other factor, with readers of the most jingoistic tabloids most likely to express similar attitudes.[51] Twenty-one per cent of the readers of the *Sun*, which had even used the headline 'Nuke Baghdad',[52] were in favour of using nuclear weapons against Iraq, compared to only 6 per cent of our sample as a whole.[53]

These findings are closely linked with others on the appeal of the British national myths of war. The statement 'we have to stand up to dictators', expressing the simplest rationale for fighting (and one to which some policitians as well as tabloid newspapers explicitly appealed), was most likely to be endorsed by those with family involvement in the war, by those who had been in the forces during the Second World War or national service, by Conservative voters – and by *Sun* and *Star* readers. Much the same groups tended to personalize war aims most strongly, by advocating the overthrow of Saddam Hussein as a war aim (but this was not entirely the same issue, as Labour voters agreed with this as much as Conservatives, and there was a strong gender gap, with women more likely than men to see Saddam himself as the problem).

It was clear that there were two supports for these positions: a view of Saddam as 'like Hitler', which appealed more to older people and Conservative voters, and a view of him as 'mad', with a special appeal to younger people and Labour voters. This picture demonstrates the complex appeal of the national myth of war, which has been reproduced with varying emphases that win support from different groups, although overall its appeal was strongest by far among readers of down-market tabloid newspapers.[54]

At the same time, however, readers of these newspapers were most likely to believe that their papers 'glorified war too much' (a statement agreed with by as many as 41 per cent of *Sun* and *Star* readers but only 7 per cent of 'quality' readers). Television coverage, too, was viewed critically by viewers who accepted many of the messages it gave about the war: 40 per cent of our sample who responded before the Baghdad bunker bombing saw it as 'glorifying war too much', while only 2 per cent saw it as 'too critical of the war'. Even after this incident, 29 per cent agreed that television glorified the war too much, but 13 per cent found it too critical.[55]

This evidence of consumer resistance to media messages, together with that of anxiety and vulnerability discussed above, qualifies the claims of one poll-sponsoring newspaper that the figures for 'approval' of the war reflected 'an extraordinary degree of unanimity, unprecedented in modern times towards any policy'.[56] This statement reminds one indeed of the conclusion reached by a study of the Falklands war, that television 'first selectively informs people's attitudes, then selectively reports on what those attitudes are, and finally ... uses this version of public opinion to justify its own approach to reporting'.[57]

Polling, like news coverage, is a process in the mediation of violence, and the Gulf war, as Giddens has pointed out, was 'the most heavily mediated, reflexively monitored war in human history'.[58] Despite this, however, it cannot be claimed that most members of British society were simply supporting the war. Given the greater contradictions surrounding responses to the war in almost all other Western societies, it is likely that the qualifications we have made to the picture of a 'supportive' society in Britain have an international relevance.

## WAR AND MILITARISM AFTER THE GULF

The Gulf war was historically important, as argued above, because of its timing and global character, rather than its duration or the number of casualties. The war expunged the idea of a purely peaceful world from the post-Cold War agenda; it demonstrated the weakness of international institutions (the United Nations authorized but did not fight the war) and the enduring dominance of American military power. It showed the continuing ability of advance Western states to gain the necessary political backing for the use of highly destructive force and the imposition of very heavy casualties on an enemy. At the same time it further exposed – even if it did not test in the manner of Vietnam – the vulnerability of societies which have become used to living without the large-scale violence of war, to the intrusion of such violence into daily life. The manipulation of information and opinion, despite its initial successes, confirmed the fragility of the legitimation of this violence in modern states.

This sense of precariousness in the apparent reinvigoration of war and militarism applies in other respects, too. The failure of Saddam Hussein and the humiliation of his overblown high-militarist state – which had already precipitated the bloodiest war of recent times before its invasion of Kuwait – is surely a major setback for militarism in the south. This judgement can be sustained, even if the uncritical optimism of American apologists like Francis Fukuyama, according to whom the defeat of Saddam is a message to every aggressively minded Third World dictator, is misplaced. The defeat of Saddam, and renewed pressure for his trial for war crimes and genocide, coincided with the re-emergence of Pol Pot, whose genocide has not prevented him receiving covert Western support.[59] American policing is likely to be selective, and there is little reason to believe that the lesson of past Western encouragement to Saddam will be fully learnt. Nevertheless, there will certainly be a demonstrative effect in cases where US interests might be threatened, and a greater element of risk in aggressive action. The intervention in Iraq's war machine which the ceasefire terms imposed certainly represents an important precedent.

There is, however, every reason to believe that, even if Saddam is eventually removed, many states will seek to build up their own versions of the military power which has been so successful in destroying Iraq. Arms sales to those who were on the 'right' side in the war will almost certainly increase. It will be difficult to deny Israel, Saudi Arabia, Egypt and even Iran; and needless to say any supply to the Arabs will have to be balanced to Israel, and vice versa. Pieties about the need to control the supply of arms are unlikely to be transformed into serious policy. The best that can be hoped for in the short term is probably an armed peace, a regional cold war, to replace the danger of hot war which has never been far away in the Middle East.

Nevertheless, the experience of the Cold War has shown that out of a long period of military stalemate can grow patterns of interdependency, cultural integration and even co-operation which may eventually lead to less dangerous international relationships. Military build-up in the Middle East may not increase indefinitely, even if the Gulf gives it a short-term boost, and it will probably not increase further elsewhere in the south, where the arms trade had already slowed down. 'The depression of the arms trade in the 1980s', according to SIPRI, 'can no longer be dismissed as a temporary aberration ... In retrospect, the arms trade patterns of the 1960s and 1970s may be seen as anomalies in the history of international relations.'[60] Clearly a new political *modus vivendi* in the Middle East, if not a solution of the region's conflicts, could provide a context in which the growth of armaments in the south slows down or is even reversed in the medium term.

In any case, as we have argued throughout this book, military build-up is not the same thing as societal militarization. Whatever else the blending of Islamic traditionalism and Western high technology in Saudi Arabia and the Gulf has produced, these are not militarized societies. Iran's Islamic society is being demilitarized, after the excesses of the revolutionary war against Iraq, even as the post-revolutionary regime rearms. Israeli society is institutionally and ideologically militarized through its permanent state of armed confrontation with the Arabs,[61] but its democracy could allow demilitarization if the conflict was defused. There is an incipient conflict in much of the Middle East, as in other newly industrializing countries, between the cultural consequences of economic change and the authoritarianism and militarism of the regimes.

The democratization of Eastern Europe and the USSR, with all its limitations, has set a very important precedent for the more developed societies of the south. Many of the same social conditions for democratic upheaval are present in the cities and towns of the Middle East, as well as in parts of Asia, Latin America and even Africa. Democratization is likely to be uneven and contradictory, and its consequences for militarism as complex as those which we have noted in the USSR. It is possible, however, that even if military build-up continues, militarism in the high, classical forms which have existed in Iran and Iraq in the last decade may come to seem an exceptional development as we enter the twenty-first century. Military governments, too – the existence of which has no necessary relation with societal militarization – may eventually become fewer, even in Africa, as they have in Latin America, if democratic pressures gather momentum.

In the USSR itself, the Gulf war was seen as providing temporary cover for a crackdown on the democrats and nationalities. The shooting of demonstrators in Lithuania in January 1991 revived memories of the crushing of the Hungarian revolution at the time of the Suez invasion in 1956. In the event, the crackdown was partly disowned by President Gorbachev, and appears in retrospect to have been just one more stage in a long-drawn-out series of confrontations. More serious, perhaps, was the fact that Gorbachev's support of the USA in the war became another serious charge against him – betraying an erstwhile Soviet ally – for the neo-Stalinist wing of the Communist party and many of its military supporters. Nevertheless it was hardly as important as other issues in this conflict, such as the loss of Eastern Europe and the acceptance of disarmament and arms control on terms which weaken the USSR more than the USA.

In the West, the Gulf war has been seen as a major check to the demobilization and demilitarization which followed the end of the Cold War. Question marks have been raised over some of the cutbacks previously announced; Britian's belated cuts, for example, announced only a week before the Iraqi invasion of Kuwait, were officially placed under review in the aftermath of the war. However, in terms of weaponry and forces, it is difficult to see that much has changed as a result of the war. The sweeping success of the coalition forces meant that very few of their weapon systems were actually destroyed in the fighting. There is no general need to renew weaponry, as after many wars, even if systems which performed particularly well will be in greater demand. In terms of strategic requirements, even the maintenance of enhanced rapid deployment forces for policing new crises in the south will not justify keeping more than a small fraction of the forces demobilized from Europe. Unless, indeed, major new threats which require policing are quickly found, the level of forces necessary may soon be seen in quite minimalist terms. Nuclear weapons will be especially redundant.

In sum, therefore, even at the levels of weaponry and troops, the Gulf is likely only to slow down, probably temporarily, and certainly not to reverse the trend towards force reductions. Future developments depend far more on events inside the USSR than on the Middle East. Only if the neo-Stalinist reaction is taken to the point of a historic defeat for the reform process, involving a radical reversal of Gorbachev's foreign policy directions, will the cutbacks in the West be halted. Even then, since there can be no restoration of the pre-1989 Soviet bloc, and since the USSR's economy has been radically weakened, any new cold war will probably be a pale version of the former conflict.

The Gulf war will do nothing to remove the large question mark over conscription in Europe, since large conscript forces are manifestly not required for global policing. It is more likely to assist in renewing some of the ideological supports of militarism, than in sustaining its declining institutional bases. This would have been truer if the Gulf victory had not been marred by its aftermath inside Iraq, which brought to the fore the contradictions the violence of war raises for post-military societies. At the time of writing, the war appears to have been double-edged in its consequences for militarism.

This should not surprise us, for the relationships of war and militarism are generally contradictory. Only the militarism of victors is ever confirmed by war; the militarism of the defeated is often fundamentally challenged. In modern wars, even those who end up on the right side have often also been defeated, as was the case for many countries in Europe in 1939–45. Only the British and Americans can celebrate the military traditions and values of that war in anything like an unequivocal way. Even the militarism of victors can be undermined, as in the widespread revulsion against war throughout the West after 1914–18.

Militarism, in an ideological sense, flourishes best in conditions in which military institutions and values are *not* tested in battle: the heyday of militarism was the decade before 1914, the culmination of a century without general conflict. In the 1990s, after two world wars and Vietnam, the legacy of disillusion with war weighs heavily on militarism, and combines with the demobilization of armed forces to reinforce the demilitarization of societies.

Militarist ideologies still flourish in some parts of Western societies, especially among the habitual victors (the UK and – Vietnam apart – the USA). Some older men, especially, cherish the memory of their heroic youth; some younger men are fascinated by the high technology of war. Some readers of hyper-patriotic papers are apparently seduced by their simple images and slogans, which keep an older militarist culture alive in a different world. Many people accept the ideological justifications for violence which are presented in the less sensational, but censored and self-censoring coverage of war on television. Large minorities of viewers, and even readers of popular newspapers, however, see these media as engaged in a glorification of war.

The war underlined, moreover, some important divisions within societies over attitudes to violence and the military. Women have been consistently shown in opinion polls as significantly less pro-war than men. Crewe has argued that, in the UK, differences between men and women on defence issues 'are very slender. Fewer than ten percentage points divide men and women in their answers to most questions. The majority of men and women take the same side on each question. There is no pitched battle of the sexes on defence.'[62] Our findings during the Gulf war, in contrast, while not supporting the idea of a pitched battle, do indicate stronger differences, especially when we take into account underlying feelings about violence as well as attitudes to formal political questions. Only 21 per cent of women 'strongly' approved of the war, compared to 38 per cent of men. Only 36 per cent of women said they were 'not concerned' about Iraqi servicemen's lives, compared to 53 per cent of men. Fifty-seven per cent of women were 'worried' about the war, compared to only 36 per cent of men.[63] War appears to accentuate the differences in attitudes to military and defence issues which exist in peacetime, and underlines that these differences should not be minimized.

The Gulf war also emphasized women's integration in military structures, with unprecedented numbers of women close to battle zones. British women reservists served in military hospitals in Saudi Arabia, and one of the 40,000 American women was among the small number of coalition prisoners-of-war taken by the Iraqis. The problem of the responsibility for the children of women soldiers in the Gulf (referred to above) raised, however, a question mark in some discussion of this new role for women. In this sense, also, the differences between the sexes in their approaches to war, which are the product of long histories of differentiated social roles and cultural conditioning, are left problematic by the experiences of the war.

Another fundamental division, documented for the first time by our research on attitudes to the war, was that between those with and without military experience or family connections with the military. Even defining those with a military connection ('warriors') in a very broad way (so that they amounted to 39 per cent of our sample), we found significant differences in attitudes to the conflict. Less than 10 per cent of warriors disapproved of the war, compared to 20 per cent of non-warriors. Breaking down this category, however, revealed more than taking it as a whole. Those who actually had family involvement in the Gulf, and men who had served in the forces in the Second World War, were far more likely to have different attitudes from the non-warriors, than were those who had some other connection with the military. The former groups were far more likely, for example, to say that they were 'not concerned' about loss of life among Iraqi soldiers. Wartime participation, rather than military participation, appeared to be the more important determinant of attitudes.[64] As the proportion of Western societies which has direct wartime or even military experience declines, the decline in the appeal of military values is likely to continue.

In the aftermath of war, both patriotism and war anxiety will fade back into popular culture. They will merge into the militarism of peacetime, in which the military is 'just a job' and war is a pretext for violent escapism or cosy nostalgia. Occasional crises force a society which has distanced itself from war to confront the reality of distant war: the Gulf war has been the most dramatic instance for two decades. Until another crisis punctures the post-militarist peace, the long decline and transformation of militarism, which we have analysed in this book, are likely to resume.

# Notes

1 At the time of writing, the Gulf conflict in its wider sense is far from complete. In what follows, I refer to events before mid-April only.
2 Chapter 1, p. 15.
3 Anthony Giddens, *The Nation-State and Violence*, Vol. 2 of *A Contemporary Critique of Historical Materialism* (Cambridge: Polity, 1985).
4 Martin Shaw, 'War and the nation-state in social theory', in David Held and John B. Thompson, eds, *Social Theory of Modern Societies* (Cambridge: University Press, 1989).
5 Joost Hilterman and Jack Geiger of Physicians for Human Rights, quoted by Ed Vulliamy, 'Doctors find Iraq is slowly dying', *Guardian* (16 April 1991).
6 Anthony Giddens, *The Consequences of Modernity* (Stanford: University Press, 1990), p. 125.
7 Ibid., pp. 120–1.
8 Julie Wheelwright, 'Women at war', *Guardian* (24 January 1991); Angela Phillips, 'Home alone', *Guardian* (6 February 1991).
9 Martin Shaw and Roy Carr-Hill, *Public Opinion, Media and Violence: Attitudes to the Gulf War in a Local Population* (Hull: Hull University Gulf War Project, Report No. 1, March 1991), pp. 9–10, 23.
10 The results of this survey will be published as Gulf War Report No. 2, 1991; a third on ideological responses to the war (based on smaller surveys of political activists, ministers of religion and anti-war activists), will also appear later in 1991.
11 See for example, *Index on Censorship*, 20, 4/5 (April/May 1991), special issue, 'Warspeak: The Gulf and the News Media', which includes a wide range of contributions and some further references; the media coverage was also the subject of a great deal of commentary in the serious press during the war.

12  Michael Mandelbaum, 'Vietnam: the television war', *Daedalus*, III, 4, (Fall 1982), pp. 157–69.

13  The shift in the coverage was recognized by significant numbers of British television viewers, according to our study of attitudes carried out during the war: see p. 206 below.

14  'Sound bites', *Weekend Guardian* (19–20 January 1991), p. 7.

15  David Pallister, 'Gulf Mediafile', *Media Guardian* (11 February 1991). The author went on to comment, however, that ITN's bull-etin of the same evening was 'incomparably better. Brent Sadler's report from Baghdad showed Iraqi pictures of civilian damage and spoke of children dying, with the corrective remark that the Iraqis had stolen the incubators from Kuwaiti hospitals.' This bulletin was a week before the bunker bombing of 13 February, which made civilian casualties a major issue, and shows that a tension in coverage of this issue was already developing in the media before this date.

16  *Yorkshire Evening Press* billboards, York city centre, 24 February 1991.

17  Raymond Whitaker, *Independent* (12 February 1991).

18  *Funday Times*, supplement to *Sunday Times*, quoted *Guardian* (7 February 1991).

19  Chapter 3, p. 82.

20  Shaw and Carr-Hill, *Public Opinion*, pp. 9–10.

21  Ibid., pp. 7–8, and charts 5a–5d, pp. 15–18.

22  Caspar Henderson, 'The filtered war', *New Statesman and Society*, 'Banned' supplement (12 April 1991), p. 16.

23  Arno Mayer, *And Did the Heavens Not Darken?* (London: Verso, 1989), p. 169.

24  Shaw and Carr-Hill, *Public Opinion*, pp. 7–8.

25  *Daily Mail*, quoted by Edward Pearce, 'Auxiliary boys' brigade', *Guardian* (14 February 1991).

26  Metropolitan Police statement, 19 February 1991, quoted *Guardian* (20 February).

27  *Independent* (6 April 1991).

28  The full list of songs, together with other information in a useful comparative survey, is given by Henderson, 'The filtered war', p. 17.

29  Maev Kennedy, 'The forgotten art of death rituals', *Guardian* (6 April 1991).

30  Nan Levinson, 'Snazzy visuals, hard facts and obscured issues', *Index on Censorship*, 20, 4/5 (April/May 1991), pp. 27–9.

31  Henderson, 'The filtered war', p. 17, and Yves Jaumin, 'Getting their own back', *Index on Censorship*, ibid., pp. 22–3.

32  Chris Hellier, 'Ozal: the second front', *Index on Censorship*, ibid., pp. 25–6.

33  Adel Darwish, 'Allah is enlisted by Arab armies', in ibid., pp. 39–41.

34  David Beresford, 'Eyewitness', *Guardian* (6 March 1991).

35 Quoted by Martin Walker, David Fairhall and Ian Black, 'Pentagon to "cut off and kill Saddam's troops"', *Guardian* (24 January 1991).
36 Michael Kelly, 'Carnage on a forgotten road', *Guardian* (11 April 1991). It has been pointed out that the majority of Iraqi troops killed were Shi'as and Kurds, among whom opposition to the Ba'athist regime was strongest; the elite Republican Guard were further to the rear (Greg Philo, letter, *Guardian* (17 April 1991)).
37 Air Vice-Marshal Tony Mason, 'Morale and civilian death', *Guardian* (7 February 1991).
38 David Gow, 'Bonn faces rise in objectors', *Guardian* (7 February 1991).
39 Reuter, 'German objectors', *Guardian* (2 February 1991).
40 Conversations with students, Hull University and Humberside Polytechnic, January 1991. The Militant Tendency (Trotskyist entrists in the Labour party) attempted to cash in on this with 'No Conscription' posters flyposted in British cities in late January.
41 Michael White, 'No rocking the warship', *Guardian* (12 January 1991).
42 A Gallup poll showed a majority of 49 per cent to 43 per cent in favour of immediate military action on the eve of war (*Daily Telegraph* (11 January 1991).
43 Madeleine Bunting, 'Divided we stand up to Iraq', *Guardian Europe* (18 January 1991).
44 Hans Magnus Enzensberger, 'The second coming of Adolf Hitler', *Guardian* (9 February 1991).
45 David Gow, 'Search for role exacerbates German identity crisis', *Guardian* (26 January 1991).
46 Shaw and Carr-Hill, *Public Opinion*, p. 13.
47 Paul Webster, 'French try to ease classroom tension', *Guardian* (24 January 1991).
48 Saeeda Khanum, 'British Muslims and the war', *New Statesman and Society* (1 February 1991), pp. 12–14.
49 Editorial, *Sunday Times* (20 January 1991).
50 Steve Platt, 'Paper flags', *New Statesman and Society* (26 January 1991).
51 Shaw and Carr-Hill, *Public Opinion*, pp. 31–3.
52 Quoted by Pearce, 'Auxiliary boys' brigade'.
53 Shaw and Carr-Hill, *Public Opinion*, pp. 7, 32.
54 Ibid., table 1, p. 6.
55 For more detailed analysis of these findings, see Shaw and Carr-Hill, ibid. (These same questions, and others about coverage of specific incidents in the war, are being asked in the follow-up survey being carried out at the time of writing, which will be analysed in Hull University Gulf War Report No. 2.)

56  *Sunday Times* (2 March 1991), reporting on the finding that its 'War Panel's' approval of the war had risen from 80 to 89 per cent.
57  Glasgow University Media Group, *War and Peace News* (Milton Keynes: Open University Press, 1985), p. 143.
58  Anthony Giddens, conference on 'Nationalism in a Post-Marxist World', London School of Economics (1 March 1991).
59  Ben Kiernan, 'Green grow the killing fields', *Guardian* (16 April 1991).
60  Aaron Kapp, 'The trade in conventional weapons', *SIPRI Yearbook 1988* (Oxford: University Press, 1988), pp. 195, 197.
61  Avishai Ehrlich, 'Israel: conflict, war and social change', in Colin Creighton and Martin Shaw, eds, *The Sociology of War and Peace* (London: Macmillan, 1987), pp. 121–42.
62  Ivor Crewe, 'Britain two and a half cheers for the Atlantic alliance', in Gregory Flynn and Hans Rattinger, eds, *The Public and Atlantic Defense* (London: Croom Helm, 1985), p. 48.
63  Shaw and Carr-Hill, *Public Opinion*, pp. 23–4. A paper on this aspect of our research is in preparation.
64  Ibid., pp. 30–1. A paper on this aspect of our research is also in preparation.

# INDEX

advertising (military)   143–5
*Afgantsi*   170
Afghanistan   96, 170
Africa   34, 40, 50, 60, 72–3,
   99, 100, 183
   military regimes in   101–4,
   209
Afro-Caribbeans (Britain)
   143
Albania   26, 35, 93
Aldershot   154
Algeria   78
*Allo! Allo!*   129, 201
American Civil War   16
Anderson, P.   17
Andreski, S.   10, 15
Angola   47, 96, 152
Argentina   61, 104, 119, 120,
   130
armament culture   14, 80–3,
   198–9
   *see also* culture
armed forces   72, 98–101
   British 114, 135–55
   *see also* military

Armenia   169
arms races
   naval (Britain/Germany)   22
   nuclear   3, 22, 51
arms spending *see* military
   expenditure
arms trade   3, 49–50, 208
Asia   27, 34, 40, 60, 72–3,
   99, 100, 101, 104, 183,
   209
Australasia   27, 34
authoritarianism (military)
   152–3
Azerbaijan   168, 169

Baghdad   198, 206
Baltic republics   171
Barnett, A.   120
Barrow-in-Furness   150
Basra   201
Belgium   35, 122
*Belgrano, General*   130
Berlin   26
Berlin blockade   34
Berlin Wall   26, 192

Blitz (London)    127–8
body count    202
Bolsheviks    176
bombing (Gulf War)    196
Bramall, Sir E.    147, 148
Brazil    50, 104
Brezhnev, L.    26
Britain    2, 22, 32, 35, 36, 37,
    39, 45, 49–50, 52, 55, 61,
    84–7, 110, 165, 173, 177
    and Gulf War    199, 203–7
    militarism in    113–55
British Army    114, 148,
    154–5
British Broadcasting
    Corporation (BBC)    133,
    198, 201
British Military Studies Group
    145
British Movement    154
British Social Attitudes
    Surveys    125–6
Brixton riots    148
brutalization (military life)    152
budgeting (military)    146
Bulgaria    26, 93
bullying (military)    153,
    170–1
*Bundeswehr* (Germany)    145
Bush, G.    111

Cable News Network (CNN)
    198
Cambodia *see* Kampuchea
Campaign for Nuclear
    Disarmament (CND)
    121–2
Canada    141
capitalism
    and East–West conflict
        (Mann)    25

and state system    32–3
and war    11, 16–18
Carr-Hill, R. A.    197
casualties (Gulf War)    194,
    196, 198, 201
    *see also* death; killing
censorship
    Falklands    133
    Gulf    197, 199–200, 201
Chamberlain, N.    120
chemical weapons    62
children (Gulf service
    personnel)    197
China    2, 49, 50, 183
Christian Democratic Party
    (Germany)    172
Christianity, military    115
Church Army    115
churches    115, 167
Churchillism    118, 120
citizen-targets    80
citizen warfare (Mann)    76
citizenship    75
    active    187–8
    and conscription    174–80
    post-military    187–8
Civic Forum (Czechoslovakia)
    166, 167
class
    conflict    19
    and defence attitudes    150
    and geopolitics (Mann)    25
    and military recruitment
        139–40
Clausewitz, K. von    44
Cold War    1, 22, 110, 155,
    168
    culture and ideology    75
    end of    vii, 1, 2–3, 23–8,
        51, 55, 62, 134, 163–4,
        165, 179, 192, 196

Second Cold War    vii, 2, 13,
    56, 134, 146
    *see also* East–West conflict
Commonwealth    110
Communism, Communist
    states    35, 183
    *see also* Stalinism
Communist Party (USSR)
    165, 171, 209
Compagnies Républicaines de
    Sécurité (CRS)    148
Comte, A.    16
Conference on Security and
    Co-operation in Europe
    (CSCE)    164, 168
Congo    35
conscientious objection
    (Germany)    203
conscription    75, 79, 164, 184
    Britain    114, 116–17, 138
    and citizenship    174–80
    Europe    83–93, 111,
    171–4, 179
    German view of    114
    and Gulf War    203, 210
    Third World    98–9
    USSR    90–3, 166, 170–1
Conscription, Law of (France)
    175
conservatism (British military)
    153
Conservative Party (Britain)
    120–4, 143, 150–1, 206
Cooper, J.    90, 92
counter-insurgency    148
Crewe, I.    150–1, 211
*Cristallnacht*    200
Croatia    91, 169
cruise missiles    121–3
cultural resources (peace)
    185

culture
    consumer    79, 84
    military    115, 126–30, 137,
    185, 188
    popular broadcasting
        (Morrison and Tumber)
        132–4
    *see also* armament culture
Czechoslovakia    92, 119, 165,
    166–8

*Dad's Army*    129
*Daily Mirror*    131
*Daily Star*    154
*Daily Telegraph*    131
death (Gulf War)    194, 201
    *see also* casualties; killing
defence    9, 11
defence policy (Britain)
    121–4, 137, 150–1
Defence Select Committee
    (Britain)    143
defence studies    6
demilitarization    23, 39, 73,
    90, 93, 109–13
    defined    13–14
    Europe    163–5
    USSR and Eastern Europe
        165–71
    Western Europe    171–4
democracy (armed forces)
    153, 176, 180
Democratic Party (USA)    174
democratization
    Third World    209
    USSR and Eastern Europe
        165–71
Denning, Lord    154
Department of Defense (USA)
    142
Desert Storm    193

deterrence   9, 11, 79
deterrence-science militarism
   (Mann)   76, 78–9
Deutscher, I.   176
development   6
disarmament   146
disciplinary boundaries   7
disembedding (Giddens)   196
*Does Khaki Become You?*   68
Doorn, J. van   74–5
Downes, C.   145

East–West conflict   25, 46, 56
   *see also* Cold War
Edgerton, D.   116
Edinburgh Festival   128
Egypt   50, 208
Eide, A.   43
El Salvador   96
elitism (military, Britain)
   138–40
*Empire of the Sun*   129
Enloe, C.   68–9, 76, 140–1
Eppelmann, R.   167
Eritrea   96
Ethiopia   96, 99
ethnic minorities (military,
   Britain)   142–3
Europe   27, 34, 56, 101
   citizenship in   174–5,
      178–9
   conscription in   83–93
   Eastern   25, 46, 57, 77, 82,
      90, 92, 112, 119, 124,
      156, 163, 171, 182, 209
   and Gulf War   203–5
   military expenditure in   46
   post-militarism in   155–7
   revolutions (1989)   vii, 26,
      166, 181, 183
   Western   25, 27, 36, 39–40,

   45–6, 57, 112, 121–2,
      156
   southern   46
European Community   27,
   37, 39, 57, 62, 164, 175,
   178–9
European empires,
   imperialism   35
European state system   32
Exocet missiles   61
exterminism (Thompson)   70,
   84

Falklands War   39, 61, 78,
   104, 136, 138, 153, 154,
   156, 204, 205, 206
   media coverage   130–4,
      198
   and national myths of war
      120–1, 123
Far East   34
femininity   188–9
feminism   177
fetishism (weaponry)   80–1
films (war)   129–30
First World War   21, 22, 32,
   33–4, 64, 95, 117, 147,
   196
flexible response   55
Foot, M.   120
football violence   154
*force de frappe*   52, 121
Fordism   65–6
France   2, 32, 36–9, 45,
   49–50, 52, 61, 78, 85,
   121, 148, 156, 201
French Revolution   32, 64,
   97, 174, 175
Freudian   80
Fukuyama, F.   207
*Full Metal Jacket*   129

fundamentalism, Islamic
119

gays (military)  142
gender  150, 188–9
  *see also* femininity; women
general elections (Britain)
  122–5
Geneva-49 (USSR)  171
genocide (total war)  21
geopolitics  25, 27
Georgia (USSR)  168, 171
Germany  22, 33, 37–9, 47,
  88, 130, 145, 154, 156,
  165, 176, 194
  demilitarization of  112,
  172–3
  East  26, 46, 90, 167, 172
  and Gulf War  203
  West  36, 39, 45, 49–50,
  85, 122, 136, 153, 172,
  174
Giddens, A.  17–19, 20,
  24–7, 76, 195, 196,
  206–7
Glasgow University Media
  Group  131–4
Gorbachev, M.  26, 38, 56,
  79, 92, 164–5, 209, 210
Gramsci, A.  65
Great Britain *see* Britain
Greece  46, 54, 87
Greenham Common  133, 154
Grenada (US invasion)  78,
  198
gross domestic product
  (military expenditure)
  45–7
*Guardian, The*  131
guerrilla wars  96–7
Gulf War  vii, 2, 38, 39, 53,

56, 60, 90, 95, 138, 141,
  157, 183
  and post-military society
  191–213
Gummett, P.  38
Gumplowicz, H.  16

Halliday, F.  41
Harries-Jenkins, G.  145
Hartley, K.  146
Havel, V.  166
Healey, D.  121
Heseltine, M.  146, 149
Hintze, O.  16
historical materialism  17
historical sociology (war)  8
Hitler, A.  194, 206
Hockey, J.  152
Hollywood  129
Home Guard (Britain)  177
homosexuality (military)  142
Honecker, E.  167
Hong Kong  42
Howard, M.  6
Hungary  26, 90, 92, 165, 209
Hussein, S.  98, 119, 193–4,
  206, 207, 208

ideology, in armament culture
  81–2
  *see also* militarist ideologies
Imperial War Museum  127–8
imperialism  36, 79
India  41, 60
Indo-China  78
Indonesia  41, 50
industrialism, industrial society
  and classical militarism  65
  as militaristic  16
  as pacific  6, 8, 11, 15–16,
  26–8

industrialism (*cont.*):
  and state system   32–3
  *see also* capitalism
industrialization (war)   20
industrialized total war   20
Inter-University Seminar on
    Armed Forces and Society
    (USA)   145
Interior Ministry troops
    (USSR)   148
international order (post-Cold
    War)   180–3, 192–3
international relations   6–7
  social movements in   24–6
  and sociology   23–8
  theory   23–8
international system   36
  *see also* state system
Iran   41, 46, 50, 53, 95, 97–8,
    194, 208
Iran–Iraq war   2, 53, 57, 61,
    62, 95, 97, 183, 192, 194
Iraq   46, 47, 50, 53, 62, 95,
    98, 183
  and Gulf War   193, 194,
    196–7, 199, 201, 202,
    203, 204, 208
Ireland   148
Islam   36, 119, 208
Israel   47, 48, 50, 61, 73, 208,
    209
Italy   49–50

Jakes, M.   167
Janowitz, M.   74
Japan   27, 34, 36, 37, 38–9,
    45, 46, 62, 85, 110, 136
Jaures, J.   176
Jeffery, K.   147
jingoism   205
Jolly, R.   141
Jordan   50

Kaldor, M.   17, 20, 43, 48–9,
    94
Kampuchea   2, 97
Kende, I.   58
Khmer Rouge   97
Khomeini, Ayatollah   95
Kiernan, V.   115, 176
killing, responsibility for (Gulf
    War)   200–1, 202
  *see also* casualties; death
*Killing Fields, The*   129
Kinnock, N.   121
Kitson, F.   148
Korea
  North   35, 50
  South   48, 50
Korean War   34, 146
Kurds (Iraq)   53, 96, 193, 196
Kuwait   41, 61, 62, 119, 193,
    196, 201, 202, 207, 210

Labour Party (Britain)
    120–4, 132, 150–1, 204,
    206
language, everyday and
    theoretical   10, 13
  *see also* terminology
Latin America   27, 40, 50, 60,
    72–3, 99, 101–2, 104,
    183, 209
LDCs (less developed
    countries)   48
Leipzig   26
lesbians (military)   142
Lewin, Lord   146
Liberal Party (Britain)   122–3
Libya   133
Linklater, A.   24
Lithuania   168, 169, 209
long peace (1945–)   3
Lovering, J.   149

*Low-Intensity Operations*
148
Luckham, R.
on Africa 102–4
on armament culture 14,
80–3, 89, 94

MacKenzie, J. M. 79,
114–15
McNeill, W. H. 16
male aggression, sub-cultures
153–4, 188–9, 211
Mann, M. 16–17, 24–7, 115
on modern militarism
76–82, 89
Marwick, A. 15
Marx, K. 16, 18–19
Marxism, Marxists 11,
16–17, 24, 26, 32, 33, 36,
45, 67, 80
Clausewitzian (Kaldor) 17
Mason, Air Vice-Marshal T.
202
mass media (war) 197–8, 202
*see also* films; media wars;
news coverage; press;
television
Mayer, A. 200
media wars 156
mercenaries 152
Middle East 34, 46–7,
49–50, 60–1, 72, 98–9,
101, 104, 194, 195,
208–10
militarism 3
armament culture and 83
classical (Third World) 23
classical (total war) 19–23,
64
conscription and 85–6
decline of 110–13

definition 9, 11–12
democratic 118–19
deterrence-science (Mann)
76–8
and Gulf War: after
207–13, in 203–7
liberal-technological
(Edgerton) 116, 117
mass 110, 115
music-hall 115, 117
national (in USSR) 170
neglect of (sociology) 5–6
nostalgia 126–30, 155–6
outward-pointing (Giddens)
18, 24
popular 21
in post-military society
108–57
revolutionary 97
socialist 77–8, 163,
174
spectator-sport (Mann) 76,
78–9, 115, 116, 198–9
militarist ideologies 12, 21,
70, 115–16, 211
militarization
definition 12–14, 71
ideological 70
power elite 67–8
societal 69
Soviet economy 164–5
thesis 3–4, 66–73
Third World 70–3,
104–5
women 68–9, 140–1
*see also* demilitarization
military
institutional *vs* occupational
(Moscos) 112
in post-military society
(Britain) 134–55
role in society 14, 73–6

military (*cont.*):
  USSR and Eastern Europe
    165–6
  *see also* armed forces
*Military Balance, The*   45
military build-up   3, 13, 72,
  208
military-democratic state   119
military expenditure   45–7
  British   135
  global   1–2
  research and development
    38–9
  Third World   47–8
  USA   40, 45, 46
  USSR   37–8, 40, 46
  Western powers   45–6
military-industrial complex
  (USA)   69, 148
military industry (Britain)
  148–50
military intervention (Britain)
  146–7
military location (Britain)
  149–50
*Military Man, Family Man:*
  *Crown Property?*   141
military mobilization   15
  ideological   21
military participation   15
  and attitudes to war   212
  and citizenship   75
military power   28, 30–62
  and economic power
    37–43
  as means of war   44, 54–62
  and political power   50–4
  and social order   20
  and world military order
    43–50
military regimes   101–4, 209
military service *see* conscription

military sociology   73–6, 145
military technology   21
militias   176–7
Mills, C. W.   67–8, 84
miners' strike (Britain)
  147
Ministry of Defence (Britain)
  142, 146, 155
*Monty Python's Flying Circus*
  201
Morrison, D.   131–4
Moscos, C.   174, 180–1
motherhood   177, 189
Muhajeddin   96, 98
Murdoch, R.   205
museums, military   127–8
Mutla Ridge   202
myths, national (war)
  119–26, 155–6, 205–6

Napoleonic wars   32
nation-state, states   24, 32,
  177–9, 189, 195
  *see also* state, states
National Front (Britain)
National Guard (USA)   143,
  148
National Health Service
  (Britain)   142
nationalism   134, 153–4, 156,
  194
  in USSR and Eastern
    Europe   165–71, 178
Nationalist parties (Britain)
  122
Nazism   118, 119, 154, 156,
  200
Netherlands   88, 136, 153,
  165, 173, 176
Neuman, S.   58
New Forum (East Germany)
  167

New Right (Britain)   132
Newly industrializing countries
   (NICs)   41, 42
news coverage (Falklands)
   130–4
Nicaragua   47, 96
*Non-Conforming Sexual
   Orientations and Military
   Suitability*   142
Non-Proliferation Treaty   53
North Atlantic Treaty
   Organization   25, 56, 86,
   87, 88, 89, 121, 123, 138,
   145, 178, 182
Northern Ireland   148
nostalgia (militarism)
   126–30, 155–6
nuclear age   23
nuclear deterrent (Britain)
   144–5
nuclear war   54–5
nuclear weapons   51–3,
   121–4
   *see also* arms races
nuclear winter   55

officer selection (Britain)
   139–40
Openshaw, S.   55
opinion polls   206–7
   Britain   125–6, 132–3,
   204, 205, 206
   Europe/USA (Gulf War)
   204–5
Organization of Petroleum
   Exporting Countries
   (OPEC)   41, 42
Otley, C.   126–7

Pacific   39, 61
Pacific Rim   27, 42

pacification (Giddens)   22,
   27–8, 195
pacifism   12
Pakistan   41, 60
Palestine   183
Panama (US invasion)   141,
   198
paramilitarization (police)
   147
paramilitary organizations
   115
Parliament (Britain)   120, 121
participation (military,
   wartime)   15, 22
patriotism   211
   Britain   115, 130–1
   USA   84
peace, peaceful society
   185–90
   *see also* long peace
peace movements   25, 89,
   121–3, 133–4, 167,
   187–8
peace studies   6, 7
Peat Marwick McLintock
   143
*perestroika*   171
Pol Pot   207
Poland   54, 92, 172
Polaris missiles   121
police (and military)   147–8
post-Cold War   62, 146, 157,
   163–4, 192, 207
post-industrial   64
post-military society   vii–viii,
   64–105
   two sides of   184–90
post-modern   66, 145
post-war   1, 3, 5–6
Powell, General C.   202
*Power Elite, The*   67, 84
Prague   167

press (Britain)
  Falklands War 130–4
  Gulf War 197, 205–6
Prussia 118

racism (military) 143
*Rambo* 129
rearmament (Britain) 146
recruitment, military (Britain)
  138–40
Red Army 176
regiments (Britain) 127,
  138–9, 145
regions (Britain) 149–50
Regular Commissions Board
  (Britain) 139–40
Republicans (Spain) 177
revolution, revolutions
  18–19, 22, 36
  Eastern Europe (1989) vii,
    26, 166, 166–7, 181
revolutionary militarism 97
riots (Britain) 148
risks (Giddens) 197
Roberts, D. 7
Rocard, M. 173
Romania 26, 87, 93, 167, 177
Ross, A. 3, 12–13, 70–3,
  93–5
Royal Air Force (Britain)
  142
Royal Military Academy
  (Britain) 138–9
Royal Navy (Britain) 138,
  142, 145, 155
Russia 33, 194
  *see also* Union of Soviet
    Socialist Republics

Salvation Army 115
Saudi Arabia 41, 61, 193,
  208, 212

schools, public (Britain)
  126–7
Scouts 126
Second World War 6, 22, 33,
  64, 66, 77–8, 111, 136,
  138, 156
  British experience/myths of
    117–19, 124, 129, 206,
    212
security firms 152
Serbia 91
sexuality 142
Shenfield, S. 90, 168
Shi'as (Iraq) 193
Shield (USSR) 165
Singapore 42
Singer, D. 44, 57, 58–60
*SIPRI Yearbooks* 45
Sivard, R. 100–2
Slovenia 91
Small, M. 44, 57, 58–60
Social Democratic Party
  (Britain) 122–3
Social Democratic Party-
  Liberal Alliance (Britain)
  123
social movements 24–6,
  187–8
Social Scientific Institute
  (Bundeswehr) 145
socialism
  and East–West conflict
    (Mann) 25
  militarized (Mann) 77–8
  retreat of 165
  state 25; *see also* Stalinism
  and total war 21
  as totalitarian 21
socialist states (war) 2
sociology
  alternatives to militarization
    thesis 73–83

historical   8
and international relations
   23–8
military   73–6, 145
and war   4, 5, 7–8, 15–19
*see also* industrialism,
   industrial society
soldiers' organizations
   (Netherlands)   176
South Africa   183
South East Asia   41
Spain   54, 173
Spanish Civil War   177
Stalinism, Stalinists   25, 26,
   163–4, 165, 168, 170,
   172, 177, 183, 209, 210
state, states   32, 181
and definition of war   9, 10
monopoly of violence
   (Giddens)   18–19
and total war   21
state power   31
state system (international)
   31–7, 181–4
Stockholm International Peace
   Research Institute (SIPRI)
   43, 45–6, 73, 208
strategic language   81
strategic studies   6
strikes (military in)   147
Sudan   47
*Sun*   130–1, 154, 205–6
superpowers   37, 51
Sweden   153
Switzerland   177
Syria   47

Tanzania   47
Task Force (Falklands)   120
Tatchell, P.   153, 177
Tbilisi (Georgia)   168
Tebbit, N.   133

technologism (armament
   culture)   80–1
technology *see* military
   technology
television   124, 130–4, 198
terminology   10
Territorial Army (Britain)
   143, 152
Thatcher, M.   119, 120, 135,
   137, 146, 153
theory, and end of Cold War
   23–8
Third World
armed forces in   94–5
arms trade and   49–50
classical militarism in   23
democratization of   209
economic situation   40–1,
   65
guerrilla wars in   96–7
limits of militarism in
   93–105
militarization   70–3,
   93–105
military expenditure   2,
   49
military regimes in   101–4
nuclearization   2
pacification and   28
policing of   183
as residual category   42
revolutions   36
states   37
total war in   95–7
transformation of   41–3
wars   2, 4, 6, 7, 43, 47,
   57–62, 95, 195
Third World War   195
Thompson, E. P.   69–70, 75,
   84, 134
Tigre   96
*Times, The*   131

total war 1, 8
  and classical militarism
    19–23
  industrialized 20
  logics of 21
  in Third World 95–7
totalitarian states,
  totalitarianism 21
trade unionism (German
  armed forces) 176
traditions
  invention of 116
  military 137, 179
Trident missiles/submarines
  121–3, 150
Trooping the Colour 128
Tumber, H. 131–4
Turkey 54, 57, 87, 201, 203
twentieth century 1

underdevelopment 6
Uganda 47
Ukraine 169
Ulster 148
unilateralism 122–3
Union of Soviet Socialist
  Republics 2, 22, 25, 26,
    27, 34–7, 38, 40, 41, 46,
    51–3, 54–6, 62, 77–8, 82,
    89, 93, 112, 123, 156,
    163, 173, 183, 193, 209,
    210
  conscription in 90–3
  demilitarization of 164–71
  empire, imperialism 35–6,
    178
  Soviet threat 119
UNITA 96, 152
United Kingdom *see* Britain
United Nations 145, 180, 207
United States of America 22,

  26, 33–7, 38–40, 41, 45,
  46, 51–3, 54–6, 61, 62,
  86–7, 93, 97, 98, 117,
  141, 142, 143, 145, 148,
  153, 157, 165, 173
empire 35–6
and Gulf War 192–3, 196,
  198, 203–5, 208, 209, 211
hegemony 36
militarism in 84, 111–12
power elite 67–8
United States Navy 155

Vagts, A. 9
values
  military 151
  peaceful 189
veterans' associations 127
Victoria and Albert Museum
  (London) 201
Vietnam 35, 41, 97
  North 35
Vietnam War 78, 97, 111,
  129–30, 156, 193, 202,
  207
  lessons of (television) 130,
    198
violence
  and definition of war 10
  football 154
  individual (ex-military men)
    152
  and nation-state 195
  responses to (Gulf War)
*Volksarmee* (East Germany)
  172
Volunteer Reserve Forces
  (Britain) 143, 144

war, warfare, wars
  citizen (Mann) 76

civil   10, 58–60
definition   9, 11–12
and development   6
economic   10
ideological   10
and industrial society
   15–19
industrialization of   16
in international relations
   6–7
media   156
neglect of (sociology)
   5–6
political   10
*see also* total war
war economies   47
war-preparation   31
definition   9, 11–12
warless society (Moscos)
   180–1
Warsaw Pact   56, 88, 89, 163,
   164, 166, 182
wartime participation   15

wartime participation ratios
   21
weapons in armament culture
   80–1
West, R.   48
Weston, D.   38
Williams, R.   5
Wintringham, T.   177
women
   attitudes to Gulf War   197,
      199, 211–12
   and war/military   140–2,
      144, 177, 188–9, 212
Women's Royal Navy Service
   (Britain)   142
world military order   43–50

Yeltsin, B.   166
Yugoslavia   26, 35, 91, 156,
   170

*Zivildienst* (Germany)   174
Zugbach, R. L. von   139–40